The History and Practice of Humanitarian Intervention and Aid in Africa

The History and Practice of Humanitarian Intervention and Aid in Africa

Edited by

Bronwen Everill
University of Warwick, UK

and

Josiah Kaplan
University of Oxford, UK

First published 2013 by
PALGRAVE MACMILLAN

Palgrave Macmillan in the UK is an imprint of Macmillan Publishers Limited,
registered in England, company number 785998, of Houndmills, Basingstoke,
Hampshire RG21 6XS.

Palgrave Macmillan in the US is a division of St Martin's Press LLC,
175 Fifth Avenue, New York, NY 10010.

Palgrave Macmillan is the global academic imprint of the above companies
and has companies and representatives throughout the world.

Palgrave® and Macmillan® are registered trademarks in the United States,
the United Kingdom, Europe and other countries.

ISBN 978–1–137–27001–6

This book is printed on paper suitable for recycling and made from fully
managed and sustained forest sources. Logging, pulping and manufacturing
processes are expected to conform to the environmental regulations of the
country of origin.

A catalogue record for this book is available from the British Library.

A catalog record for this book is available from the Library of Congress.

Contents

Foreword

Jennifer Welsh

It is a great pleasure to provide an introduction to this interdisciplinary work. I am, indeed, very admiring of the interdisciplinary attempt. Several years ago, in collaboration with an international lawyer and a philosopher, I decided to create the Oxford Institute for Ethics, Law and Armed Conflict, where we live interdisciplinarity every day. And while it is fantastic to get the momentum to have discussions like this, it does require time and a willingness to listen to how different things are conceived.

My comments come with the health warning that I am a political scientist, so I come at the issue of humanitarian intervention from that perspective. In my own work, however, I have always been very interested in the historical roots of current norms – and in some cases, law – and also the intersection with law. In my own work on classical thinkers and intervention, my colleagues and I have considered Mill, Kant, Mazzini, Burke, Grotius, and a number of other thinkers who have grappled with ideas of intervention from a moral, political and legal perspective. It is thus interesting that while the phrase 'humanitarian intervention' may not appear in their works, and while we all need to be aware of the Skinner edict to not read back meaning, Vitoria nonetheless discusses 'rescue of innocents', or in Grotius' case, actions to protect persecuted populations.

In the discipline of international relations, the period of the nineteenth century is interesting from two perspectives. First, this was the era in which a very particular practice of saving foreign nationals arose, and which took on the narrow legal term 'humanitarian intervention' for much of the late nineteenth century and early twentieth century. By the same token, however, this same era saw the practice developing of what we might today recognize as a more twenty-first century conceptualization of humanitarian intervention – as actions to protect persecuted minorities, predominantly, but not exclusively, Christian. Several texts from political science explore this point, including, somewhat controversially, Gary Bass's *Freedom's Battle*, in which the author attempts to develop an argument in favour of humanitarian intervention, and Martha Finnamore's work, which explores the rise of humanitarian ideas and rationale.

In my own work, particularly in the introduction to my edited book on humanitarian intervention and IR, I have grappled with a particular definition of humanitarian intervention which has arisen in law and practice during the post-1945 period. On the one hand, international lawyers have attempted to narrow this phenomenon to something very, very specific: namely, action *without* the consent of the host state, firstly, of a military nature, secondly, unilateral. By unilateral, I mean that it necessarily has to be only one state engaging in it, but *not* authorized by the UN Security Council. This rationale for unilateralism is, in turn, rooted in the fact that actions which are authorized by the UN Security Council under Chapter 7 are considered by lawyers to be acts of collective security. They may have a rationale that humanitarian crises or threats to civilians constitute a threat to international peace and security, but they are conceived by international lawyers as acts of collective security. In my view, this conceptualization, while very helpful from a legal standpoint, is of limited utility in providing us, as analysts, in understanding a far broader category of activity. I therefore diverge from that definition in a couple of ways.

One, I recognize that the non-consent of the host state is something very tricky to demand. In certain cases, consent will exist, but it will be coerced in some significant ways. Or missions may evolve from peacekeeping missions which originally possessed consent for the original placing of forces – as in Bosnia – but which have lost that consent at a later stage. I suggest that, while playing around with the notion of whether there is consent or not is incredibly important analytically, if we want to examine a body of cases, we may want to recognize that strict requirement of no host-nation consent is actually quite a difficult precondition to demand.

At the time of this writing, the debate surrounding humanitarian intervention in Libya's ongoing civil war represents a very interesting footnote, because in my reading this is actually the very first time the Security Council has authorized the use of force for humanitarian purposes without the consent of the host state. This development differs from previous issues of consent surrounding military intervention in Somalia, East Timor and Rwanda in a number of ways. In the first case in Somalia, there is a very good argument to be made that there was not actually a coherent agent that that could give consent. And in the latter two cases, consent was *technically* achieved, but under implicit coercion. In the case of East Timor, the Indonesian government did consent to Australian-led action in 1999, although I would argue that it was heavily coerced by the threat of reneging on IMF loans. And in the case of Operation Turquoise, a UN peacekeeping operation was already operating on the ground. With this context in mind, Libya is actually quite significant because it is arguably the first time the council's actions might be conceived as nothing other than explicitly coercive.

Consent is only one piece of the definition of humanitarian intervention which, I suggest, we may wish to relax. The second is that we may not want to only consider humanitarian intervention in terms of those that do not have Security Council authorization, or the authorization of a regional body that then gets Security Council authorization. This is because, again, I believe this encourages the risk of overlooking cases where humanitarian justifications, or humanitarian motives, were the *primary* justification of the mission. Such operations are different than, for instance, an intervention for the purposes of eliminating threats to peace and security which are related to civil war, or even arguably the possession of weapons of mass destruction.

This point brings up the thorny issue of motives. Can we only call humanitarian interventions those which have a pure humanitarian motive? Two points here are worth raising. One is that there will be many cases where more than one motive may be at work. And of course, that is a reality in politics. Cases exist – I would argue Australia's impetus in East Timor is a good example – where a mix of humanitarian rationales and particular reputational and economic interests drive international involvement. Somalia, I would argue, is conversely one of the hardest cases to say there were strong competing *national* interests – here, I think humanitarian motives, whether or not they were realistic or carried out appropriately, were nonetheless primary. Another case where humanitarian motives are very dominant is the intervention at the end of the first Gulf War in 1991, to protect Kurds in Northern Iraq. Here, a series of considerations about the end of that conflict clearly drove the US calculus. But there was also good evidence to suggest that the first Bush administration was highly influenced by humanitarian concerns. These were partly reputational, tied to the fact that the US had just gone to war to remove a regime, and now faced massive humanitarian suffering which compelled responsible action. But these motives are very difficult to disentangle.

I find it interesting that when political scientists speak to philosophers about this phenomenon of mixed motives, they are often very puzzled as to why we tie ourselves in knots about this question. Philosophers often say to me, 'well, in moral philosophy, we accept the phenomenon of mixed motives, that individuals act for a variety of reasons. So why are you so worried about having only one motive?' I think it is an interesting point, albeit one that still leaves remaining questions about motives, the difference between motive and intent, and the importance of making sure that the intention is a humanitarian outcome, regardless what the variety of motives might be. The fact that an *a priori* intention to bring about a positive humanitarian outcome should dominate the way in which you conduct the operation is important, and I believe we should be very worried if the intent is perhaps not that. Others may contend that this is a false distinction, but I feel it can be drawn out further.

Lastly, I would like to consider this issue of selectivity and consistency. In discussions of humanitarian intervention, one often finds, among those who are opposed to enshrining this notion as a legitimate practice, three kinds of argument. The first two, I think, are very powerful. The last one, regarding consistency, is one I wish to challenge.

The first argument is that we should be very wary about extending the number of legitimate exceptions to the ban on legitimate force that exists in the UN charter. That there is a very strong prudential argument in favour of saying that the use of force should be illegal, as one's starting position, and that one only moves away from this, if one is not a pacifist, in conditions of self-defence and collective security. According to this argument, the suggestion that a third category of humanitarian action exists is, in a way, opening the gate to numerous wars for ignoble purposes. I have a lot of sympathy for that argument. I would simply say, however, that actually what we have seen in practice is not rampant interventionism: there has actually been very little, comparatively, humanitarian intervention, considering the number of cases of mass atrocities against populations.

The second reason that is often given for why we should be cautious about whether humanitarian outcomes actually result, is the negative long-term consequences of intervention, and the enduring fact that war and the use of force is extremely unpredictable. There are, indeed, authors who would argue, quite compellingly – Robert Jackson is an example of this – that the greatest threats to human life and human rights have occurred in the context of armed conflicts and their aftermaths, something taken up in several chapters of this book. So be careful what you unleash. And I do think that that is a very powerful argument.

The last argument, about consistency and selectivity, is that we should not condone this practice, because we will not be able to do it everywhere. It will be practiced selectively. It is this argument which I wish to challenge a little bit. I should start by saying that selectivity *is* extremely damaging to legitimacy. If one wishes to make the case that in exceptional circumstances force, including imminent threat or the commission of mass atrocity crimes (beyond human rights violations on a more localized or lower level), should be condoned as a last resort in those cases, one confronts a very powerful norm in the form of territorial integrity and self-determination. Intervention, simply put, is always disruptive of some very powerful norms, which in my view rest on some very powerful normative foundations. I find that the proponents of humanitarian intervention tend to tar the opponents with a brush that says 'all you're concerned about is your own regime security. You don't want this norm because you're afraid of what's going to happen to you'. I actually think, however, that some deeper arguments about self-determination, territorial integrity, and notions of sovereign equality exist which need to be taken seriously. In this context, the selective practice of humanitarian interventions will make those arguments stronger, and will harm the legitimacy of the principle.

That being said, I do have some sympathy with Tony Blair's retort that just because you cannot intervene everywhere does not mean you should not intervene where you can. On the whole I am supportive of that statement, but I think we need to add a caveat to it: namely, the justifications for why you cannot intervene must be very good reasons. Beyond this, I would classify such reasoning into two categories. The weaker arguments, in my view, are ones about capability. If you take humanitarian intervention seriously, or if you take the notion that there exists a responsibility to act in these instances, than in my view you need to take responsibility seriously. In such very extreme instances, you must develop the capability to act. And there are many states and actors in international society today who are not doing that. Kok-Chor Tan makes the very interesting argument that we currently have an 'imperfect' responsibility to protect, one which is not allocated to any agent in particular, and which depends on many agents who do not have the capability to act on this responsibility. To this end, I want to make the provocative argument that if we are *not* going to develop the capability, then we should not call it a responsibility – one which is discretionary, and a right.

The argument I find more persuasive is one drawn from just war theorizing: that the existence of these massive violations of human rights, or their imminent commission, only provides a right cause to act, rather than dictates one *should* act. There are a number of other considerations that need to come into play before such a decision is made: about proportionality – whether you can act in a way that is proportionate; about reasonable prospects of success – what kind of damage

you will do in the course of intervening; and about proper authority –
is this something that is being done by one state without the sanction of important regional neighbours or the international community?
Those considerations are paramount. In considering these questions,
some of the cases where we have seen selectivity (i.e. non-intervention)
have been less compelling. In Chechnya for instance, decision-makers
faced the very difficult calculation which weighed placing a very high
value on the lives of Chechen civilians against the prudence-inducing
prospect of escalating a conflict with a very powerful state, that is,
Russia. Some might say, 'ah, that's a political scientist speaking, someone who is thinking about power'. To which I plead absolutely guilty.
But I raise Chechnya only as an example: my point is to suggest that
we should very meticulously interrogate the reasons for selectivity, and
to cast doubt on any blanket endorsement which claims 'you can act
somewhere, but not other places' is appropriate.

My final point is, of course, that all of these preceding points conceive
of humanitarian intervention as the use of military force. I do share with
legal scholars the belief that actions of another kind, such as those that
involve interference and humanitarian aid and humanitarian assistance,
should be called 'humanitarian action' rather than humanitarian intervention. I do, however, acknowledge that there is certainly a school of
thought which says we should conceive of this more broadly, which
I acknowledge has validity.

Acknowledgements

The editors would like to acknowledge the generosity of the British Academy, which provided a small grant to make a workshop on 'Humanitarian Intervention: History, Theory, Policy and Practice' and this book possible. We would also like to thank Nuffield College, Oxford, for hosting the workshop. Many thanks to the contributors for their time and patience in putting the final product together, and in negotiating across disciplinary boundaries. And finally, thanks to Christina Brian and Amanda McGrath at Palgrave Macmillan, for their invaluable help in the publication process.

Contributors

Michael Aaronson is Director of CII – the Centre for International Intervention – at the University of Surrey. He was chief executive of Save the Children, UK, and previously a member of the UK Diplomatic Service. His early career was as a relief worker with Save the Children in Nigeria.

Nina Berman is Professor of Comparative Studies at The Ohio State University. She recently published *German Literature on the Middle East: Discourses and Practices, 1000–1989* (2011). Her current book project is *Transnational Dynamics: Land, Charity, and Romance in German-Kenyan Relations*. She collaborated with Klaus Mühlhahn and Patrice Nganang on the forthcoming anthology, *German Colonialism Revisited: African, Asian, and Oceanic Experiences* (University of Michigan Press).

Christopher Clapham is based at the Centre of African Studies, Cambridge University. He is a specialist in the politics of Ethiopia and the Horn of Africa, and his books include *Haile Selassie* (1969) and *Transformation and Continuity in Revolutionary Ethiopia* (1986), with a large number of articles on Ethiopian and African politics.

Richard Drayton is Rhodes Professor of Imperial History at King's College London. He is the author of *Nature's Government: Science, Imperial Britain and the 'Improvement' of the World* (2002), is co-editor of the *Cambridge Series in Imperial and Postcolonial Studies* and is on the editorial board of the *Journal of Imperial and Commonwealth Studies*.

Bronwen Everill is Assistant Professor of Global History at Warwick University. Her research focuses on humanitarian engagement with Africa between the eighteenth and twentieth century. She is the author of *Abolition and Empire in Sierra Leone and Liberia* (Palgrave Macmillan, 2013).

Claude Kabemba is Executive Director of the Southern Africa Resource Watch. He received an MA in International Relations from the

University of Witwatersrand, where he is currently a PhD candidate. Before joining SARW in November 2006, he worked at the Human Sciences Research Council and the Electoral institute of Southern Africa as a Chief Research Manager and Research Manager respectively. He has also worked at the Centre for Policy Studies as a researcher.

Josiah Kaplan recently completed his DPhil at Oxford University, where he researched issues related to global peace operations burden-sharing, peace enforcement, security sector reform, and African security. He has worked in Sierra Leone with UNDP, with UNDPKO and UNICEF in New York, and with the Overseas Development Institute in London.

Claire Leigh is an adviser on governance and international development. She received an MPhil in International Relations from Oxford University and is currently a Research Fellow at the Overseas Development Institute (ODI). Prior to joining ODI Claire worked for the Africa Governance Initiative in both Rwanda and Liberia, and for the Prime Minister's Strategy Unit under Gordon Brown.

Christopher Saunders is Emeritus Professor at the University of Cape Town, where he taught for many years in the Department of Historical Studies. A graduate of Balliol and St. Antony's Colleges, Oxford, he has published widely on aspects of recent Southern African political history.

Kathleen Vongsathorn recently completed her DPhil at the University of Oxford. She is currently a postdoctoral research fellow at the Max Planck Institute for the History of Science, and has a related article in the *Journal of Imperial and Commonwealth History* on the rhetoric that philanthropists employed in order to sell leprosy as a humanitarian cause in the British Empire.

Jennifer Welsh is Professor of International Relations at Oxford University and co-director of the Oxford Institute for Ethics, Law and Armed Conflict. Her books include *Edmund Burke and International Relations* (1995) and *Humanitarian Intervention and International Relations* (editor, 2003).

Introduction: Enduring Humanitarianisms in Africa

Bronwen Everill and Josiah Kaplan

From the colonial era to the present, European and American relationships with Africa have been reified in terms of 'humanitarianism'. This edited volume critically examines such relationships, questioning their underlying structures both in the nineteenth century and today. We adopt a unified concept of humanitarianism which sees humanitarian military interventions as part of a series of related activities – or 'interventions' – in African societies, which includes not only military action, but also economic aid, political support and state-building and assistance. In doing so, the text contributes to a growing interdisciplinary literature that takes a critical look at the West's humanitarian and security relationship with Africa.

Our unique perspective, focusing on the contemporary continuities with nineteenth-century imperial engagements with the continent, moves this literature beyond its predominate engagement with later grounding in European humanitarian movements such as the Red Cross, towards earlier historical roots in the anti-slavery movement and Britain's anti-slavery naval patrols off the West Coast of Africa. The case studies reveal how concepts of humanitarianism uniquely grounded in Western colonial history have shaped today's aid industry, state-building and governance initiatives and military interventions in Africa.

This book brings together an interdisciplinary range of experts in African affairs, highlighting regional case studies across sub-Saharan Africa, as well as more thematic issues, such as the evolving definitions of 'humanitarian' interventionism. These authors explore each case study in both historical and contemporary perspective, drawing on common themes and paradigm shifts in discourse, theory and practice surrounding humanitarianism and humanitarian interventions. All

1

engage with the core question of what constitutes a 'humanitarian' intervention over time in a particular region.

History, policy, theory and practice are all part of the bigger picture of humanitarian assistance and intervention and are necessary for understanding not only the driving forces behind Western interventions in Africa premised upon humanitarian grounds, but also how the people, states and humanitarian, political, and military organizations involved in such endeavours see their role. In exploring this theme, we hope to illuminate both our present understanding of contemporary humanitarian intervention practice in Africa and our understanding of its historical origins.

Definitions

The terms 'humanitarianism' and 'humanitarian intervention' both require a brief introduction. 'Humanitarianism' arose as a concept in the enlightenment and subsequent evangelical revivals of the late eighteenth and early nineteenth century.[1] Based on 'an image or an idea of human nature that made humanitarian feelings insistently "natural"', humanitarianism arose out of an earlier project that attempted to define what was human.[2] As Karen Halttunen writes, 'in the context of the bourgeois "civilizing process", compassion and a reluctance to inflict pain became identified as distinctively civilized emotions, while cruelty was labelled as savage or barbarous'.[3] Although military interventions had been taking place between European states for centuries before, often on the grounds of misgovernment, 'tyranny' or religious sympathy, a more widespread, popular humanitarianism emerged with Europe's contact with new worlds in the expansion – and contraction – of empires.[4] This was an important aspect for the development of the universalism of humanitarianism, as, combined with a missionary revivalism, 'sympathy' was now crucial to the self-definition of European empires as they came into contact with 'barbarous others'.

Read in the loosest way, 'humanitarianism' might be seen as a philosophical stance which can inform one set of actors' relationship to and interactions with another set of actors based on 'sympathy' or 'irresistible compassion' in light of what is perceived to be 'obvious suffering'.[5] As the universalism of humanitarian sympathy expanded and critiques were levelled against those who seemed to be merely participating in 'spectatorial sympathy', increasing calls to actually intervene on behalf of those suffering coincided with the evangelical revivals and imperial crises of the late eighteenth century to produce an interventionist movement for the abolition of the slave trade and slavery in Africa and the New World.[6] These interventions were frequently military – as with the Anti-Slavery Naval Squadrons off the West African coast – and relied on both the universalization of Western sympathies and a recasting of the sovereignty of non-Western actors. Interventions necessarily challenge sovereignty because they are attempting to impose a vision of universal humanity on another group without their consent.[7]

Humanitarian intervention, while driven by the motives of sympathy and universalism, is not the only form of humanitarianism to arise out of the late eighteenth century, however. Humanitarian action in the nineteenth and twentieth centuries also included a variety of governance, economic, trade, medical, and social interventions by a variety of actors focused on 'development' and the civilizing mission. Typically, these were connected projects, as military intervention led to the provision of missionary or NGO aid and ultimately to state-building and 'development'. These actions were not only linked by a process, but also by their shared role in inserting outside actors between the state and the individual, a theme that the interdisciplinary contributions in this volume allow to come through. This volume will deal with the unified concept of humanitarianism which sees humanitarian military interventions as part of a series of related activities – or 'interventions' – in African societies, which includes military action, economic aid, political support and state-building and assistance.

In the contemporary discourse of International Relations (IR) and its related disciplines (such as international security and international legal studies), the term 'humanitarian intervention' itself remains vigorously contested.[8] Generally speaking, 'humanitarian intervention' within this literature is used most commonly to refer to military actions undertaken by states or coalitions of states, which rely on the threat or direct use of coercive force to achieve humanitarian goals. Thus Adam Roberts defines 'humanitarian intervention' as

> coercive action by one or more states, involving the use of armed force in another state without the consent of its authorities, and with the purpose of preventing widespread suffering or death among the inhabitants.[9]

In practice, much debate over the last 20 years of scholarship and practice has been dedicated to defining where past interventions have fallen within the terminological 'grey area' of military actions stretching from a traditionally pacific UN Charter Chapter 6 peacekeeping mission to peace enforcement, stabilization operations and full-scale conventional warfare.[10] Two fundamental criteria have helped distinguish 'humanitarian interventions' from other forms of military operation, namely (1) such operations are 'humanitarian', in that the intervening force in question is motivated by a humanitarian impetus, and (2) they feature some form of coercive interference in the affairs of another state. Both criteria are briefly described here.

First, to qualify their actions as 'humanitarian intervention', the intervening actor(s) must possess a sincere and authentic *humanitarian justification* for interfering in the affairs of another state. Here, again, criteria for 'humanitarian action' remain the subject of intense contestation, with scholars, policymakers and organizations providing a number of different criteria of what constitute sufficiently justifiable humanitarian imperatives. The International Commission on Intervention and State Sovereignty (ICISS), for instance, describes a 'humanitarian' intervention as one which responds to large-scale loss of life through acts such as genocide or ethnic cleansing. Conversely, it does not consider the overthrow of democratically elected governments or environmental disasters as sufficiently 'humanitarian' justifications.[11]

States themselves may act out of a sense of selfless ethical responsibility in the face of what they perceive to be unignorable humanitarian offenses, or may be compelled to honour legally binding treaty obligations (such as the UN Convention on the Prevention and Punishment of the Crime of Genocide). They may also adopt the rhetoric of humanitarianism to justify their use of force, when in reality they are driven by national economic, political or security self-interests. Complicating matters further, such motivations are rarely kept separate in practice – governments and coalitions in the past have routinely intervened on self-interested grounds but achieve humanitarian outcomes.[12] As such, Weiss writes, 'the ethical humanitarian rationale' behind intervention 'need not be exclusive or even foremost' to the decision calculus of the intervening actors. To qualify as a 'humanitarian intervention', however, such motivations must at least 'be explicit and prominent'.[13]

The second distinguishing criterion of armed humanitarian interventions is that they seek to interfere in the internal affairs of another state without first requiring the consent of the sovereign or dominant authority to be deployed. This issue of consent represents a central axis of debate within the contemporary study of humanitarian intervention within IR. It is here that interventionist norms premised on humanitarian grounds, such as the rapid expansion of the Responsibility to

Protect (R2P) norm in international law, clash with powerful and well-entrenched norms of state sovereignty and consent that have otherwise long defined the post-Westphalian international order for the past several centuries and which continue to lie at the heart of both customary international law and the UN Charter.[14]

A state may, however, give consent ambiguously, or else be forced to give consent under coercion from external powers. A vacuum of power may also exist in which no single authority possesses a claim to sovereignty with which to grant such consent. Welsh, noting that ' "non-consent" is in practice very difficult to maintain – particularly when consent is ambiguous or coerced' – provides a definition of humanitarian intervention which eschews a strict requirement of consent. As she writes, humanitarian intervention involves 'coercive interference in the internal affairs of a state, involving the use of armed force, with the purpose of addressing massive human rights violations or preventing widespread human suffering'.[15]

These terminological debates are important to understanding the concept of humanitarian intervention, but tend to presume it as an exclusively military phenomenon in nature. Military humanitarian intervention, however, while driven by the motives of sympathy and universalism, is far from the only form of humanitarianism to arise out of the late eighteenth century. Humanitarian action in the nineteenth and early twentieth centuries also involved the establishment of new governance structures, economic interventions, consumer interventions, medical and social assistance and the loosely defined 'development' of states.

Indeed, in IR scholarship other authors have persuasively defined 'humanitarian intervention' in broader terms, encompassing a more expansive conceptualization of interference in the affairs of another state or territory for humanitarian motives. Authors such as Tesón, Scheffe, Ramsbotham and Woodhouse allow for non-forcible means of intervention, without military action.[16] Such actions include, for example, the threat or use of economic sanctions, coercive diplomacy, crisis management and other means by which an external actor's will is imposed upon another state or actor for humanitarian motives without the use of force.

Moreover, these sorts of intervention actions need not be taken only by states. The modern shift among humanitarian organizations, which Fox describes as 'overtly political [...] politically conscious aid strategy', represent a force of non-state actors who engage in interventionist behaviour in Africa and throughout the developing world traditional for humanitarian motives.[17] Such interventionist NGOs – typified most notably in organizations like MSF which reject traditional norms of neutrality as long practiced by groups such as the Red Cross – are less commonly included in the discussion of humanitarian intervention, but under broader conceptualizations of the term in fact constitute some of the international communities' most active participants in such actions.[18] These organizations also have strong historical precedents for their own forms of intervention and action, which stem from the late eighteenth-century missionary and anti-slavery projects in Western Africa and which, themselves, often predated or occurred alongside larger imperial interventions in the nineteenth century.

The literature

In the growing literature seeking to connect modern humanitarianism, intervention, aid and assistance to its historical roots, the focus has primarily been on either of two types: seeking the origins of humanitarian assistance through either tracing the roots of the Red Cross or similar organizations or tracing the roots of humanitarian intervention's international legality, the definitions of sovereignty and the precedents for military intervention on 'humanitarian' grounds.[19]

In this volume, however, we seek to advance the study of these phenomena as historically connected projects which reveal the contradictory nature of the universalisms that humanitarianism – and its associated actions – claims. Humanitarianism is an active philosophy; belief in the universality of the human condition and 'human sympathy' requires that the holder of that belief act. Therefore, this book seeks to explore the contradictions that arise from such actions in practice, be they assisting in state-building projects for post-conflict countries, providing relief in times of crisis or engaging in military action. By tying together the historical experiences of these humanitarian actions with contemporary practices and theoretical understandings, it is hoped that the relationships between these aspects of humanitarianism and the corresponding ambiguities that arise are made clear. Kenneth Cmiel, writing in 2002, pointed to the growing literature on the history of human rights, much of which either focused on the development of a language of 'universal rights' in the Enlightenment or skipped forward to look at the latter half of the nineteenth century. When examining the historical roots of modern humanitarian intervention and assistance, many scholars and journalists alike have looked to the development of Henry Dunant's International Red Cross movement and Florence Nightingale's work in Crimea. The Red Cross provides an especially interesting starting point, as its continuity from the mid-nineteenth century to the present allows for an examination of continuity over time with regard to policies of impartiality in war, definitions of humanitarianism and importantly for historians, records!

Journalist Linda Polman's controversial book, *War Games*, highlighted the continuing problems faced by the Red Cross and other organizations in delivering humanitarian relief impartially. Polman's book responded to Cmiel's criticism that much of the history of human rights in particular did not ask what he perceived to be the 'hard questions': 'what if all the activism didn't really matter? What if all the brutality that human beings do to each other continues?...What if claims made in the name of universal rights are not the best way to protect people?'[20] While the historiographical debate in the 1990s centred on the historical foundation for humanitarianism and human rights, more recently the literature has been moving in the direction of asking these hard questions. Recent work on the Red Cross has raised questions about the ability of humanitarian intervention to remain aloof from the practical concerns of governance, politics and accountability in times of war. Heather Jones's article, for example, explores the problems of perceived impartiality in the Red Cross during the First World War.[21] She argues that while the International Committee of the Red Cross (ICRC) remained neutral, national committees were implicated in preferential treatment for their own soldiers and poor treatment of enemy combatants.

These examinations of the roots of humanitarian movements and their relationship with governance and political involvement are interesting in that they reveal the tensions inherent in involving oneself in conflict, resolution and reconstruction. However, the majority of these interventions tend to be intra-European and specifically involve wartime intervention and assistance. As models for the types of humanitarian intervention and assistance and understandings of human rights that are predominant in Africa now, they are weak. What is needed instead is an understanding of the kinds of ongoing humanitarian intervention and assistance in African polities that has been taking place since the late eighteenth century, including economic, political and military interventions on behalf of people deemed to be in need of humanitarian assistance.

In the first chapter of his influential history of humanitarian intervention, primarily focused on Europe, Gary Bass cites the British anti-slavery naval campaign off the coast of West Africa as a prime example of *genuine* humanitarian intervention, one which challenges critiques of humanitarian intervention as a historically cynical enterprise in support of empire or national interest. Bass explains that 'There really is such a thing as humanitarianism; it is not just veiled imperialism; governments can sometimes be made to send troops not because of self-interest but because of a genuine sense of humanity.'[22] Historians such as Robin Law, Allen Howard, Michael Turner and Howard Temperley have, however, demonstrated that the humanitarian aims, while generally unselfish, were often misguided or ineffectual.[23] Christopher Fyfe, A. G. Hopkins and Robin Law all argued that the colony represented Britain's first foothold in the moral scramble for Africa.[24] By framing anti-slavery as a national moral imperative, Britain was essentially bound to expand into Africa, first in West Africa as a result of the Sierra Leone settlement, but later, using the same arguments, into East Africa. Demonstrating the gap between intention and reality, this literature highlights the failure of a succession of governors to eradicate slavery in Africa. Allen Howard, echoing the discoveries of these historians, argues that the growth of legitimate trade actually led to more enslavement within Africa, as slaves were used in the production and transportation of palm oil.[25] He also charts the routes used by experienced slave traders to avoid capture by British vessels, highlighting the futility of the humanitarians' ambitions. Richard West points out the negative effects of the humanitarian campaign on the freed slaves – the long trip to Sierra Leone and the Mixed Commission Courts, the wait in the ship hold during the trial and the less-than-salubrious conditions of the King's Yard refugee camp.[26]

The language that pervades in both the economic and humanitarian strain of this literature is that of 'unintended consequences', a familiar trope to those in IR dealing with humanitarian intervention and assistance today. Aidan Hehir, for instance, writes that 'a scepticism towards and even a rejection of, humanitarian intervention does not necessarily constitute an immoral or even amoral outlook; genuine concerns remain about the effects that such action has, with many arguing that humanitarian intervention and assistance does more harm than good'.[27] Jennifer Welsh argues that those consequences could include 'the impact on the norms of territorial integrity and non-intervention, the creation of unrealistic expectations on the part of oppressed peoples, the negative side effects arising from the use of force and the potential for long-term "occupation" by the intervening power'.[28] Although these authors are referring specifically to *military* intervention, the same consequences can be seen throughout the whole range of humanitarian intervention and assistance, from food aid, to refugee provision, to state-building activities. In fact, in a recently published book on the history of humanitarian intervention, Brendan Simms and D. J. B. Trim argue that 'to confine "debates about humanitarian intervention and assistance to its military dimensions" will be too often to separate "arbitrarily... issues that in practice overlap" '.[29]

There has been a recent proliferation of work calling into question our understanding of humanitarian aid and the development system that has grown up in Africa over the past 20–30 years. This literature, however, tends to remain isolated within its own disciplinary constraints. History scholarship, like Simms and Trim's recent book, fills in much of the historical background for humanitarian intervention and assistance, focusing in particular on Europe. Most of the other writing on this subject is from a political science perspective, and does not engage fully with the historical legacies and continuities, while the historical literature fails to push forward the implications of the history.

The fields of IR, politics and history stand to directly benefit from the depth of perspective offered by a broader historical view of the continuities and evolution of humanitarian intervention and assistance since the colonial era – including debates in IR regarding the R2P discourse, neo-liberal models of post-conflict state-building and directions in aid sector reform. Indeed, a recent 'critical turn' in humanitarian intervention and assistance studies indicates the presence of a growing movement within IR which has begun to draw from colonial history and postcolonial critical theory in order to deconstruct prevailing normative assumptions regarding Western humanitarian intervention and assistance rhetoric and practice. Current debates regarding models of military intervention and assistance and the 'R2P' discourse,[30] post-conflict state-building and aid sector reform overlap directly with the study of humanitarian intervention and assistance and imperialism.[31]

Indeed, a recent body of critical work on humanitarian intervention and assistance and peacekeeping studies – embodied in works of leading scholars such as Pugh, Paris, Orford, Barkawi and Laffey, among others – points to the growing trend of research willing to engage in earnest with colonial history and postcolonial theory as a means of deepening the field's understanding of such ambitious intervention and assistance projects.[32] These authors have made important initial inroads in highlighting the strong neo-colonial dimensions of contemporary humanitarian intervention and assistance, as well as the enduring legacies of colonial-era policies in shaping modern armed conflicts and socio-economic imbalances throughout Africa and the broader Global South. Orford, for instance, chronicles the complex linkages between the Rwandan genocide, an authoritarian state apparatus directly inherited from Rwanda's colonial past and short-sighted policies of the international development community which fostered its modern development.[33]

Paris similarly deconstructs peacekeeping and peacebuilding operations to show their utility as vehicles of prevailing Western hegemonic global culture – one which enshrines 'rapid liberalization' and 'hasty democratization' as sacrosanct norms, while simultaneously excluding promising alternative models for conflict resolution that nonetheless clash with the neo-liberal consensus.[34] And Bellamy argues the presence of a 'hidden normative [liberal] agenda' beneath ostensibly technical, 'value-free' Western-initiated humanitarian interventions which nonetheless carry with them a range of 'potentially unseen, negative consequences' for the societies into which they are deployed.[35]

Building upon such calls for greater critical insight into humanitarian intervention and assistance and peacebuilding projects, a number of authors have advocated for increased engagement with normative approaches to the study of intervention and assistance and peacekeeping and a greater role for critical theory, including postcolonial perspectives.[36] This so-called critical turn in humanitarian intervention and peacekeeping studies is still small in comparison to the wider IR literature, but it is rapidly growing in influence and depth.[37] Such developments are a welcome and long-overdue addition to IR's body of work on contemporary humanitarian intervention and assistance, both in the context of Africa and throughout the Global South. IR is an exceptionally diverse branch of study, ranging across both political science and a number of interdisciplinary frames and as such any statements about the discipline as a whole carry with them an inevitable caveat against over-generalization.

Nonetheless, it is fair to say that the modern study of relations between international actors has long shown an uneasy relationship between its study of humanitarian intervention and assistance and its own Eurocentric normative foundations. IR scholarship, particularly within the subdisciplines of international security studies and international legal studies, today claims a large and well-developed body of applied research dedicated to describing and improving the practice of contemporary military and economic humanitarian intervention and assistance. Yet this same literature remains limited by its one-sided focus on what Cox classifies as 'problem solving' research, which eschews more critical, deconstructive avenues of inquiry in favour of predominantly instrumental, positivist scholarship.[38]

In particular, Paris notes, the humanitarian intervention and assistance literature is narrowly focused on 'the design, conduct and outcome of [intervention and assistance] operations', but ultimately 'pay[s] relatively little attention to the broader implications of peace missions for our understanding of international politics'.[39] One direct result of this imbalance is that many Eurocentric biases continue to be reproduced in present-day descriptions of the international space and the subaltern. With Western Great Power politics and the Westphalian state traditionally serving as the central point of reference, the periphery of the Global South, particularly Africa, has long been relegated to a subordinate subject of focus and defined largely in relation to the core.[40] Ashley points to the realist tradition – still dominant within IR – as particularly prone to 'silence regarding the historicity of the boundaries it produces, the space it historically clears and the subjects it historically constitutes'.[41]

Within this body of positivist, 'problem-solving' research, 'the agent of emancipation is almost invariably the West, whether in the form of Western-dominated international institutions, a Western-led global civil society, or in the "ethical foreign policies" of leading Western powers'.[42] A dearth of postcolonial critical research within contemporary security studies and international legal studies, however, has until recently left IR often ill-equipped to confront such deeply entrenched premises with rigour. Yet liberal and even post-positivist traditions fail to address themes of imperialism, colonialism and postcolonialism with consistency.[43] 'IR's central categories of sovereignty and the states-system generate a systematic occlusion of the imperial and global character of world politics, past and present.'[44] Acharya and Buzan are blunter still: IR's substantial body of theoretical scholarship today still remains 'produced by and for the West' and rests 'on an assumption that Western history *is* world history'.[45]

As a result, authors such as Bellamy accuse the body of scholarship dedicated to humanitarian intervention and assistance of believing 'itself to be untainted by ideology, power and the dominance of knowledge'.[46] Indeed, humanitarian intervention and assistance launched by the international community – most often meaning Western-based institutions such as the UN Security Council, World Bank, IMF, NATO and Northern NGOs – are routinely portrayed by the literature and in popular Western imagination as emancipatory struggles from the core to bring stability and order to African subjects residing in the ostensibly 'anarchic' Southern periphery.[47]

Moreover, analysis of contemporary African conflicts and issues of socio-economic underdevelopment on the continent suffer from a widespread lack of historical grounding with regard to the colonial era. As Orford explains, the unique legacies of colonialism present in African politics today, alongside the explicit parallels between colonial and contemporary Western intervention and assistance in the Global South, represent the very same histories 'that are taken out of the story of peacekeeping and humanitarian intervention' by such scholarship. Left in their place instead is often 'a much simpler and more powerful story of a civilized West faced with the disintegration of African states and their descent into barbarism'.[48]

In short, then, IR's study of humanitarian intervention and assistance and its relationship with the colonial era, across a range of its subdisciplines, requires critical strengthening. The study of humanitarian intervention and assistance today demands, in particular, sustained engagement with postcolonial theory and greater historical awareness of the enduring legacies of colonialism in the state of contemporary conflict and underdevelopment. It is here that increased interdisciplinary engagement between imperial historians and IR scholars can have the greatest impact.

Such calls for greater interdisciplinarity find support with IR scholars who have long advocated for greater engagement between their discipline and international or global history.[49] With the recent 'critical turn' in humanitarian intervention and assistance and peacekeeping scholarship, there exists an ideal and timely opportunity to bring together international historians and IR scholars in order to exchange interdisciplinary dialogue on humanitarian intervention and assistance and in so doing, enrich both fields. Not only can historical perspectives directly inform emerging theory-building and applied policy analysis within IR, but the modern examples of humanitarian intervention and assistance can provide analogies which will help inform historians' understanding of the often very personal motivations, as well as the organizational dimensions at play in policy and practice directing intervention and assistance of the nineteenth and early twentieth centuries.

This implies a more thoughtful agenda than simply using colonial history as a tool to catalogue the more glaring examples of modern neo-colonialism, or engaging in what Paris decries as overly sweeping 'hyper-criticism' of the entire liberal peacebuilding and humanitarian intervention and assistance agenda.[50] Rather, a greater understanding of the nuances and complexities of colonialism can serve to better problematize a full range of assumptions IR holds regarding humanitarian intervention and assistance and thus deepen its understanding of the phenomena itself. Historians meanwhile can benefit from a contemporary ethnographic look at how the decision making about conducting an intervention takes place, how humanitarian movements begin, what motivates humanitarian actors and how the role of Western and African agency affects processes of humanitarianism in nuancing their own understandings of the relationships between imperialism and humanitarianism in the past.

There exists, in short, a unique and timely opportunity to bring together historians and IR scholars in order to exchange interdisciplinary dialogue on humanitarian intervention and assistance, and in so doing, enrich both fields. By combining these fields and bringing in those with on-the-ground policy experience in African humanitarianism and intervention and assistance, this book aims to connect new research in history, IR, politics, development studies and policy implementation as it pertains to Western intervention and assistance in Africa. Not only do historians provide directly applicable 'lessons' from colonial history for IR and policy-making in contemporary practice, but those modern examples of intervention, aid and assistance, governance reform, and development can help to shape how historians conceive of prior interventions and the motivations of actors involved in them.

Outline of the book

In the first chapter, 'Freetown, Freretown and the Kat River Settlement: Sites of Nineteenth Century Humanitarian Intervention and assistance and Precursors to Modern Refugee Camps', Bronwen Everill lays out the comparative history of three 'freed slave' settlements to investigate the development of a pattern for dealing with refugees in the British Empire that has survived into the present. This chapter demonstrates the long history of a military-assistance-governance model for dealing with humanitarian crises. When a humanitarian crisis was identified, military power would be used (in some cases) to defend the oppressed population. However, the British Empire and humanitarian agencies and missionary societies that operated within the empire soon became aware of the need for follow-up care and the establishment of new systems of governance. Military and humanitarian goals soon developed into full-fledged refugee settlements, with many of the problems and issues that face contemporary refugee settlements.

In Chapter 2, Kathleen Vongsathorn looks at the development of ideas of humanitarian medical intervention and its relationship to imperialism, state sovereignty and international aid organizations. In combating leprosy in Uganda, colonial and postcolonial medical missions saw their goals as universal. However, the relationship of leprosy to ideas about the civilizing mission exaggerated the extent of this disease and affected the perception of it and the direction of humanitarian aid in the region. These medical interventions came up against the state and demonstrated the relationship of non-military interventions to the legacies of imperialism. Subsequent humanitarian medical interventions have been affected by this particular mission and reflect the issues that surround ideas of morbidity in Africa.

Nina Berman's chapter 'Contraband Charity: German Humanitarianism in Contemporary Kenya' looks at the culture of charity and asks the question whether charity is perceived as a right or a responsibility and whose right or responsibility it may be. She begins with a study of the influence of Albert Schweitzer on German conceptions of humanitarianism in Africa. Her chapter then examines the role of contemporary external interventionists – specifically from Germany – who have operated in Kenya with or without the government of Kenya's support. Her chapter brings the question of paternalism, power and African agency to the fore, albeit at the 'micro-intervention and assistance' level, looking at the long history and contemporary practice of individual German actors in African charity.

The fourth chapter, 'Reading' British Armed Humanitarian Intervention in Sierra Leone, 2000–2' examines the imperial narrative at the heart of the British understanding of the 2000 intervention and assistance in Sierra Leone. This intervention has been viewed as a new paradigm for 'clean' and effective unilateral military interventions. Kaplan contests this narrative. He applies postcolonial historical analysis to the readings of British intervention and assistance in order to understand how military humanitarian intervention has been recast from the nineteenth- and twentieth-century paradigms, but also how it continues to follow in many of their patterns.

Christopher Clapham's chapter on the Horn of Africa investigates the history and policy of the military interventions that have taken place in this region. His focus is on the 1984–5 famine and on Operation Restore Hope. The chapter presents the long-standing image of the Horn as a place of acute Western humanitarian interest, but also as a site of continual negotiation between local and global actors. In particular, the relationship between intervention, sovereignty and human welfare have been famously complex in this region and help to highlight the role of local politics in wider humanitarian actions.

Claude Kabemba combines historical analysis of the Congo's role in the heart of multiple humanitarian interventions with a contemporary assessment of the DRC's struggles with intervention and aid. Kabemba investigates the differences between the humanitarian intentions and humanitarian outcomes in the Congo's nearly continuous encounter with humanitarian interventions – both military and non-military. In particular, he draws out the relationship of indigenous actors to the humanitarian intervention agenda, looking at Mobutu and Kabila as key players in the humanitarian interventions.

Chapter 7 looks at a broader history of twentieth-century Southern African intervention in 'Humanitarian Aspects of Intervention by the United Nations in Southern Africa'. Chris Saunders uses a comparative approach to investigate the language of the mandates regarding use of force in order to understand the questions of how humanitarian these missions were. He draws out another theme of the book, looking at the primary motives of the United Nations and the UN military forces, tying into the broader question raised throughout the chapters of the contrast between intent and outcome. He also investigates the role of neo-liberalism and the issues of mission creep in a variety of specifically UN interventions from Congo in 1960 through to Angola and the Democratic Republic of Congo in 2011.

In Chapter 8, we turn to a practitioner's perspective. In 'The Nigerian Civil War and "Humanitarian Intervention"' Michael Aaronson argues that the principle of humanitarian action has been damaged by the political appropriation of humanitarian intervention. Humanitarian action, or the impartial relief of human suffering, faces a problem of diminished legitimacy, foreshadowed by the interventions – or failures to intervene in crucial areas – in Nigeria. This chapter ties together the history of the intervention with the subsequent layers of policy and practice that emerged. Aaronson shows that the wrong set of conclusions was drawn from 'Biafra', which led to the development of a new set of ideas about humanitarian intervention in Africa that harked back to the imperial role of military intervention instead of focusing on what he argues could have been the effective provision of neutral, impartial, humanitarian assistance coupled with effective diplomacy and third-party mediation.

Offering another perspective from the policy and practice side of the field, Claire Leigh's chapter explores the origins and ironies of recent trends in the development sector towards country ownership and good governance. Drawing on case studies from Rwanda and Liberia, the chapter offers a critique of the opportunities and challenges of current state-building and governance initiatives in post-conflict African countries.

Finally, Richard Drayton offers conclusions from the perspective of an imperial historian. He reflects on the liberal and neo-liberal story of 'development' and 'progress' that is ever present in the humanitarian intervention and assistance narrative. His discussion develops some of the themes of power and intentions as well, expanding on the legacies of imperialism in intervention and assistance and suggesting policy changes that might address these legacies. This chapter ties together the larger overall picture of imperial power relations and the history of armed interventions to draw conclusions about contemporary practice and the prospect for humanitarian engagement going forward.

Themes

This study brings together for the first time a collection of work that critically examines the interventionist relationship with Africa from a historical, theoretical and practical perspective, drawing on the expertise of the various contributors, but also tying together diverse experiences and disciplinary fields to portray a holistic picture of the paradigm that has informed humanitarian work in Africa for the past 200 years. In bringing together these connected fields, several themes emerged in our understanding of the long history of humanitarianism and humanitarian intervention and assistance.

One major theme that emerges is the contested nature of 'humanitarianism' in conflict, post-conflict and state-building. Aaronson's chapter most clearly illustrates the danger of the use of 'humanitarianism' in African engagements, but each of the chapters explores the use of that term in different intervention contexts. As humanitarian military intervention and assistance progresses into the post-conflict humanitarian aid work and interventionist state-building, does it cease to be a 'humanitarian intervention and assistance'? Can a military 'humanitarian intervention' be undertaken without a full awareness of the post-conflict aid work and state-building interventions and humanitarian assistance that will be necessary? How intrusive can an intervention and humanitarian assistance be before it crosses the line into 'imperialism'?

The most obvious link between imperial and postcolonial humanitarian intervention and aid is the liberal and neo-liberal argument for

development and 'progress'. Hegemonic Western authority is perpetuated through the paternal relationship between intervener and 'intervened', developer and developed. This raises the issue of sovereignty
and power in the decisions to intervene and highlights the coercive
nature of the humanitarian project. All of the chapters use case studies to tie together the various themes of the book, revealing that the
nature of humanitarian intervention and assistance in Africa has always
been an unstable mix of military, assistance and governance that relies
on an uneven balance of power between the humanitarian intervener –
be they individuals, as in Berman's study of Kenya; non-governmental
agencies, as in Everill, Aaronson and Leigh's chapters; or militaries, as in
Saunders' and Kaplan's chapters – and African relief recipient.

A striking sub-theme is how language and discourse relegates the
opponents of neo-liberal projects to marginal status. This is tied to
the mentality of the intervener and the perpetuation of the 'Image of
Africa' problem.[51] Humanitarianism serves a function in Western identity creation that is tied into Orientalist – or in this case 'Afrientalist' –
discourses. This is particularly clear in the case studies presented by
Kaplan, Everill, Leigh and Berman, but is a constant theme throughout. In examining the mentality of the intervener, however, questions
arise about the motivation and intent of the intervener, as well as how
to measure the consequences of intervention and assistance.

This has been an important theme of African (and African diaspora) writing on the subject of humanitarianism in Africa. Africans
are and have been complicit in the culture of humanitarianism and
humanitarian intervention, but they have also been some of its
most outspoken critics. Edward Wilmot Blyden, the Liberian Pan-
Africanist, W. E. B. Du Bois wrote that although people like Albert
Schweitzer could 'train Negroes as assistants and helpers' the idea
would be to train independent and self-sufficient doctors and missionaries in a new Africa that 'does not continue to be dependent
on European charity'.[52] More recently, Zambia's Dambisa Moyo contributed a new voice to this argument with her controversial *Dead
Aid*, in which she argued that international humanitarian aid was sti-
fling endogenous African economic growth as African states became
increasingly dependent on what Du Bois would term 'European
charity'.

Another African critique reflects the frustration with lessons not
learnt. Edward Wilmot Blyden, the Liberian intellectual, wrote in 1887
that among European missionaries and their committees and boards at
home, there was 'a constant necessity ... to find what may hold the public ear, in the impatient demand for immediate visible results'.[53] More

recently, George Ayittey, of Ghana, criticized the failure of the humanitarian aid missions to Africa throughout the 1980s and 1990s to learn lessons from their mistakes, noting that although allowing thousands to die in a preventable conflict is 'cruel', 'to barge into an African crisis situation without any understanding of the complexities of the issues involved and without any clue as to what the long-term solution should be ... is even crueller'.[54] A number of the chapters in this volume touch on these problems and their repetition in various forms from the time of colonialism to the present, highlighting both Philip Curtin and Chinua Achebe's accounts of the rise of an 'image of Africa' that has dominated European and American thinking about the continent and, we would argue, the shape of humanitarian engagements with the continent.

This work does not aim to be the last word on the relationships between humanitarianism, imperialism, and intervention and assistance. Its contributors do hope, however, to provide a range of case studies and a fresh, interdisciplinary approach that reveals a way into a new understanding of the continuities and differences in policy and practice of humanitarian intervention. The volume offers a frank exchange of views, analysis and recommendations that highlight the often-contentious debates about the role of humanitarianism in Western engagement with Africa. These examples, covering two centuries, show that despite changing practices and an ever-broadening awareness of the limitations of humanitarianism, the fundamental paradigms that have functioned since the imperial age continue to underpin the dynamics of intervention and assistance in Africa.

Notes

1. The rise of this 'humanitarian' ethos is described in Alan Lester, 'Obtaining the "Due Observance of Justice": The Geographies of Colonial Humanitarianism', *Environment and Planning D: Society and Space*, 20 (2002): 278–9; Andrew Porter, ed., 'Trusteeship, Anti-Slavery and Humanitarianism', in *The Oxford History of the British Empire, Volume III* (Oxford: Oxford University Press, 1999), 198–220; Boyd Hilton, *The Age of Atonement: The Influence of Evangelicalism on Social and Economic Thought, 1795–1865* (Oxford: Clarendon Press, 1988); Christopher Leslie Brown, *Moral Capital: Foundations of British Abolitionism* (Chapel Hill, NC: University of North Carolina Press, 2006), 26–7.

2. Norman S. Fiering, 'Irresistible Compassion: An Aspect of Eighteenth-Century Sympathy and Humanitarianism', *Journal of the History of Ideas*, 37.2 (1976): 196; D. J. B. Trim, ' "If a Prince Use Tyrannie Towards His People": Interventions on Behalf of Foreign Populations in Early modern Europe' in

D. J. B. Trim and Brendan Simms, eds, *Humanitarian Intervention: A History* (Cambridge: Cambridge University Press, 2011), 29–66.
3. Karen Halttunen, 'Humanitarianism and the Pornography of Pain in Anglo-American Culture', *The American Historical Review*, 100.2 (1995): 303.
4. Trim, 'If a Prince Use Tyrannie', 29–66.
5. Fiering, 'Irresistible Compassion', 195.
6. Halttunen, 'Humanitarianism and the Pornography of Pain', 308; Brown, *Moral Capital*, 26–7.
7. D. J. B. Trim and Brendan Simms, eds, 'Towards a History of Humanitarian Intervention', in *Humanitarian Intervention*, 5.
8. Jennifer Welsh, ed., *Humanitarian Intervention and International Relations* (Oxford: Oxford University Press, 2004), 3; Anthony Lang, ed., 'Humanitarian Intervention: Definitions and Debates', in *Just Intervention* (Washington, DC: Georgetown University Press, 2003), 1–7.
9. Adam Roberts, 'The So-Called "Right" of Humanitarian Intervention', in Horst Fischer and Avril McDonald, eds, *Yearbook of International Humanitarian Law 2000*, Vol. 3 (The Hague: T. M. C. Assert, 2000), 3–51.
10. See, for instance, Trevor Findlay. *The Use of Force in UN Peace Operations* (Oxford: Oxford University Press, 2002).
11. International Commission on Intervention and State Sovereignty (ICISS), *The Responsibility to Protect* (Ottawa, ON: International Development Research Centre, 2001).
12. Thomas Weiss. *Humanitarian Intervention*, 2nd edn (Malden, MA: Polity Press, 2012), 6–15.
13. Ibid., 8.
14. See Welsh, *Humanitarian Intervention*, for a fuller discussion. See also Gene Lyons and Michael Mastanduno, eds, *Beyond Westphalia: State Sovereignty and International Intervention* (Baltimore, MD: Johns Hopkins University Press, 1995).
15. Welsh, *Humanitarian Intervention*, 3.
16. David Scheffer, 'Towards a Modern Doctrine of Humanitarian Intervention', *University of Toledo Law Review*, 23 (1992): 266; Fernando R. Tesón, *Humanitarian Intervention: An Inquiry into Law and Morality*, 2nd ed. (Irvington-on-Hudson, NY: Transnational Publishers, 1997); Tesón, 'Collective Humanitarian Intervention', *Michigan Journal of International Law*, 17 (1996): 325–7; 'OliverRamsbotham and Tom Woodhouse', in *Humanitarian Intervention in Contemporary Conflict: A Reconceptualization* (Cambridge, MA: Polity Press, 1996), 115–231.
17. Fiona Fox, 'Conditioning the Right to Humanitarian Aid?', in D. Chandler, ed., *Rethinking Human Rights: Critical Approaches to International Politics* (Basingstoke: Palgrave Macmillan, 2002), 19–37.
18. Aidan Hehir, *Humanitarian Intervention: An Introduction* (Basingstoke: Palgrave Macmillan, 2010), 18–19. See also Ian Smillie and Larry Minear, *The Charity of Nations: Humanitarian Action in a Calculating World* (Bloomfield, CT: Kumarian Press, 2004), 225–242.
19. Gary Bass, *Freedom's Battle: Origins of Humanitarian Interventionism* (New York: Alfred Knopf, 2008); Michael Barnett, *Empire of Humanity: A History of Humanitarianism* (Ithaca, NY: Cornell University Press, 2011), Chapters 2–4; Welsh, *Humanitarian Intervention*; Trim and Simms, eds, 'Towards a History of

Humanitarian Intervention', 2–12; Simon Chesterman, *Just War or Just Peace? Humanitarian Intervention and International Law* (Oxford: Oxford University Press, 2001).

20. Kenneth Cmiel, 'The Recent History of Human Rights', *The American Historical Review*, February 2004 <http://www.historycooperative.org/journals/ahr/109.1/cmiel.html> (13 June 2011).

21. Heather Jones, 'International or Transnation? Humanitarian action during the First World War', *European Review of History*, 16, no. 5 (2009), 697–713.

22. Bass, *Freedom's Battle*, 19.

23. Robin Law, ed., *From Slave Trade To 'Legitimate' Commerce: The Commercial Transition in Nineteenth-Century West Africa: Papers from a Conference of the Centre of Commonwealth Studies, University of Stirling* (Cambridge: Cambridge University Press, 1995), 23; Howard Temperley, *White Dreams, Black Africa: The Anti-slavery Expedition to the River Niger 1841–1842* (New Haven, CT: Yale University Press, 1991), 141; Michael J. Turner, 'The Limits of Abolition: Government, Saints and the "African Question", C. 1780–1820', *The English Historical Review*, 112.446 (1997): 334–5.

24. A. G. Hopkins, 'Britain's First Development Plan for Africa', in Robin Law, ed., *From Slave Trade To 'Legitimate' Commerce*, 246; Robin Law, *From Slave Trade to 'Legitimate' Commerce*, 23.

25. Allen M. Howard, 'Nineteenth-Century Coastal Slave Trading and the British Abolition Campaign in Sierra Leone', *Slavery & Abolition*, 27.1 (2006): 25.

26. Richard West, *Back to Africa: A History of Sierra Leone and Liberia* (London: Jonathan Cape, 1970), 76–7.

27. Hehir, *Humanitarian Intervention*, 258.

28. Welsh, *Humanitarian Intervention*, Introduction.

29. Simms and Trim, *Humanitarian Intervention*, 7, quoting Paul Williams, review of Jennifer Welsh, *Humanitarian Intervention and International Relations*, in *International Affairs* 80 (2004): 541.

30. Welsh, *Humanitarian Intervention*; J. L. Holzgrefe and Robert Keohane, eds, *Humanitarian Intervention: Ethical, Legal and Political Dilemmas* (Cambridge: Cambridge University Press, 2003).

31. Stephen Krasner, 'Shared Sovereignty: New Institutions for Collapsed and Failing States', *International Security*, 29.2 (2004): 85–120; Richard Caplan, *International Governance in War Torn Territories: Rule and Reconstruction* (New York: Oxford University Press, 2005). Julien Barbara, 'Rethinking Neo-Liberal State Building', *Development in Practice*, 18.3 (2008): 307–18; Dambisa Moyo, *Dead Aid: Why Aid Is Not Working and How There is Another Way for Africa* (New York: Farrar, Straus and Giroux, 2009).

32. See, for instance, Michael Pugh, 'Peacekeeping and Critical Theory', *International Peacekeeping*, 11.1 (2004): 39–58; Roland Paris, 'Peacekeeping and the Constraints of Global Culture', *European Journal of International Relations*, 9.3 (2003): 441–73; Anne Orford, *Reading Humanitarian Intervention* (Cambridge: Cambridge University Press, 2003); and Tarak Barkawi and Mark Laffey. 'The Postcolonial Moment in Security Studies', *Review of International Studies*, 32 (2006): 329–52.

33. Orford, *Reading Humanitarian Intervention*, Chapter 3.
34. Paris, 'Peacekeeping and the Constraints'; Pugh, 'Peacekeeping and Critical Theory'.
35. Alex Bellamy, 'The "Next Stage" in Peace Operations Theory?', in Alex Bellamy and Paul Williams, eds, *Peace Operations and Global Order* (New York: Routledge, 2005): 19.
36. Esref Aksu, *The United Nations, Intra-State Peacekeeping and Normative Change* (Manchester: Manchester University Press, 2003); Oliver Richmond 'UN Peace Operations and the Dilemmas of the Peacebuilding Consensus', *International Peacekeeping*, 11.1 (Spring 2004): 83–101; Tom Woodhouse and Oliver Ramsbotham, 'Cosmopolitan Peacekeeping and the Globalization of Security', *International Peacekeeping*, 12.2 (2005): 139–56.
37. Virginia Fortna and Lise Howard, 'Pitfalls and Prospects in the Peacekeeping Literature', *Annual Review of Political Science*, 11 (2008): 288.
38. Robert Cox, 'Social Forces, States and World Orders', *Millennium: Journal of International Studies*, 10.2 (1981): 126.
39. Roland Paris. 'Broadening the Study of Peacekeeping Operations', *International Studies Review*, 2.3 (2000): 27.
40. Stephen Krasner. 'Rethinking the Sovereign State Model', *Review of International Studies*, 27, special issue (2001): 17–42.
41. Richard Ashley, 'The Geopolitics of Geopolitical Space: Towards a Critical Social Theory of International Politics', *Alternatives*, 12.4 (1987): 403–34.
42. Barkawi and Laffey, 'The Postcolonial Moment', 350.
43. Ibid., 334. See also Terry Terriff, Stuart Croft, Lucy James, and Patrick Morgan, *Security Studies Today* (Cambridge: Polity, 1999) and Uday Singh Mehta, *Liberalism and Empire: A Study in Nineteenth Century British Liberal Thought* (Chicago, IL: University of Chicago Press, 1999).
44. Tarak Barkawi and Mark Laffey, 'Retrieving the Imperial: Empire and International Relations', *Millennium*, 31 (2002): 110.
45. Amitav Acharya and Barry Buzan, 'Why is there no Non-Western International Relations Theory?', *International Relations of the Asia-Pacific*, 7.3 (2007): 288.
46. Bellamy, 'The "Next Stage"', 19.
47. Orford, *Reading Humanitarian Intervention*, 55.
48. Ibid., 157.
49. See, for instance, Paul W. Schroeder, 'History and International Relations Theory', *International Security*, 22.1 (1997): 64–74; Colin Elman and Miriam Fendius Elman, eds, 'Symposium: History and Theory', *International Security*, 22.1 (1997): 5–85; and John Lewis Gaddis, 'International Relations Theory and the End of the Cold War', *International Security*, 17.3 (1992–1993): 5–58.
50. Roland Paris, 'Saving Liberal Peacebuilding', *Review of International Studies*, 36 (2010): 337–65.
51. Philip Curtin, *The Image of Africa: British Ideas in Action, 1780–1850* (Madison, WI: University of Wisconsin Press, 1962); Chinua Achebe, *An Image of Africa* (London: Penguin, 1977, 2010).

52. A. A. Roback, ed., *In AlbertSchweitzer's Realm: A Symposium* (Cambridge, MA: Harvard University Press, 1962), 243–55.
53. Edward Wilmot Blyden, *Christianity, Islam and the Negro Race*, 2nd edn (Baltimore, MD: Black Classic Press, 1888), 55.
54. George B. N. Ayittey, *Africa in Chaos* (New York: St Martin's Press, 1999), 13.

1
Freetown, Frere Town and the Kat River Settlement: Nineteenth-Century Humanitarian Intervention and Precursors to Modern Refugee Camps

Bronwen Everill

In 2005, a former rock star announced that 'Every single day, 50,000 people are dying, needlessly, of extreme poverty. More than were dying at the time of Live Aid. Dying of AIDS, dying of hunger, dying of diseases like TB and Diarrhoea. Dying, often for want of medicines which we can buy over the counter in a chemist', continuing on that this was 'the starting point for THE LONG WALK TO JUSTICE – we will not tolerate the further pain of the poor while we have the financial and moral means to prevent it'.[1]

Pre-dating Geldof's announcement by over a century, F. W. Fox addressed the Aborigines Protection Society outlining a similar approach to Africa:

We have to lend a listening ear to the cries of the suffering and oppressed, from whatever part of the Continent they may arise, we have to declare to the nations of Great Britain, Germany and other European countries, that the Bible shall not be forced into Africa, by the bullet and at the point of the sword, that African explorations and discoveries can be efficiently and effectually carried out in the future, without the destruction of so much human life and the shedding of so much human blood, as has been the case in the past, that commerce shall not be conducted at the expense of the happiness and prosperity of the helpless and innocent and that European and other traders shall not fatten upon the miseries of the people by the importation and sale of fire-arms and poisonous spirits. In a word the principles of Freedom Justice and Brotherhood must be promulgated and enforced by moral influences and forces, so as to uproot oppression, injustice and rapine, which have too long reigned everywhere supreme on the African Continent.[2]

Despite the changes in the intervening centuries – most notably the end of European colonialism in Africa – these two quotations share more than hyperbolic style. They share an approach to Africans and Africa that is grounded primarily in the humanitarian movement. At the height of the new 'globalization' craze of the early twenty-first century, human rights campaigners, humanitarians and INGOs seized upon the role of global economic structures in creating poverty in Africa. At the same time, historians were examining the lineages of that globalization in the imperialisms of the nineteenth century. Frederick Cooper notes that

> [w]hat was most 'global' in the nineteenth century was not the actual structure of economic and political interaction, but the language in with slavery was discussed by its opponents: a language of shared humanity and the rights of man ...used first to expunge an evil from European empires and the Atlantic system and, from the 1870s onwards, to save Africans from their alleged tyranny towards each other.[3]

This language and attitude towards Africa emerged as a by-product of the anti-slavery campaign in Britain.[4]

This chapter will explore the rise of a certain type of humanitarian interventionist institution that also emerged from the anti-slavery movement: the anti-slavery settlement. The idea of the anti-slavery settlement, first proposed in the late eighteenth century on both sides of the Atlantic, spread beyond its initial remit throughout the nineteenth century. It began as a government–missionary joint project in Freetown, Sierra Leone, with non-British iterations in Liberia and Gabon. Its initial success – and the perceived success of similar projects in North American and Australian settler contexts – spawned a distinct project in South Africa, introduced as a response to settler encroachment on indigenous lands and wars along the colony's border. By the late nineteenth century, the model had spread to East Africa, with the renewed campaign against the slave trade. By the twentieth century, the model was fully formed and was a recognized way for both colonial governments and missionaries to deal with displaced populations, ultimately giving rise to the modern refugee camp.

Of course there were other European and colonial influences feeding into British models for settling displaced peoples, particularly coming from the Indian subcontinent, Australia and New Zealand, North America and from those fleeing the pogroms and wars of Europe in the late nineteenth and early twentieth century. However, the conscious use of African examples by colonial officials, humanitarians in the metropole and missionaries on the ground in dealing with African freed slaves and other displaced groups was notable – and is notable in its absence from discussions of refugee policy development in discussions of humanitarian interventions, which primarily focus on European refugee camps in the Second World War.[5] In fact, Malkki argues that there was 'not a more encompassing apparatus of administrative procedures' for dealing with refugees until 'the standardizing, globalizing processes of the immediate postwar years'.[6] However, this seems to overlook the 'globalizing processes' of empire formation, which were pervasive throughout the nineteenth century and which dealt extensively in the humanitarian realm. Zolberg, Suhrke and Aguayo also focus exclusively on European refugees as the origin for modern refugee camps.[7] Despite Malkki's (and others') reluctance to identify the roots of humanitarian tools in the imperial period, the description of what post-war refugee sites represented belies their imperial origin:

> The segregation of nationalities; the orderly organization of repatriation or third-country resettlement; medical and hygienic programs and quarantining; 'perpetual screening'... and the accumulation of documentation on the inhabitants of the camps; the control of movement and black-marketing; law enforcement and public discipline; and schooling and rehabilitation.[8]

These tools of governance, control and humanitarian action were in use, however, long before the Second World War and, in fact, most likely have more to do with the shaping of responses to African displaced populations than European post-war developments.[9] Although European refugee camps have an obvious lineage in Europe, African sites should have an African refugee lineage as well. An analysis of the deeper history of humanitarian relief and settlement plans in the sites that are the focus of this chapter reveals the gradual development of the model and its emergence *as* a model for humanitarian intervention in Africa.

Although this work is framed in the discipline of history, it takes a comparative, case study approach to the sites under observation. The reason for this approach is not to suggest that these sites are the same, or to neglect the historical specificity of each of their situations. However, it is valuable to use a political science approach and look at them as establishing a 'model' of engagement with refugees not least because the missionaries and humanitarians involved in their establishment consciously built a model from previous experiences and thought of their own project as fitting into that model and adding to it. They were consciously developing a paradigm for dealing with displaced Africans throughout the nineteenth century and the creation of these sites – Freetown, Kat River and Frere Town – established that model, as well as contributing significantly to its continued implementation into the twentieth (and twenty-first) century.

This chapter builds on the significant body of historiography on the links between anti-slavery and imperial expansion in Africa to argue that the paradigm for Western engagement with Africa, established in the eighteenth century as one based on humanitarian interventions, has remained continuous.[10] This chapter looks particularly at three settlements – Freetown in Sierra Leone; Frere Town in Kenya; and the Kat River Settlement in South Africa – as three sites which helped to form British thinking about human rights, refugees, governance and forms of humanitarian state-building. It will begin with the history of these three settlements, before moving on to look at them comparatively with regard to metropolitan and colonial writing about them and then finally, drawing out brief, preliminary ways in which these sites provide parallels with modern refugee and state-building interventions in Africa. Although the sites are separated by vast distances on the continent, by changing realities and priorities in the metropole and the colonies and by the groups who advocated their settlement, they demonstrate the development of a standardizing approach to the settlement of refugees from slavery that expanded to all refugees and has continued to inform the processes of refugee resettlement to the present. Looking at them in comparison allows us to draw out the parallels in behaviour and attitudes and see the change and continuity over the long nineteenth century.

History of the settlements

In the late eighteenth century, working together with the evangelical Clapham Sect, who were pushing for the abolition of the slave trade in parliament, the anti-slavery advocate Granville Sharp helped to raise money and interest in a new 'Province of Freedom' on the Freetown peninsula in Sierra Leone. The settlement was intended to be a utopian settlement for 'Black Poor' from London. Although the first settlement faced obstacles including disease and violent disputes with indigenous populations, the experiment was not abandoned. Instead, the Sierra Leone Company (1791) took over administration of Sierra Leone. The company was run by a group of humanitarians including members of the Clapham Sect – William Wilberforce, Thomas Clarkson, Henry Thornton – but it combined humanitarian aims with the attempt to make the colony economically self-sufficient through the introduction of 'legitimate commerce'. Finally, in 1808, the company dissolved and reformed itself as the humanitarian organization, the African Institution, handing official authority over the colony to the British government, but continuing to act in an advisory capacity.

The colony had expanded with the settlement of the roughly 1200 Black Loyalists who fought with the British in the American Revolution, had been transported to Nova Scotia and were brought to Sierra Leone by John Clarkson. In 1800, 500 Maroons, a group of free black Jamaicans joined them. In 1807, both Britain and the US abolished the slave trade and began operating squadrons along the west coast of Africa to capture slave ships. The population of Freetown grew quickly as slave ships were impounded by the navy and the slaves on board – referred to as 'recaptives' or 'Liberated Africans' – were integrated into Sierra Leone society.

In Freetown, the African Institution and the Church Missionary Society (CMS) had an important role ensuring that the humanitarian aims of the freed slave settlement would be tightly connected to the governance of the colony. The CMS was founded in 1804 with the goal of promoting the spread of the Gospel in Britain's colonial territories and the board of the CMS frequently overlapped with the African Institution and other anti-slavery organizations. Together with an early governor of the colony, they were vital institutions in the development of the anti-slavery settlement model. Governor Charles MacCarthy (1816–24) created a 'parish plan' for administering the colony in districts run by CMS missionaries. MacCarthy expanded the colony into the interior, establishing a number of 'parishes' run by CMS superintendents responsible for administering the smaller settlements, providing education and conducting religious duties. Each of these parishes housed a CMS manager who would oversee the apprenticeship of Liberated Africans in various necessary trades.[11]

Under MacCarthy's governorship in the 1810s and 1820s, new Liberated Africans were assigned to a village where they were required to stay (movement between villages or out of the colony was restricted). There they were encouraged to marry local women, contribute labour to the colony and expected to attend church on Sundays and mission schools throughout the week with their families, thereby promoting the development of 'civilization' among recaptives and indigenous groups. The CMS managers in turn relied heavily on the 'class leaders' or self-selected 'kings' to mediate their authority in the parishes and organize labour for the villages, particularly after Governor MacCarthy's death and the scaling back of colonial investment in the parishes. Despite the initial attempts to mix up the Liberated Africans, villages increasingly became ethnically homogeneous as 'Aku' (Yoruba), Egba and 'Ibo' (Igbo) recaptives moved to areas populated with their countrymen.[12] The Aku had their own king (King John Macaulay) who was recognized as their leader by the Freetown government and dealt with as the representative of Aku interests, responding to their requests for education provision, jobs and rations for new arrivals.

Despite the entirely different nature of the British settlements in South Africa and Sierra Leone, beginning in 1829, startlingly similar policies to the MacCarthy plan of humanitarian resettlement were attempted in the Kat River settlement of recently emancipated Khoi in the Eastern Cape. Although this settlement was not strictly an anti-slavery measure, it introduced the idea that another oppressed group could benefit from the same type of methods being used concurrently in Freetown. Given the amount of correspondence, collaboration and competition between the British missionary societies, it seems likely that this attempt at resettlement was part of a wide-ranging idea of reform through settlement circulating in the empire at this time. The names of some of the districts within the settlement – Buxton and Wilberforce – hint at the connections its founders and missionary operators felt to the wider humanitarian project.

Ordinance 50, which was ratified in 1828, freed the Khoi from their service to colonists and, while it did not recognize them as full participants in civic and political society, its advocates claimed that it provided them 'additional protection ... in the same manner as orphans, apprentices and soldiers have additional protection afforded them in England'.[13] This coincided with the expulsion of the Xhosa from their land near the Kat River. A contemporary report described the early settlement as consisting of 'chiefly of Hottentots from the missionary institutions of Bethelsdorp and Theopolis, bastards from the districts of

Bavia's River and Zwagershoek and some Gonahs who had been suffered to remain after the expulsion of Macomo'.[14] But the settlement acted as a continuing draw to those in need of land throughout the period and economic refugees were numerous. In other words, the settlement was a response to the needs of some 5000 Africans, displaced by the arrival of Afrikaner and British settlers.

The settlement was founded in 1829 as a barrier between the white Cape Colony and the Xhosa and it relied on the Khoi to act as intermediary settlers.[15] Here, the nature of the 'refugees' was slightly different, since at first they were chosen by virtue of their respectability and later were joined by mostly economic refugees, seeking access to land on which to farm. The 'respectable' included Wesleyan converts and families from mission stations, as well as some of the locally termed 'Bastaards' – many of mixed Khoi and Dutch or German ancestry, who had already taken up Dutch 'civilization'.[16] Some of these were given responsibility for running districts within the settlement, including Andries Botha, a Gona who was put in charge of those remaining Gonas who were not expelled with Maqoma and the Xhosa.[17] As with the Freetown model, the LMS and colonial government relied on 'native' leaders to act as intermediaries and take positions of representative authority in explaining decisions and ensuring the smooth operation of settlement governance functions.

Despite the different reason for the displacement of these resettled Africans, many of the humanitarians' goals for the settlement were similar. The London Missionary Society (LMS) took the role assigned to the CMS in Sierra Leone, advancing Christian conversion, education and 'legitimate' production in the form of agriculture.[18] The agent for the LMS in Cape Town reported that 'The progress of the settlement in agricultural pursuits, cattle breeding, rearing of horses, the establishment of schools, the spread of civilization, sobriety and the formation of missionary, bible, temperance and teetotal societies was rapid.'[19] Development and progress rested on the ability to monitor, educate and separate the oppressed population and provide them with the benefits of civilization, much like the Freetown scheme on which the Kat River settlement was modelled.

In the mid-1860s, the campaign against the slave trade began to shift from West to East Africa. The popularity of David Livingstone's evangelical and anti-slavery work and explorations revived interest in the anti-slave trade crusade just as the West African trade was finally coming to an end. As the trade gained more and more publicity through the early 1870s, the anti-slavery movement embraced it as a new field of operation. The naval campaign began, however, before any provisions were made for the Africans who would be freed from the trade. As Lindsay Doulton has written,

> [m]any believed that, having embarked on the campaign of slave-trade suppression, Britain was bound by a continued sense of responsibility to provide protection to the Africans it had freed. This widely-held view was summed up by Clement Hill (clerk in the African department of the Foreign Office) in 1873 when he stated 'It is clear that Great Britain...who has taken on herself the duty of liberating slaves, is bound, even at a large cost, to see that they are not sufferers by her acts'.[20]

As a result of the perceived failures of the naval squadron on the East African coast, in 1872, the *Quarterly Review* suggested, under the advice of David Livingstone, that 'the most beneficial measure which could be introduced into Eastern Africa would be the moral element which has done so much for suppressing the Western slave-trade ... after all, the suppression of the trade around the English settlements on the West Coast is mainly due to the existence there of settlements of free Christian Negroes'.[21] At a public meeting in 1874, the Bishop of Ripon supported a resolution to continue fighting the East African slave trade in the same way as the West. He consciously invoked the legacy of Freetown and its model settlement:

> His lordship, in supporting the resolution, urged that it committed the meeting to far more than a mere suppression of the Slave Trade. The slaves captured on the West Coast of Africa were nobly dealt with by the then Government, which gave them grants of lands at Sierra Leone and their moral and religious education was also cared for. They should urge the Government to deal in a similar way with the slaves captured on the East Coast and afford opportunities to those who were earnestly bent upon it of promoting their welfare, of instructing them in agriculture, general education and in religion. The results which had followed the work in Sierra Leone were a great encouragement to do this and why should they not have a second Sierra Leone on the Eastern Coast, where the liberated slaves might be taught the arts of civilization and embued [*sic*] with those Christian principles which would enable them to attain happiness in this world and everlasting happiness in the next.[22]

The settlement – named Frere Town for its champion, Sir Bartle Frere – was established near Mombasa. The CMS was given responsibility for running the school, a church and other institutions designed to help freed slaves back onto their feet and give them employment skills in agriculture, or as labourers. Discipline was a major part of the settle-ment, with a rotating council of elders employed by the CMS agent to dispense justice, keep the settlement clean and orderly and ensure compliance with rules about entry and movement. The purpose of the settlement, as reported back to Lord Derby, was that 'while every guar-antee is afforded that education will not be disregarded, the slave will be taught the duty of earning his own livelihood, as well as shown the way in which to do so in the most advantageous manner'.[23] Once again, practical labour, training, health, sanitation and religion were champi-oned as the groundwork for development, progress and civilization, this time with conscious invocation of the Sierra Leone model.

Comparative sites

In comparing these three settlements, established throughout the nine-teenth century, commonalities emerge in the process of military inter-vention, the creation of a refugee 'victim' group, the establishment of a model settlement for them and in the onset of disillusionment. The *Quarterly Review*, in 1873, summarized the sentiment of the anti-slavery activists' intentions in following through the military inter-vention in the slave trade with support for the displaced Africans who were its victims: 'We have constituted ourselves in the eyes of Heaven and of the world, the protector of the Negro and we can-not shake off at will the responsibility which such a protectorship involves.'[24] The initial military interventions in the slave trade in West and East Africa created a problem of displaced liberated slaves. The only way to prevent their re-enslavement was to establish settlements for the refugee Liberated Africans and provide them with protection, if nothing else. In South Africa, the military interventions by the colo-nial state were undertaken to protect colonial settlers from resisting Xhosa as they took over their land. But internal displacement followed these wars and resulted in certain opportunities for other oppressed groups.

State-building took place in the wake of the conflicts in order to provide a home for the refugees, but also to create something new. Freetown, Frere Town and Kat River were all imagined as model com-munities, an opportunity for humanitarians to experiment with utopian state-building. Although there were practical state-building projects underway – the infrastructure projects, education provision and choice of representatives to act as intermediaries for the colonial or missionary governments – there were also plans for developing and improving life for the freed slaves and displaced people at the settlements. Each of these cases shows the continuity of the language being used over the course of the nineteenth century. In the best enlightenment model of the time, Granville Sharp planned Freetown's governance structure to reflect what he imagined medieval Anglo-Saxon England's state to be, with tithing-men and hundredors elected as representatives on a rolling basis. Kat River was equally utopian, with the initial families hand-picked for their exemplary status as churchgoers in order to provide an example for those who followed. In Frere Town the humanitarians and government stressed that they were trying to establish a self-sufficient society by introducing the formerly enslaved Africans based there to 'useful' labour.[25] The goals of the settlements were to introduce a refuge for the formerly enslaved or persecuted, to provide them with tools, homes and land, to train them in skills as well as the 'modern' values of Britain (including sanitation, proper clothing, domestic roles, Christianity and literacy).

Another common, *unintended* consequence of setting up these refugee settlements was the impact of these settlements on the local populations. In understanding the internal dynamics of the West and East African slave trades, or the relationship between settlers, Xhosa and Khoi in South Africa, humanitarians in the metropole frequently made decisions about who the 'victims' were and who the 'oppressors' were based on vague information or sources involved with their own biases. For instance, the settlement of the 'victimized', formerly oppressed Khoi could only take place because the Xhosa had already been evicted from Kat River. As Alan Lester writes of the project, 'Ironically, it was this callous expulsion [of Maqoma and his followers by colonial troops] that provided humanitarians with their first opportunity to construct a model settlement from scratch – one designed to demonstrate the progress that the freed Khoi were capable of making.'[26] By establishing these settlements and training and educating their inhabitants, British 'humanitarians' (be they missionaries, governors or anti-slavery activists) created new governance structures and shaped the polities in which they were located, as well as introducing a new, sometimes foreign, group of elites who had the benefit of 'modern' British education and connections. Much of the time the LMS, CMS, British and Foreign Anti-Slavery Society, Aborigines' Protection Society and other humanitarian organizations applauded the 'civilization' of these former refugees. But in other cases, humanitarians were similarly disappointed by the independent behaviour of these supposed innocent 'victims' whom they were helping.

Crucially, the establishment of these settlements did not mean that freed slaves conformed to the methods of the humanitarians that ran them, or shared their goals. As Elizabeth Elbourne has argued, the Khoi adopted and adapted Christianity and the Christian missionaries' message as a means of adapting to their own community crises in the early nineteenth century.[27] The settlements existed as dynamic communities where some were actively involved in the Christian mission and civilizing project and others were more reluctant. In the most glaring case, refugee former slaves in Sierra Leone were accused of slave trading themselves. For instance,

> Judge Jeffcot, Chief Justice of Sierra Leone, officially declared in 1831, that the colony *'established for the express purpose of suppressing this vile traffic, was made a mart for carrying it on'*. Parliamentary enquiries put the fact beyond all doubt, that instances have occurred in the colony of persons being actually spirited away and sold as slaves, by their fellow colonists.[28]

In 1833, Governor Findlay described Thomas H. Parker, a former police magistrate, as having been 'dismissed in consequence of his having been accused of the crime of aiding and abetting in the slave trade'.[29] Since many of the accused slave traders were Africans recently moved from the surrounding area in the slave trade, they may have had connections to slave trading in the region prior to their own enslavement or had no other means of supporting themselves after their initial government rations expired.

These accusations could usually be swept under the carpet of the apprentice system that prevailed for teaching Liberated Africans skilled labour, but other forms of resistance to humanitarian discipline were also in evidence. Despite restrictions on movement into and out of the Freetown parishes, the Liberated Africans clearly migrated between them, eventually creating the highly ethnic villages that developed later in the century. Records from Frere Town also demonstrate that discipline was a source of debate between the Liberated Africans, missionaries and government. In a case where a Frere Town youth was sentenced with whipping by the mission appointed elders (chosen from 'respectable' members of the community), the Mombasa Magistrate responded that

[a]s a result of all these changes a large proportion of the population of Freretown is getting beyond the powers of a Missionary
Authorities [sic] to control and this decadence from a Missionary
point of view, will continue unless Freretown is to be regarded as a
separate entity and estranged from the ordinary regulations and priv-
ileges governing the Township of which Freretown forms no small
part... I must protest most strongly against what Mr. Binns is now
attempting to bring about namely, that my Court is to be a facile
means of [supporting] the waning power of the Mission Authorities
over the members of their flock and of maintaining unimpaired the
dignity of the elders and of other self constituted parochial bodies in
Freretown irrespective of the laws under which we 'others' live.[30]

Discipline, management and order were all deemed as necessary aspects
of the settlements because they helped to inculcate values of ordered
civilization and helped to develop governance structures in the new
model communities. When Liberated Africans in Freetown and Frere
Town transgressed these disciplinary boundaries or contravened the
humanitarian goals and methods, they demonstrated that they were
not helpless 'victims', challenging the narrative of British intervention
in Africa.

What was more embarrassing for the humanitarians was the escalation of violence in Kat River. What this revealed was the danger of
settling refugees near the very people they were fleeing; in this case,
the colonial settlers. In the 1830s and 1840s, settlers from nearby towns
began to enforce dress codes and building codes and began ' "clearing"
squatters from government land around the town', sending them to
Kat River, where there was growing disenchantment with the decreasing amount of land, food and level of wealth over the course of the
1840s.[31] But High Commissioner Smith and Kat River Settlement superintendent J. H. Bowker thought the best way to police this settlement
was to fine, tax and evict settlers who did not follow the rules. The LMS
agent complained about 'the framing of a Vagrant Act, under the acting-
governorship of Colonel Wade, an act which contained the essence of
despotism, which exhibited the strong prejudice entertained against the
natives by the colonists'.[32] In 1850, they approved a police raid of the
settlement to remove any Xhosa, who were unauthorized to be there,
but also raiding and burning down the houses of legitimately settled
Xhosa.[33]

After the intervention in the colony's legal definition of the Khoi,
the humanitarians were bound to provide a new settlement area and

'protect' them; but this meant a definition of who was a 'victim' of European oppression and therefore worthy of protection and who was a violent resister who belonged outside of European protection. There was a sense that by choosing settlers who were recommended by missionaries, or by rewarding colonial service with land in the settlement, the LMS was creating and maintaining a barrier land of loyal Africans who would support the colonial project. As Robert Ross concludes, there was an 'impossibility of drawing a fixed line between the Xhosa and Khoi' combined with the economic instability of the settlement and 'the assumption by many white colonists that the Kat River colonists were indeed disloyal'.[34] In fact, it was with mixed feelings that a jury convicted Andries Botha of treason after his involvement in one of the outbursts of war between the Colony and the Xhosa in which the Khoi residents of Kat River (and the LMS missionaries) were persecuted by settler vigilantes. Botha was accused of being involved in the Xhosa rebellion, as were a number of other Khoi who joined after years of grievances against raids and poor treatment. Although convicted of treason – a crime carrying the death penalty – the jury recommended mercy 'for his former loyalty, good conduct and services'.[35] Botha did not receive the death penalty, serving a jail sentence in its place and suggesting how strong the humanitarian designations of 'victims' and 'loyalists' were.

Finally, the fraught relationships between the colonial governments and the humanitarians and missionaries presented problems for each of the settlements. In the period before the extension of the British Protectorate in East Africa, there were debates over who had the ultimate authority over the freed slave settlements. In 1889, Sir Charles Evans Smith produced a Blue Book on the subject of runaway slaves in Mombasa, in which he had addressed a letter

> to the missionaries of the various denominations who have established themselves in the neighbourhood of Mombasa, in which I endeavoured to impress upon them the necessity in their own interests, of their endeavouring earnestly and loyally to put a stop to the practice which has hitherto existed of the harbouring runaway slaves within the limits of their various Stations.

The response of the missionaries at Frere Town, led by Reverend Mr. Carthew, Smith reports, 'shows how completely he fails to appreciate the local conditions under which he has to conduct his important work'. Finally, Smith wrote that 'I have warned the Superintendent of the Church Missionary Station at Frere Town and I have asked him to communicate the warning to the Heads of other Missions in the neighbourhood, that if the missionaries persist in maintaining this system, which has existed for so many years past, it will be impossible to answer either for their own personal safety, or, indeed, for the continuance of the Mission Stations.'[36] The humanitarians felt that their priorities lay with providing a refuge for fleeing slaves, educating, feeding and clothing them. The Imperial British East Africa Company officials believed that the priority was to maintain a good working relationship with the Arab and Swahili traders on the coast and, if possible, use their influence to gradually introduce the idea of abolishing slavery.

Even after the establishment of the colonial government, problems remained between the freed slave settlements and the local government. In 1912, the head of the Frere Town mission, Reverend Binns, complained that the Mombasa government, which was ostensibly responsible for the area around Frere Town, had neglected its duties and now

> the roads have not been cared for by the Government neither have they policed this side as far as I know. There are often disturbances in the Swahili shambas but there is no one to move in these matters... the Shihiri shops and meat market outside our land over which we have no control... seems to be in a very unsanitary condition.[37]

Although the government investigated the claims, they decided that it would be best just to have the shop owners near the settlement 'undertake the cleaning themselves', highlighting the government's unwillingness to intervene on behalf of the settlement.[38]

A persistent lack of funding and the use of humanitarian organizations by governments to cut costs plagued these attempts at refugee provision and state-building. After MacCarthy's governorship, Freetown rarely saw sustained infrastructure investments in the nineteenth century. When it did occur, it was so noteworthy as to receive praise from the Liberated Africans themselves. In 1838, they petitioned Britain to recognize the good work of Lieutenant Governor Campbell writing that because of him 'civilization' had been achieved through public health initiatives, swamp drainage, bridge building, street naming and dwelling numbering and the clothing of Liberated African refugees as they arrived in the colony.[39] This was a rare case, however, as governors were constantly attempting to cut expenditure and outsource their costs to humanitarian organizations. Even the Kat River settlement, which was run very inexpensively, was government outsourcing of a kind: the humanitarians saw it as a model community of Liberated Khoi farmers; the governor of the Cape saw it as a buffer between the colonial settlers and the displaced Xhosa.[40]

The CMS authorities in Frere Town were given some free reign by the Imperial British East African Company representatives and later by the Protectorate Government. The CMS and British authorities relied on each other – the CMS needed the British protection; the authorities needed the goodwill and publicity of the CMS and their humanitarian allies, the Aborigines' Protection Society and the British and Foreign Anti-Slavery Society. But CMS missionaries, paid only by the CMS, were asked by the government to act as parish superintendents, teachers and representatives of the Liberated African Department. Frere Town, despite its pledge to make the Liberated Africans 'self-sufficient' farmers, was constantly short of funds for supporting its work with recently arrived Liberated Africans. Appeals to the Foreign Office for as little as £5 per Liberated African were turned down and the CMS complained of 'the very great expense necessarily incurred by the Society in maintaining and clothing nearly four hundred Freed Slaves'.[41] Although the colonial governments in each of these settlements relied on the missionary societies to feed, clothe and manage displaced populations, tensions between the governments and the missionaries continuously ran high as they disagreed about sources of funding and the division of responsibility.

Refugee camp legacy

The perceived success of these sites contributed to a proliferation of humanitarian settlements across the continent. In South Africa, the shifting domestic politics pitted British humanitarians against the Afrikaner nationalists, who they believed were oppressing native populations and engaging in the Indian Ocean slave trade. F. W. Cheeson wrote to Fowler and Charles Buxton in the 1870s arguing for a policy of 'civilization' for those Africans presently enslaved by the Boers 'to organize measures for their defence and to settle down to agricultural pursuits'.[42] Anti-slavery refugee sites in British East Africa (eventually Kenya), particularly flourished in the early twentieth century. The Frere Town experiment yielded further settlements along the Swahili Coast in Malindi, Tezo, Pumwani and Mjombani. During the First World War, the British East African government was resettling fugitive slaves from German East Africa.

By the time of the Italo-Abyssinian crisis in the 1930s, the British had expanded their policy of settlements to accept Ethiopian refugees. This refugee settlement arose as 'the sudden concentration of six thousand Abyssinians of mixed origin necessitated many administrative measures, apart from the major problems of food, water, health, sanitation and public safety'. British officials took account of 'All the organization necessary for a small town was evolved in some form or another: fire stations were set up, milk and vegetable markets established and local Bye Laws framed and administered.' Learning from their previous problems in East and Southern Africa, officials also made note of the fact that the local population might be hostile to the Ethiopians and 'No strangers were permitted and the permits of all Alien Somalis were endorsed "Not to visit Refugee Camp"'. Showing the continuity of involvement, despite the settlement's evolution into what could be fully recognized as a modern refugee camp, missionaries were still heavily involved in health, sanitation and education. The Kenya government called on missionaries from the region and 'the services of Mr. Alan Smith of the Sudan Interior Mission were obtained and under his direction a school was started in December'. He and his team set up a school that 'embraces both the children who were forced to join the refugees en route from Abyssinia and who had neither parents nor relations in the Camp' and provided them a place to 'live in the School grounds'.[43] Missionaries and government continued to work on the model begun in Freetown that was based on a partnership in providing necessities (housing, rations, sanitation, some form of work) and improving lives (education, health care).

Beyond the historical examples of continuity, however, this investigation of these three common sites of humanitarian intervention in the nineteenth century is meant to suggest the persistence of certain visions of engagement with Africa. Although the model evolved over the course of the twentieth century, several key elements remained intact from the earliest incarnation to the present day. The language and methods of intervention, resettlement and 'victimhood' remained strikingly similar. This aligns with Fanon, Curtin and Achebe's descriptions of the continuity of engagement with Africa, with the language and methods of governance formed in the imperial exchange.[44] Other scholars have begun to recognize these continuities in modern development theory by using postcolonial theory to investigate contemporary language and economic models.[45] This chapter has presented a different way of examining the continuities and differences: by examining three sites of settlement for displaced peoples as the imperial model was developed over the course of the nineteenth century.

However, the plans and their problems should also bring some contemporary parallels to mind. Modern parallels in Africa highlight why it may be important to look to the long history of refugee resettlement in Africa to illuminate our understanding of contemporary practice. The emphasis on providing practical education continues in any number of INGO education campaigns across Africa, with a focus, as Malkki notes, on education provision in refugee camps. And the continuing funding problems that faced all of the nineteenth century projects arise when today's refugee camps – like Kakuma in Kenya – become a city or 'state' unto itself. The raids on Kat River bring to mind the security problems that faced refugee camps in Goma, as Hutu militias perpetrated nightly violence; or the Ghanaian police raids on Liberian refugees in Buduburam Refugee Camp.

Beyond the refugee settlement itself, it is also clear that the humanitarian practices share continuities with those used in Freetown, Frere Town and Kat River. The utopian post-conflict state-building continues in Liberia and Rwanda and continues to some extent to fail in the Democratic Republic of Congo (DRC). The problems of 'outsourced' humanitarian relief from governments in Kat River or Freetown continue in places like Nigeria and South Africa today, where governments no longer in crisis rely on NGO and INGO actors to run health and education programmes.

In both the historical and contemporary engagement with African refugees, the idea of Africa as a site for intervention remains constant. These intervention ideologies and the process of military intervention, refugee settlement, and governance and state-building have endured in modern engagement with Africa. Although not every refugee settlement proceeds from Western intervention, nor does every military intervention lead to governance and state-building, the processes of their implementation and their intent in casting the West as the protector of the refugee victim, remain paradigmatically linked, despite changes in terminology and details of practice over the past two centuries.

Notes

1. Bob Geldof, Press Release, 1/6/05, http://www.live8live.com/media/index. shtml#.
2. Rhodes House Library, Oxford (RHO) MSS Brit Emp S22 G1, Address by F. W. Fox on African Affairs at the Annual Meeting 21 May 1890 of the Aborigines Protection Society.
3. Frederick Cooper, 'What is the Concept of Globalization Good For? An African Historian's Perspective', *African Affairs*, 100 (2001), 204.

4. Philip Curtin, *The Image of Africa: British Ideas in Action, 1780–1850* (Madison, WI: University of Wisconsin Press, 1962).
5. For instance, Lisa H. Malkki, 'Refugees and Exile: From "Refugee Studies" to the National Order of Things', *Annual Review of Anthropology*, 24 (1995), 495–523.
6. Ibid., 498.
7. Aristide R. Zolberg, Astri Suhrke and Sergio Aguayo, *Escape from Violence: Conflict and the Refugee Crisis in the Developing World* (Oxford: Oxford University Press, 1989), 5–26.
8. Malkki, 'Refugees and Exile', 498.
9. Colonial governance and discipline is discussed, for instance, in Anupama Rao and Steven Pierce, eds, 'Discipline and the Other Body: Humanitarianism, Violence, and the Colonial Exception', in *Discipline and the Other Body: Correction, Corporeality, Colonialism* (Raleigh, NC: Duke University Press, 2006), 1–35; for more on modern understandings of this tendency towards discipline in development, see David G. Williams, 'Governance and the Discipline of Development', *The European Journal of Development Research*, 8.2 (1996): 157–77.
10. A. G. Hopkins, 'Economic Imperialism in West Africa: Lagos, 1880–92', *Economic History Review*, 21 (1968): 580–606; *An Economic History of West Africa* (London: Longman, 1973), 124–66; 'Britain's First Development Plan for Africa', in Robin Law, ed., *From Slave Trade To 'Legitimate' Commerce: The Commercial Transition in Nineteenth-Century West Africa: Papers from a Conference of the Centre of Commonwealth Studies, University of Stirling* (Cambridge: Cambridge University Press, 1995), 247–8; Law, *From Slave Trade to 'Legitimate' Commerce* (Cambridge: Cambridge University Press, 1995), 23–6; Howard Temperley, *White Dreams, Black Africa: The Anti-slavery Expedition to the River Niger 1841–1842* (New Haven: Yale University Press, 1991), 141; Michael J. Turner, 'The Limits of Abolition: Government, Saints and the "African Question", C. 1780–1820', *The English Historical Review*, 112.446 (1997): 334–5; Allen M. Howard, 'Nineteenth-Century Coastal Slave Trading and the British Abolition Campaign in Sierra Leone', *Slavery & Abolition*, 27.1 (2006): 25; Richard West, *Back to Africa: A History of Sierra Leone and Liberia* (London: Jonathan Cape, 1970), 76–7.
11. CMS Archives CAI E5, MacCarthy to Pratt, 15 June 1816; Bronwen Everill, *Abolition and Empire in Sierra Leone and Liberia* (Basingstoke: Palgrave Macmillan, 2013), 21–2; Lamin O. Sanneh, *Abolitionists Abroad: American Blacks and the Making of Modern West Africa* (Cambridge, MA: Harvard University Press, 1999), 192; Christopher Fyfe, *A History of Sierra Leone* (Oxford: Oxford University Press, 1962).
12. John Herskovits Kopytoff, *A Preface to Modern Nigeria: The 'Sierra Leonians' in Yoruba, 1830–1890* (Madison, WI: University of Wisconsin Press, 1965), 21–2.
13. *Report from the Select Committee on Aborigines: Minutes of Evidence*, evidence of Colonel Wade, quoting J. Philip, 318, as cited in Alan Lester, *Imperial Networks: Creating Identities in Nineteenth-Century South Africa and Britain* (London: Routledge, 2001), 34.
14. J. Rose Innes, Cape Town, 30 May 1851 in Rev. James Read, Junior. *The Kat River Settlement in 1851: Described in a Series of Letters Published in 'The South African Commercial Advertiser'* (Cape Town, 1852), v.

15. Tony Kirk, 'Progress and Decline in the Kat river Settlement, 1829–1854', *The Journal of African History*, 14 (1973): 412; Robert Ross, 'Ambiguities of Resistance and Collaboration on the Eastern Cape Frontier: The Kat River Settlement 1829–1856', in Jon Abbink, Mirjam de Bruijn and Klaas van Walraven, eds, *Rethinking Resistance: Revolt and Violence in African History* (Leiden & Boston: Brill, 2003), 120–1.
16. J. Rose Innes, Cape Town, 30 May 1851 in Read, *The Kat River Settlement in 1851*, v; Kirk, 'Progress and Decline', 413.
17. Kirk, 'Progress and Decline', 412.
18. Lester, *Imperial Networks*, 37.
19. The Rev. Wm. Thompson, Agent for the LMS, Cape Town, 27 March 1851, in Read, *The Kat River Settlement in 1851*, x–xi.
20. Lindsay Doulton, 'The Royal Navy's Anti-Slavery Campaign in the Western Indian Ocean, c. 1860–1890: Race, Empire, and Identity' (unpublished PhD thesis, University of Hull, 2010), 219.
21. Sir Bartle Frere. *Articles on the East African Slave Trade &c. 1872–83, The Quarterly Review*, vol. 133 (London: RHO, July and October 1872), 552.
22. East African Slave Trade Committee, *First Report of the Proceedings of the East African Slave Trade Committee* (London, July 1874), 17.
23. Euan-Smith to Derby, 18 July 1875, India Office *Letters from Zanzibar*, as cited in Moses D. E. Nwulia, *Britain and Slavery in East Africa* (Washington, DC: Three Continents Press, 1975), 155.
24. Frere, *Articles on the East African Slave Trade*, 536.
25. Nwulia, *Britain and Slavery*, 154.
26. Lester, *Imperial Networks*, 35.
27. Elizabeth Elbourne, 'Early Khoisan Uses of Mission Christianity', *Kronos*, 19 (1992): 3–27; Elizabeth Elbourne and Robert Ross, 'Combating Spiritual and Social Bondage: Early Missions in the Cape Colony', in Richard Elphick and Rodney Davenport, eds, *Christianity in South Africa: A Political, Social, and Cultural History* (Berkeley, CA: University of California Press, 1997), 33.
28. Samuel Cornish and Theodore Wright, *The Colonization Scheme Considered in its Rejection by the Colored People – In its tendency to uphold caste – In its Unfitness for Christianizing and Civilizing the Aborigines of Africa, and for Putting a Stop to the African Slave Trade: In a Letter to the Hon. Theodore Frelinghuysen and the Hon. Benjamin F. Butler* (Newark, NJ: Aaron Guest, 1840), 22–3.
29. National Archives (UK), CO 267/119, 5 March 1833 (Governor Findlay).
30. Kenya National Archives (KNA), AP/1/229 Frere Town Policing of case pf Benjamin, 1904, Room 1, Shelf 276, Box 5, Response to Mr. Binns' accusations on behalf of the Frere town elders against the Magistrate of Mombasa from Magistrate to His Honour Judge Hamilton, 3 December 1904.
31. Lester, *Imperial Networks*, 156.
32. The Rev. Wm. Thompson, Agent for the LMS, Cape Town, 27 March 1851 in Read, *The Kat River Settlement in 1851*, x–xi.
33. Lester, *Imperial Networks*, 157.
34. Ross, 'Ambiguities of Resistance and Collaboration', 122.
35. *Trial of Andries Botha, Field-Cornet of the Upper Blinkwater, in the Kat River Settlement for High Treason in the Supreme Court of the Colony of the Cape of Good Hope on the 12th May 1852 and subsequent days* (Cape Town: Saul Solomon & Co., 1852), 224.

36. KNA, MSS/61/599 (CMS/1/599), Church Missionary Society Correspondence.
37. KNA, PC/COAST/1/19/54 Frere Town Conservancy Rates 1912, Room 2, Shelf 1303 Box 113, From Binns to the Acting Provincial Commissioner, Mombasa, 21 July 1912.
38. KNA, PC/COAST/1/19/54 Frere Town Conservancy Rates 1912, Room 2, Shelf 1303 Box 113, District Commissioner, 21 September 1912.
39. *Addresses, Petitions, &c. from the Kings and Chiefs of Sudan (Africa) and the Inhabitants of Sierra Leone, to his Late Majesty, King William the Fourth* (London: Privately Printed, 1838), 14–15.
40. Lester, *Imperial Networks*, 36.
41. National Archives (UK), FO 84/1484 Kirk to Derby, 10 January 1877.
42. F. W. Cheeson, *The Dutch Republics of South Africa; Three letters to R. N. Fowler, Esq., M. P. and Charles Buxton, Esq, M.P.* (London: William Tweedie, 1871), 10.
43. KNA, PC/NFD/1/4/2 Isiolo District Annual Report, 1937 (p. 173) Ethiopian Refugees.
44. Frantz Fanon, *The Wretched of the Earth* (Harmondsworth: Penguin, 1961, 1967); Curtin, *Image of Africa*; Chinua Achebe, *An Image of Africa* (London: Penguin, 1977, 2010).
45. Stefan Andreasson, 'Orientalism and African Development Studies: The "Reductive Repetition" Motif in Theories of African Underdevelopment', *Third World Quarterly*, 26.6 (2005): 971–86.

2
Public Health or Public Good? Humanitarian Agendas and the Treatment of Leprosy in Uganda

Kathleen Vongsathorn

From the eighteenth century, when increased European contact with Africa led to high death rates among European explorers and colonizers in West Africa's tropical climate, Africa has often been associated in the minds of Westerners with sickness, death and disaster.[1] Over the last three decades, media discussions of the African HIV/AIDS epidemic have continued to perpetuate stereotypes of African disease, ignorance and blame.[2] It is then left to Western humanitarians, with their 'salvation agenda', as Alex de Waal terms it, and their supposedly superior technology, morality and customs to save Africa from itself.[3] Yet what is often missing from discussions of medical humanitarianism are the mistakes that Western humanitarians have made in past and current health crises in Africa, or at the very least, the failure of Western humanitarians to use their resources in such a way as to most effectively promote the health of the largest number of Africans.

From the beginnings of biomedical intervention in Africa, humanitarians have pursued their own political and moral agendas. Missionaries were usually the first and then the most widespread providers of biomedicine in colonial Africa, opening dispensaries, general hospitals, maternity centres, leprosy settlements and schools for the training of African medical orderlies, nurses and midwives. For missionaries, the provision of biomedicine had dual motivations: it attracted Christian converts, often when other evangelical methods were unsuccessful, and it fulfilled a Christian responsibility of benevolence, to heal the body as well as the soul.[4] After the First World War, colonial governments became increasingly involved in healthcare as well, embarking upon their own medical programmes and supporting and intervening in those of missionary medical institutions. For the government, medicine was a means of promoting public health and, perhaps more importantly, justifying colonialism through the provision of technology and expertise that Africans supposedly could not supply themselves. Benevolence and humanitarianism were important arguments for colonialism amidst growing criticism of the imperial endeavour.[5] The men and women involved in these humanitarian acts had limited resources and competing demands to juggle, including their own political, moral and economic priorities and the need to attract donors in Europe and America. As such, the actual health needs and wants of African patients were often the last consideration.

This chapter highlights some of the motivations, continuities and consequences of medical humanitarian intervention in Africa by examining leprosy work in colonial and postcolonial Uganda. In Uganda, leprosy received humanitarian attention that was far out of proportion with its actual morbidity and mortality statistics, at the expense of other, more destructive illnesses that could have been treated more effectively and at less expense. Moreover, concerns of evangelization and the 'civilizing mission' led to a system of leprosy control that was extremely limited in scope, such that biomedicine never reached more than a small percentage of all the country's leprosy sufferers. In the name of public health, Uganda's colonial leprosy control programme was a disaster, but in the name of humanitarianism, it was an inspiring pursuit in the relief of suffering. This chapter examines some of the religious, political and economic reasons that medical humanitarianism was diverted from the greatest public health threats to the perceived greatest public good and the repercussions and continuities that these choices have had for humanitarianism in the present, not just for leprosy, but also for the relationship between humanitarianism and such epidemic diseases as HIV/AIDS and tuberculosis.

Suffering, Christianity and the role of humanitarians in expanding leprosy treatment

Medical humanitarians have a long history of placing emphasis on specific diseases that is unwarranted by the diseases' morbidity and mortality statistics and then handling the treatment of that disease ineffectively for religious, moral and political reasons of their own. In colonial Uganda, leprosy is perhaps the best example of this combination of unfortunate circumstances.

Large-scale leprosy work in Uganda began in 1930, with the Anglican Church Missionary Society's (CMS) founding of an in-patient leprosy settlement at Kumi, in eastern Uganda. Over the next four years, leprosy settlements proliferated: in 1931, the CMS opened another settlement on Lake Bunyonyi in south-western Uganda and in 1932 and 1934, the British and Irish Catholic Franciscan Missionary Sisters for Africa (FMSA) followed suit by opening two leprosy settlements in central Uganda, at Nyenga and Buluba respectively.

Leprosy as a popular humanitarian cause

Leprosy was a popular humanitarian cause for most of the twentieth century and indeed leprosy has a long history of importance as a charitable cause, dating back to medieval Europe. In the modern time period, leprosy's attractiveness to humanitarians resulted from its millennia-long association with Christianity and the perceived vulnerability of leprosy sufferers to stigma and pain. The propaganda of secular and religious humanitarian organizations, including charities and missions, frequently mentioned the compassionate example that Christ set in the New Testament. Christ ignored injunctions forbidding contact with leprosy sufferers, touched and healed leprosy sufferers and urged all Christians to 'cleanse the lepers', which was interpreted as healing them physically and spiritually.[6] Uganda's leprosy missionaries wrote of Christ as their inspiration to pursue leprosy work, stating that healing leprosy sufferers was 'the most Christ-like work anyone can do'.[7] In addition to describing leprosy sufferers as objects of Christ's special compassion, leprosy charities portrayed these afflicted individuals as the most vulnerable people in the world, more so even than slaves.[8] There was special emotional, religious and humanitarian benefit to be found in the care of those perceived most vulnerable and a myth of leprosy's universal stigmatization lent itself to the perception that all leprosy sufferers faced ostracism and stigmatization.[9] Moreover, in its advanced stages, leprosy could be accompanied by debilitating and disfiguring symptoms and dramatic descriptions of some of these symptoms lent further credence to the notion of the 'leper' as a helpless sufferer.

From the missionaries' perspective, leprosy also offered a unique opportunity for evangelization. Unlike other mission enterprises, such as mission hospitals, which patients visited for no more than a few days or a few weeks, leprosy patients often stayed in the settlement for years, usually with limited family contact. This sustained residency was an unusual opportunity for evangelization and Uganda's leprosy missionaries therefore preferred the idea of treating leprosy sufferers as in-patients, rather than as out-patients.[10] Leprosy treatment also drew people into contact with the missions who otherwise never would have been reached, as many patients travelled long distances from districts where Christianity had not yet spread.[11] Moreover, the leprosy sufferer's conversion to Christianity was perceived as particularly sincere. Missionaries believed that 'God gives a special compensation and consolation to those who suffer', and none suffered more than the leprosy patient, who was capable of a relationship with God to which the missionaries could only aspire.[12]

Benevolence and the 'civilizing mission' were also important motivators of leprosy humanitarianism, for missionaries, secular organizations and government officials alike. As one missionary wrote, 'It is the special privilege and joy of the medical work that it meets the need of the down and outs, most wretched and unfortunate of men, women and children.'[13] And another added, 'For the sake of humanity ... we appeal to you to send a donation.'[14] As welfare gained importance in the colonial agenda after the First and Second World Wars, the prevention of debilitation through leprosy became a duty of the government. It was also an opportunity to justify colonialism, as the colonizers and missionaries offered care and biomedicine that Ugandans supposedly would not and could not provide.[15] In-patient leprosy settlements had the added benefit of being ideal venues for the enactment of the 'civilizing mission', in that they fashioned and educated useful subjects of the British Empire.[16]

Leprosy's growth as a medical and humanitarian interest in Uganda

Estimates of leprosy's incidence in Uganda were variable throughout the colonial time period, depending upon the extent of government and mission medical work and the intervention of external leprosy humanitarians. In 1908, only six leprosy patients were reported as attending government dispensaries or hospitals, out of a total 53,078 recorded medical visits, which led the department to report that leprosy 'is rarely met with in this Protectorate', though 'natives' reported its existence neighbouring areas not yet under administration.[17] At this time, leprosy work in Uganda was a small-scale affair. There was only one leprosy camp, opened by the French Catholic White Fathers missionaries in 1911, which housed but did not treat about 30 leprosy sufferers.[18]

Around 1918, Native Administrations (NAs) began using money from their own budgets to create small leprosy camps in their districts. Shortly thereafter, in 1921, the medical department reported 'That leprosy is widely spread throughout the Protectorate has long been known', though in fact their records of leprosy's incidence were no higher in 1921 than in 1912, the 33 cases out of 97,810 treatments recorded were only treble the proportion of leprosy patients recorded in 1908.[19] As the NA 'leper camps' grew in size, along with 'increased facilities for diagnosis and treatment', so too did the medical department's tally of leprosy's incidence in Uganda. In response to a survey that the British Empire Leprosy Relief Association (BELRA) sent to all British colonies, Uganda's medical department estimated that there were 6000 leprosy sufferers in Uganda, a rate of two per mille.[20] BELRA's secretary, Reverend Frank Oldrieve, pointed out to Uganda's governor that this was actually five times the incidence of leprosy in India, which had heretofore been most strongly associated with the problem of leprosy in the British empire.[21]

In 1931, BELRA's medical secretary, Dr. Robert Cochrane, finished another leprosy tour of Uganda and following his visit there he reported an estimated 20,000 leprosy sufferers in Uganda, or roughly four per mille. When East Africa's newly appointed interterritorial leprologist, Dr. Innes, completed a survey of leprosy in Uganda in 1948, he estimated at least 100,000 leprosy sufferers, or 20 per mille.[22]

If we use 1931 as a benchmark, there were certainly other diseases with higher morbidity rates than leprosy. In each of their annual reports, Uganda's medical department listed the number of patients they had contact with who were suffering from any given illness. In 1931, there were 3822 cases of leprosy noted at government institutions, with an additional 345 in-patients at the CMS' 2 leprosy settlements, as compared to 50,293 cases of malaria, 47,598 cases of yaws, 64,591 cases of syphilis and 41,310 cases of bronchitis.[23] These are only the highest disease returns for 1931; there are dozens of other ailments for which Ugandans sought biomedical treatment more frequently than leprosy, such as gonorrhoea, scabies and diarrhoea.[24] If we assume that leprosy patients were as likely to attend dispensaries and hospitals for treatment as malaria, yaws and syphilis patients, a reasonable assumption given that leprosy was stigmatized only in a minority of Uganda's ethnic groups, then leprosy's incidence was only 8 per cent of that of malaria and yaws and 6 per cent that of syphilis. Supposing that the estimate of 20,000 leprosy sufferers was correct, then at the very most there would have been one sufferer of leprosy to every three sufferers of syphilis. Even within the leprosy settlements, most patients suffered from intercurrent illnesses. A 1948 survey of disease incidence at the Lake Bunyonyi leprosy settlement had 40 per cent of the patients suffering from yaws.[25] If leprosy's mortality rates were to be compared against those of other diseases, it would rate with even less importance, for leprosy was a chronic disease that most patients lived with for decades. The average death rate in Uganda's leprosy settlements in 1946 was 24.8 per mille, as compared to 20.3 per mille in the whole Protectorate and most of these deaths were from intercurrent illnesses such as malaria.[26]

Comparing the incidence of leprosy to other diseases present in Uganda is particularly enlightening when considered against the government's expenditure on health. In 1931, with only two mission leprosy settlements in existence, the government granted £1000 for 'leprosy relief measures', which was half what they supplied to the CMS for their maternity work and midwifery training. These grants represented an enormous imbalance of spending, given that the infant mortality rate was 209.71 per mille and the maternal mortality rate was 14.6 per mille. To further put the exorbitance of the leprosy grant into perspective, it amounted to £2.45 per leprosy in-patient, whereas the grant for the government's European and Asiatic hospitals amounted to £0.13 for each patient seen, or £0.84 per in-patient admission.[27] Incidentally, there were fewer new cases of sleeping sickness than leprosy in 1931. The fact that the government granted an even larger sum towards sleeping sickness than leprosy, £3958, evinces some sense of the government's consistently skewed medical spending priorities.

High spending on leprosy was characteristic of Uganda's medical department throughout the late colonial period. In 1947, for example, the medical department awarded £4498 for the four mission leprosy settlements, which was used for the treatment and care of 3000 in- and out-patients. This grant amounted to 1 per cent of the medical department's entire annual budget, yet when compared against the number of patients treated that year at government hospitals and dispensaries, over two million, proportionally speaking they ought to have received only 0.13 per cent of the funding.[28] And these medical department grants entirely exclude the settlements' other sources from money, such as NAs, missions and British and American charities.

The in-patient model of leprosy treatment in Uganda was quite expensive, but if that expense had an appreciable effect on the incidence of leprosy in Uganda, then such spending might have been justified by the goals of public health. Public health, after all, was a goal touted by the colonial government and the eradication of leprosy was touted at various times by missionaries and other humanitarian organizations. However, the plan of leprosy control jointly pursued by all of these actors was not effective in treating the widest possible number of leprosy patients or in limiting the incidence of the disease. Estimates of leprosy's incidence only went up as time passed, from 4 per mille in 1931 to 20 per mille in 1948. Admittedly, this does not necessarily indicate an actual increase in the incidence of leprosy in Uganda, as estimates of leprosy increased as wider surveys of leprosy took place and biomedical provision spread across Uganda. In the late 1940s, both CMS leprosy settlements did receive higher proportions of leprosy patients from outside the nearest districts. This could indicate that the incidence of leprosy had decreased in these districts, but it could just as easily mean that everybody who was willing to enter a leprosy settlement had already done so, since entrance was voluntary.

The pursuit of public health?

From 1930 to 1951, leprosy control in Uganda was approached through the creation of in-patient settlements where leprosy patients would undergo several years of biomedical treatment and palliative care until the symptoms of their disease were halted. At the time of Uganda's 1948 leprosy survey, 3000 leprosy sufferers were receiving treatment at four missionary settlements, the majority as in-patients and a few hundred as out-patients. This meant that the thousands of pounds spent by humanitarians and the government went to the treatment of only 3 per cent of all Uganda's leprosy patients. Of Uganda's estimated total of 100,000 leprosy sufferers, Dr. Inness estimated that 20,000 were infectious, so at best there were still 17,000 men, women and children who continued to spread leprosy across most of the Protectorate.

Given the constraints of medical interventions in colonial Africa, in terms of money, staff and the cooperation of sick individuals, it might be tempting to conclude that in spending large amounts of money to treat a small fraction of leprosy patients, Uganda's humanitarians were doing the best that they could with the resources they had available. However, this was not the case. From the first conceptualization of large-scale mission leprosy work in 1927, tensions existed between various government officials, missionaries and doctors in Britain over whether the most effective policy of leprosy control was being pursued.

When the CMS Dr. Wiggins arrived in Uganda to undertake leprosy work in 1927, he was initially inclined to follow the medical department's recommendation to treat leprosy with a segregated in-patient settlement, primarily because it would be less costly in terms of money and staff.[29] However, local chiefs and the district commissioner did not believe that segregation was a practicable means of attracting the maximum number of leprosy patients for treatment and so, on their advice, Wiggins instead planned the creation of six out-patient treatment centres, spread across the Teso region of eastern Uganda.[30] He believed that, in the end, if leprosy patients could be treated closer to their homes, one of the greatest difficulties of leprosy control policy would be alleviated: persuading leprosy sufferers to segregate themselves for biomedical treatment.[31]

By January 1929, Wiggins had also proposed the founding of an in-patient leprosy settlement for children, as parents were too often 'apt to be slack at bringing them up for treatment'.[32] With staggeringly high numbers of out-patients attending for treatment and an in-patient facility on the horizon, in February 1929, six months after he commenced leprosy treatment in Teso, Wiggins announced that the work had grown too much for one doctor to handle, even with assistance from his nurse daughter and Ugandan orderlies.[33] Wiggins' first hope was that the CMS, supported by British leprosy charities, could fund another mission doctor for the Teso leprosy work. Although the CMS medical committee expressed themselves appreciative of 'the rapid expansion of this work under the supervision and organization of Dr. Wiggins', they did not feel that they were in a position to supply or support another doctor and moreover: 'leprosy relief work on such a large scale is properly the function of the Government'. They would, however, 'be prepared to encourage a scheme for the development of a Central Leprosy Colony'.[34] Although out-patient leprosy treatment was more effective for public health, in-patient leprosy treatment was more effective for evangelism and the CMS had no qualms about recommending a downsizing of Teso leprosy work, since after all, the public health was the responsibility of the government.[35]

Dr. Wiggins' last hope was that the government would fulfil their responsibility for the public health of Ugandans by taking over the out-patient leprosy clinics that he had started, leaving in-patient leprosy treatment in the more willing hands of the mission and British charities. However, in a personal meeting, the DMSS told Wiggins that the government could not take over any of the out-patient centres, or provide extra medical staff in Teso. Wiggins concluded that 'the campaign against Leprosy in this district is entirely in our [the mission's] hands and future work must be planned according to the staff at our disposal'.[36] Although the central medical department would not financially support the recurrent annual cost of out-patient leprosy treatment, they did agree to contribute a special, one-time grant for the foundation of an in-patient leprosy settlement. So, Wiggins proposed that the government's funds go to the foundation of an in-patient leprosy settlement for infectious adults, while the children's leprosy settlement, which was a more attractive fundraising prospect, would be the financial responsibility of the Mission to Lepers and CMS. The out-patient leprosy centres were thus closed, in favour of two large in-patient settlements.[37]

While the out-patient treatment centres were fully functioning, albeit with the mild compulsory measure of a fine for those patients who did not regularly attend for treatment, which the DMSS later forbade, Wiggins was treating more than 2000 patients a week and more than 3000 total leprosy patients, including irregular attendees.[38] The leprosy settlement he founded at Kumi and Ongino, however, did not grow much larger than 1200 combined over the entire colonial period.[39] So although Wiggins' initial methods of drawing patients were imperfect, out-patient treatment clearly had the potential to reach more leprosy sufferers than in-patient settlements. Indeed, as early as 1932 missionaries had to begin turning prospective leprosy patients away from the settlements, because they did not have the space or money to accommodate them.[40] Government officials in other parts of Uganda agreed with this assessment; when CMS missionaries began discussing plans to open a leprosy settlement in south-western Uganda, the district medical officer encouraged the facilitation of leprosy treatment at government sub-dispensaries instead.[41] The district commissioner agreed and wrote that 'local treatment centres, whether attached or not to existing Dispensaries, would be at first by far the least expensive, the most suitable and, with care, not difficult to popularise', for young and more easily curable patients would be far more willing to come for regular treatment.[42] At this point, however, the CMS missionaries had received approval for an island settlement from the former provincial commissioner and although attempts were made, no colonial officers were able to obstruct the founding of the settlement.

Various colonial government officials continued to question the efficacy of an in-patient leprosy control model for the next 20 years, in light of the government's perceived responsibility to promote the public health of Ugandans. In response to an inquiry from the chief secretary, most likely prompted by the visit of a BELRA leprologist, the Director of Medical Services (DMS) wrote in 1938 that

> I agree that the leper settlements are doing excellent work. This must be regarded more as philanthropic than as preventive medicine since although no doubt a number of infectious cases are segregated in these institutions it cannot be claimed that more than a

small proportion of infectious lepers are admitted or that segregation is early enough to prevent others being infected before these cases are removed from contact with the general community...The hope of any appreciable reduction of leprosy in Uganda lies in the wider extension of rural sanitation and health education. If there is any money available for leprosy, I should prefer to see it spent on preventive medicine and education rather than on leper settlements which are costly methods of inadequately tackling a problem which is probably less serious in this Protectorate than many others such as tuberculosis.[43]

In 1943, after a sleeping sickness outbreak at the Buluba leprosy settlement, the colonial government considered moving the leprosy settlement and again the idea of out-patient treatment centres in lieu of an in-patient settlement was brought up. The district medical officer noted that the number of leprosy patients under treatment was 'so small compared with the number at large in [Busoga]'. The DC thought the solution was out-patient treatment, writing that 'I should have thought that if we could have leprosy cases treatment centres dispensed over the district as we have sub-dispensaries, we should have greater numbers attending for treatment because the dislike of the people for any walks from their homes is natural.'[44] The provincial medical officer replied that the government had neither the staff nor the petrol to allow the treatment of leprosy at a number of sub-dispensaries and the 'future of leprosy control must be left for better times'.[45] A string of similar criticisms and uncertainties culminated in 1948 with Dr. Innes' final report on leprosy in Uganda. In addition to pointing out the small percentage of leprosy patients under treatment, Innes stated that the settlements were 'poorly sited strategically', that only eight medically trained Europeans were actively engaged in leprosy work and that the new, highly effective sulphone drugs were not being used.[46]

Innes' criticisms confirmed a tension that had existed between the missions and various government officials for more than a decade, over whether the resources granted to the missions for leprosy treatment were being used as effectively as possible. From the government's perspective, effective leprosy treatment meant rendering the largest possible number of leprosy patients non-infectious, so that they would not continue to spread the disease. CMS missionaries in particular also expressed a desire to limit the spread and incidence of leprosy, especially among children. For example, when writing of his plans to found a leprosy settlement at Lake Bunyonyi, CMS Dr. Sharp wrote that he hoped for 'all curable cases

[to] be cured and the spread of this disease in Kigezi be stayed'.[47] Several years later, Sharp wrote to his DC that

[t]he migration of so many lepers to the Colony must result not only in the alleviation of much suffering, but also in a marked diminution in the number of healthy persons becoming infected all over the District. It may well be hoped that, as this migration is encouraged to continue, Kigezi District will in a few years cease to be the hotbed of leprosy that it has been in the past.[48]

A missionary nurse at the CMS' Kumi settlement wrote of their attempt to follow medical recommendations as to the best way to control leprosy:

At a conference of medical men in Cairo recently, it was stated that the most successful treatment of leprosy was that carried out among children and of those the early cases. These two facts therefore have led us to our chief methods of treatment: first preventative, by isolating as far as we can all infectious cases; and secondly, concentrating very much on the treatment of the children.[49]

According to statements like this, missionaries agreed with government officials that leprosy settlements should be used to decrease the incidence of leprosy. However, other mission priorities ultimately interfered with this public health goal.

In assessing whether leprosy missions were actually capable of decreasing the incidence of leprosy, it is first necessary to consider whether biomedicine actually had the ability to halt leprosy's spread. During the colonial period leprosy doctors and nurses generally believed that if 'early cases' were given biomedical treatment, appropriate care and a nourishing diet, the progress of leprosy could be halted and the infectious patient rendered non-infectious.[50] Whether or not this was true is open for debate. Until 1947, the predominant biomedicine used in the treatment of leprosy was *chaulmoogra* oil, injected intradermally into infected areas of the skin. The efficacy of this treatment was doubted even in the 1920s, when biomedical doctors began advocating its use, and as it has since been discredited, it is difficult to assess the extent to which missionaries were truly capable of healing leprosy.[51]

Given the questionable efficacy of the biomedical treatment available for the first two decades of Uganda's leprosy settlements, to a certain extent low annual discharge rates from the settlements were to be expected. In order to maximize the number of patients who could be effectively treated and rendered non-infectious, the mission settlements were meant to preferentially admit infectious and early cases of leprosy, especially children. However, the missionaries had different priorities for their patient populations and they found it difficult to turn away patients in the advanced stages of the disease, even if they were not infectious and treatment would do little to improve their condition. As one CMS missionary wrote:

> The majority were poor, filthy and helpless enough... two of them were smothered in ulcers from head to foot, their poor little bodies maimed and legs doubled under them, so that unless... an operation is performed, they will never be able to walk... Another old woman... was literally smothered from head to foot in large patches of leprosy. Another woman, with her poor old face eaten away. It is useless for me to try and describe such pitiful sights. Lepers! No, no one has any time for them in their villages and I am afraid that there are some people elsewhere who think that it is much nicer to treat the acute sufferers, who quickly respond to treatment, in preference to these poor creatures.[52]

In the children's half of their leprosy settlement at Kumi, the CMS missionaries did preferentially admit patients in the early stages of the disease; fewer than 15 per cent showed signs of visible disability.[53] Kumi was therefore referred to by visiting leprologists as a model leprosy settlement, 'run on the best possible lines; and the methods used are worthy of careful study by those concerned with leprosy relief and control'.[54]

On the other hand, half of the adults at Ongino and half of all the leprosy patients at Lake Bunyonyi evidenced disability and in 1933, the majority of patients at Nyenga were not physically capable of cultivating their own food.[55] Many of these disabled patients would have fallen under the government's category of 'burnt-out' cases and when overcrowding became an issue, the government asked missionaries to admit only 'infectious cases and active cases likely to be benefited by skilled anti-leprosy treatment'.[56] This issue was most contentious at Buluba, because of the combination of overcrowding and the high degree of influence that the local NA had over the settlement. Government officials felt that the work of Buluba was handicapped by the presence of these 'burnt-out' cases and instructed Buluba to discharge their 'burnt-out' cases in 1943, after a sleeping sickness outbreak limited the amount of land available for cultivation and drastically increased the upkeep costs of the in-patients. The FMSA missionaries complied, but afterwards continued to admit these advanced cases, which government officials occasionally commented on with disgruntlement.[57]

The issue of the care and housing of 'burnt-out' cases came up at a number of meetings of BELRA's Uganda Branch throughout the 1940s. At a 1943 meeting:

> Attention was drawn to the existing tendency to retain such cases in institution partly from laudable motives of sympathy with the afflicted, but also because it was in many cases extremely difficult to arrange for their reception.

> It was pointed out that the advantages of discharging non-infectious cases as soon as it was safe to do so lay not only in the erection of more accommodation for active lepers but in the encouragement given to all, by the reasonable expectation of early release, to remain in the institutions until treatment has been completed.

> It was further agreed that the care of those burnt out cases was not a primary responsibility of the committee and after discussion it was resolved: 'That the attention of Government should be drawn to the necessity for the erection of institutions for the care of the disabled, infirm and helpless, without undue delay.'[58]

Such institutions were labelled the responsibility of the NA and not something for the medical department or missionaries to worry about. The missionaries, however, disagreed and the CMS settlements, in particular, continued to harbour large numbers of 'burnt-out' cases. This resulted in a very low discharge rate: in 1946, 5.6 per cent of the patients at Kumi were discharged and 4.2 per cent of the patients at Lake Bunyonyi. The FMSA settlements, on the other hand, which had more competition for space because of their size and which were more subject to the will of the government, discharged far more patients in this year: 20 per cent at Nyenga and 32 per cent at Buluba.[59] These higher discharge rates did not mean that the FMSA actually treated more leprosy patients that the CMS. The opposite was true, given the greater size of the CMS settlements, which treated a total of 1575 patients in 1946, as compared to 525 at the FMSA settlements. Moreover, clinically speaking, a leprosy patient was only an 'arrested' case if two years of observation passed without any symptoms of the disease reoccurring.[60] There were a high number of voluntary readmissions to the FMSA settlements as a result of the FMSA's policy of paroling patients before the observation period had elapsed. The CMS preferred that this two-year observation period elapse while the patient was still within the settlement, especially in the case of child leprosy patients, and this also contributed to their lower discharge rates. Regardless of the medical discharge policies of each mission, higher discharge rates and more admittances could be achieved, which the missionaries knew and ignored.

Humanitarian pressures and the over-emphasis of leprosy

In spite of these continuing government concerns over the efficacy and expense of in-patient leprosy treatment, the government continued to provide a large portion of each settlement's financial support. Combined, the Protectorate government and NAs supplied approximately half of each settlement's annual budget, throughout the colonial period.[61] Part of the reason that the government supported the leprosy settlements so heavily was because there were humanitarian and political benefits for them in doing so, as discussed earlier in the chapter. The other reason was the pressure applied on them by missionaries and external humanitarian organizations.

In 1927, the government found itself being pushed into action by missionaries and a secular humanitarian organization, after 20 years of diffidence on the issue of leprosy. Reverend Oldrieve visited as part of a larger tour that he made through British East and West Africa, on behalf of BELRA.[62] BELRA was founded in 1923 as the first explicitly secular humanitarian organization addressing the issue of leprosy in the Britain and its colonies, and in promoting their leprosy work throughout the empire, BELRA's leaders found that

> [t]he most effective way of influencing medical administrators in the Colonies...has been by personal contact with the Association's experts. With the cordial co-operation of home and overseas Colonial officials, the Association from the first arranged tours of their secretaries in the colonies...The results thus achieved will serve to illustrate the leprosy problem of the Empire, both as to what has already been achieved and, more important still, as to what awaits solution through future work.[63]

Oldrieve's leprosy tour of Uganda was the first in a series of BELRA visits that took place over the colonial period and it was calculated to stimulate a leprosy control programme in the Protectorate, though as yet BELRA had relatively little money to offer in assistance. Oldrieve's tour did indeed have some of the intended effect, creating a small ripple in Uganda's government, though not an entirely enthusiastic one.

Anticipating Oldrieve's arrival, DMSS Chell prepared a report on leprosy in Uganda and the outline of a potential leprosy campaign, which he forwarded to provincial commissioners for comment, so that when Oldrieve arrived they might 'place before him some scheme capable of introduction to combat the disease'. The DMSS, at least, was inclined to pursue leprosy work, writing that the figures on leprosy, 'if true, show the need for immediate action'.[64] Set in motion by Oldrieve's visit, the DMSS began the first coordinated government attempt to plan a policy of leprosy control in Uganda, involving central, provincial and district medical and administrative officers. Whatever his personal opinions may have been, Chell's successor, DMSS Keane, tried to quell colonial administrative officers' dissent towards the foundation of in-patient leprosy settlements because

> [i]t will be most disastrous to the cause of leprosy in Uganda if any idea of opposition, by the Government generally or by the Medical Department, to the British Empire Leprosy Relief Association or to any of the doctors concerned in treating Leprosy, is allowed to gain ground.

> There is unfortunately no question that the London British Empire Leprosy Relief Association with the best intentions is communicating freely and independently with local doctors as well as with the Uganda Branch Council.[65]

In one instance, after a meeting between missionaries and government officials over the leprosy settlement at Lake Bunyonyi, he wrote to the DC that 'If the [minute record] reaches Dr. Sharp or Dr. Smith unamended a wrong impression and perhaps misunderstanding might be created and this I am sure you wish to avoid at all costs', particularly because he was sure that 'Dr. Sharp will report to Sir Leonard Rogers on arrival in London.'[66] Sir Leonard Rogers was an eminent leprologist and one of the founders of BELRA.

Contact between Uganda's leprosy missionaries and BELRA representatives in England created tensions and difficulties for government officials on numerous occasions over the years. In 1929, there were several months of protracted debate over Dr. Wiggins' use of compulsion in Teso out-patient leprosy treatment. The DMSS was against compulsion and backed by the governor, their greater authority prevailed in ending the practice. However, DMSS Keane attributed the length of the debate and the resentment that was created to the influence of BELRA. Dr. Wiggins, he wrote, was 'an emissary partly of Sir Leonard Rogers, is naturally a strong upholder of his ideas', and

> [i]t must be recognised too, that British Empire Leprosy Relief Association, London, is communicating directly with individual workers here. Their acts, although well-intentioned, do rather detract from the object of the local Council. One result is that certain workers here get few benefits from the parent Association while others get a great deal. The Secretary of the British Empire Leprosy Relief Association has written an apology on the matter but the practice still continues.[67]

Gradually, it became accepted practice for BELRA grant requests to go through the Uganda Branch Committee, but occasionally missionaries tried to circumvent this process by appealing directly to London. For example, in 1946 when Buluba's FMSA missionaries hoped to get a larger grant than they believed the Uganda Committee would allow them for the installation of a water pump, they appealed directly to BELRA's London office.[68] When the members of the committee found out about this, they were considerably annoyed and such instances highlight the possibilities for manipulations and tensions to arise because of the interventions and priorities of different humanitarian actors.

There are numerous other instances when the contact between Uganda's missionaries and BELRA representatives created tensions or problems for government officials and pushed them to spend more money on leprosy and exert more compulsion than they felt was wise, at the expense of people suffering from other diseases. In 1929, for example, 'District Commissioners are constantly being asked for assistance to force lepers in for treatment and to force segregation', contrary to instructions from the medical department.[69] After a visit from BELRA's medical secretary in 1938, the chief secretary asked the DMS Kauntze to write a report on government assistance for the mission leprosy settlements and he wrote:

> Pneumonia and gonorrhoea are much greater dangers to the community than leprosy; pneumonia is the cause of the largest number of deaths in hospital and gonorrhoea and its complications beside leading to sterility in women is the cause of great morbidity and suffering. Recently new drugs have been produced which give most satisfactory

results in these cases. However large the sums given to leper settlements, a demand for still further extension will be made since only a fraction of the total cases of leprosy in the country are dealt with in these settlements. From the point of view of the greatest good, it would appear to be more advantageous to buy the new drugs for pneumonia and gonorrhoea referred to above than to increase grants for a disease which will undoubtedly disappear with an improved standard of living and hygiene.[70]

He observed that 'Shs.59/- a head was expended upon lepers, as against Shs.9/- a head upon all other types of patient and suggested that the results achieved were disproportionate to the expenditure.'[71] However, district administrators informed the DMS that in 1937, they had committed five years of building grants to the leprosy settlements and they could not withdraw financial support.[72] Humanitarians could influence colonial government officials to spend money even against their better judgement, especially when it often took only one or two officials to agree to a grant.

The gradual eradication of leprosy

After Dr. Innes' strict censures of leprosy control in Uganda in 1948, the colonial government decided that if they were going to expend money on leprosy, they would do so more effectively, in the better interests of Uganda's public health. In 1947, the first biomedical treatment definitively proven to effectively treat leprosy was discovered: sulphone drugs. As the leprosy settlements began using these drugs, between 1948 and 1950, the time needed for the treatment of each patient shrank rapidly, usually to less than two years. This allowed for the possibility of radically changing leprosy treatment, as most patients could be healed and rendered non-infectious within a shorter period of time and the in-patient settlements could treat a larger number of individuals. A leprologist for Uganda was appointed in 1951 and in addition to the in-patient leprosy settlement, African local governments started opening small leprosy villages, where leprosy sufferers could receive medication.[73] Kumi and Buluba began formal training programmes for Ugandan leprosy orderlies, who would supervise these leprosy villages and out-patient dispensary treatment.

Under new schemes of leprosy control, more leprosy sufferers did come into contact with biomedicine, but these leprosy assistants could not always be relied upon to give adequate treatment to all the patients

under their care and the leprosy villages quickly degenerated into ter-
rible conditions.[74] The efficacy of leprosy control in any given area
depended upon a proactive district leprosy officer, who could arrange
for assistants to travel all over the countryside on motorbikes to give
medication regularly to any leprosy sufferers.[75] In the postcolonial
time period, there were several individuals whose teams of leprosy
orderlies were quite effective in reducing the incidence of leprosy in
specific regions, with generous financial assistance from humanitarian
organizations such as the German Leprosy Relief Association.

Between 1951 and the 1990s, leprosy was almost entirely eradicated
in Uganda, more or less under the helm of a handful of missionary
nurses and Ugandan doctors and the Ugandan leprosy assistants that
they trained, with the financial backing of foreign humanitarians. In the
1980s, as leprosy was gradually disappearing, the networks of leprosy
treatment were re-tasked into leprosy and tuberculosis programmes,
as the leprosy and tuberculosis bacilli are very similar. Today, these
leprosy and TB officers primarily treat HIV/AIDS patients suffering from
tuberculosis.

Continuities, consequences and conclusions

The seeds of leprosy control that were planted in 1927 eventually led
to the eradication of leprosy in Uganda and in the meantime those
leprosy patients who were able to obtain leprosy treatment at the mission settlements were able to benefit from palliative care, biomedicine
and technical training, which often improved the future course of their
lives. Missionaries, external humanitarian organizations and the government officials who supported leprosy work as a humanitarian endeavour
approached in-patient leprosy treatment with the best of intentions and
undoubtedly had a positive influence on the lives of several thousand
people.

This chapter by no means wishes to detract from the service that
humanitarians and their Ugandan staff provided in improving the
futures of these thousands of people and the personal sacrifices that
many of them made in this endeavour, Ugandans and Europeans
alike. After visiting the hospitals that remain at three of these former
colonial leprosy settlements, I am full of admiration for the achievements of these hospitals and their past and present staff. The fact
remains, however, that for most of the colonial period, humanitarians
approached leprosy treatment in a manner that they knew would
reach only a small minority of all the leprosy sufferers in Uganda,
not only because of their limitations of staff and resources but also

because in-patient leprosy settlements better suited their ideals for evangelization and the civilizing mission. They had opportunities to pursue different policies of leprosy control and chose not to follow them.

Consequently there were many more thousands of leprosy patients who never had the opportunity for biomedical treatment and even more thousands of people suffering from other ailments such as gonorrhoea and pneumonia who did not receive the less costly biomedical treatments that could have had a more positive effect on their health than could the treatment available for leprosy treatment before 1948. This was largely due to the perceived religious and social benefits of caring for supposedly vulnerable leprosy sufferers in settlements, rather than out-patient clinics, and the political pressure brought to bear on the colonial government by British humanitarians.

Today's humanitarians to Africa still face this dilemma of whether to use finite resources to treat a relatively small number of sufferers of a particular disease, instead of preventing transmission of that disease, or, alternatively, treating larger numbers of people more cheaply for a different, equally destructive disease. In *The White Man's Burden*, economist William Easterly discusses exactly this problem in relation to the fight against HIV/AIDS in Africa. Although he points to health as the area in which humanitarian aid to Africa has enjoyed the most conspicuous success, he also points out the failure of humanitarians to prevent the onset of the AIDS crises, even though many were aware of the epidemic's increase through the 1980s and early 1990s. The aid community began addressing the issue of HIV/AIDS only after so many millions had become infected that the problem became visible to the Western world.[76]

Although leprosy never carried the morbidity and mortality risks of AIDS, even with a relatively small population of leprosy patients, it was a very visible disease with obviously disfiguring symptoms that captured the imagination and made leprosy sufferers the object of pity. Compassion, Easterly argues, has often been a guide to humanitarian aid, but not always an effective one, because it can lead people to focus on solutions that cost more lives than they save. A large portion of the aid community's resources are being funnelled into anti-retroviral treatment for HIV patients who are already suffering, when encouraging preventive measures instead would cost less and arguably save even more lives. Furthermore, there are other diseases, such as malaria, tuberculosis and diarrhoea, that kill two and a half times as many Africans and some of these diseases are far more cheaply prevented and treated than HIV and AIDS.[77]

Similar again to the religious and social choices that humanitarians made in colonial Uganda by choosing in-patient leprosy treatment, many of today's humanitarians approach aid with a 'salvation agenda'.[78] The PEPFAR campaign launched by America's Bush administration in 2003 is a prime example of the moral and political agenda of donors negatively affecting the health of African recipients. Influenced by evangelical Christian supporters of the Bush administration, PEPFAR encouraged HIV prevention education through abstinence-only, even though successes in reducing HIV/AIDS in Senegal and Uganda had demonstrated how effective condom use could be in preventing the spread of HIV.[79] This is reminiscent of immorality policies at Uganda's mission leprosy settlements: if a patient was caught having sex outside of marriage, they were expelled from the settlement and cut off from the biomedical treatment that it provided.

In conclusion, humanitarians, and medical humanitarians in partic- ular, have great capacity to do good in Africa, saving lives through the prevention and treatment of myriad diseases. But humanitarian organi- zations and the governments and donors who so often support them do not always make the choices that are in the best interests of Africans' public health, though they might believe them to be for the public 'good', especially if good is defined in terms of morality. This pattern, of specific, visible diseases that evoke special compassion being approached in such a way as to treat fewer people expensively, rather than more people cheaply, is not new to the modern humanitarian landscape. The precedents of moral and social agendas influencing the health choices of humanitarians and of political agendas necessitating a certain degree of government compliance and assistance to humanitarians were set dur- ing the colonial period and continue today. In some cases, the same charities are involved, such as Oxfam and the Red Cross, who made annual donations to the missions and leprosy-specific charities that supported Uganda's leprosy work starting in the 1940s.

Though it may be with the best of intentions, Western humanitarians have a history of approaching African health and deciding which dis- eases are worthy of attention and in what ways that attention should be focused, without reference to the wishes and needs of the poor who are actually suffering. There is a great sense of blame for the HIV/AIDS epi- demic that is attributed to Africans, with their supposedly uncontrolled sexuality and 'backward' habits. But fewer people examine the role that the Western world has played in creating contemporary Africa's health crises, through colonialism and uneven humanitarian aid in the past.[80] This chapter has sought to show that even with the best of intentions, medical humanitarians have long approached the health of Africans with their own priorities, even purposefully choosing to save fewer lives in order to fulfil these agendas.

Notes

1. Philip Curtin, *The Image of Africa: British Ideas and Action, 1780–1850* (Madison, WI: University of Wisconsin Press, 1962), 71.
2. Joseph R. Oppong and Ezekiel Kalipeni, 'Perceptions and Misperceptions of AIDS in Africa', in E. Kalipeni, Susan Cradock, Joseph R. Oppong, and Jayati Ghosh, eds, *HIV & AIDS in Africa: Beyond Epidemiology* (Oxford: Blackwell Publishing, 2004), 47–8.
3. Alex de Waal, *AIDS and Power: Why There is No Political Crisis – Yet* (London: Zed Books, 2006), 63; Michael Adas, *Machines as the Measure of Men: Science, Technology, and Ideologies of Western Dominance* (Ithaca, NY: Cornell University Press, 1989).
4. Peter Williams, 'Healing and Evangelism: The Place of Medicine in Later Victorian Protestant Missionary Thinking', in W. J. Shiels, ed., *The Church and Healing* (Oxford: Blackwell, 1982), 276; A.F. Walls, ' "The Heavy Artillery of the Mission Army": The Domestic Importance of the Nineteenth-Century Medical Missionary', in W. J. Shiels, ed., *The Church and Healing* (Oxford: Blackwell, 1982), 290.
5. Frank Prochaska, *The Voluntary Impulse: Philanthropy in Modern Britain* (London: Faber and Faber, 1988), 81; David Hardiman, ed., 'Introduction', in *Healing Bodies, Saving Souls: Medical Missions in Asia and Africa* (Amsterdam: Rodopi, 2006), 20.
6. Matthew, 10:8.
7. Rosa May Langley, 'Miss Langley's Account of Answered Prayer', *Ruanda Notes*, 43 (1933): 12.
8. LEPRA Office, Colchester, England, British Empire Leprosy Relief Association Annual Report, 1935.
9. Zachary Gussow and George Tracy, 'Stigma and the Leprosy Phenomenon', *Bulletin of the History of Medicine*, 44.5 (1970): 425–49.
10. Leprosy Mission Archives, Brentford, England (Leprosy Mission), 118/16, Letter from Dr. Wiggins to Anderson, Secretary, Mission to Lepers, 1 January 1929.
11. 'The Healing Fellowship', *Mission Hospital*, 43.500 (September 1939): 236.
12. Rosa May Langley, 'Report of Happenings among the Lepers', *Ruanda Notes*, 54 (October 1935): 15; Rosa May Langley, 'News of the Lepers', *Ruanda Notes*, 41 (July 1932): 16–17.
13. Leonard Sharp, 'Dr. Sharp's Letter', *Ruanda Notes,* 43 (1933): 27.
14. Mother Kevin, 'Mother Kevin's Worldwide Appeal for the Lepers', *The Universe*, 19 January 1934.
15. Prochaska, *The Voluntary Impulse*, 81; Anna Crozier, *Practising Colonial Medicine: The Colonial Medical Service in British East Africa* (London: I.B. Tauris, 2007), 61; Hardiman, 'Introduction', 20; Jinja District Archives, Jinja, Uganda (JDA), Medical Leprosy, Letter from Senior Medical Officer, Jinja, to District Commissioner (DC) Busoga, 26 September 1930; JDA, Medical

Leprosy, Memo from Director of Medical Service (DMS) Buchanan containing summary of BELRA Meeting Notes from July 1943; Leonard Sharp, 'Kigezi', *Mission Hospital*, 32.364 (May 1928): 103.

16. T. O. Beidelman, *Colonial Evangelism: A Socio-Historical Study of an East African Mission at the Grassroots* (Bloomington, IL: Indiana University Press, 1982), 21; Brian Stanley, *Bible and the Flag: Protestant Missions and British Imperialism in the Nineteenth and Twentieth Centuries* (Leicester: Apollos, 1990), 157–61; University of Birmingham Special Collections (Birmingham), CMS/G3/AL Adelaide Kent 1938.

17. Uganda Medical Department Annual Report (London: Government Printer, 1908), 38.

18. Uganda Medical Department Annual Report (London: Government Printer, 1921), 13.

19. Uganda Medical Department Annual Report, 1921, 13, 20; Uganda Medical Department Annual Report (London: Government Printer, 1912), 11.

20. Uganda National Archive, Entebbe, Uganda (UGA), A46/2374, Replies to the Questionnaire of the British Empire Leprosy Relief Association, June 1924.

21. UGA, A46/2374, Letter from Frank Oldrieve to Sir W. F. Gowers, 20 September 1926.

22. Robert G. Cochrane, 'Leprosy in Uganda', *Leprosy Review*, 2.2 (1931): 59; United Kingdom National Archives, London, England (UKNA), CO/685/15, Uganda Medical Department Annual Report, 1931, 29–31; UGA, J6/25I, Dr. Innes Report 12; UKNA, CO/685/31, Uganda Medical Department Annual Report, 1948, 15.

23. 'Annual Report Number', *Mission Hospital*, 36.415 (August 1932).

24. UKNA, CO 685/10, Uganda Medical Department Annual Report, 1931, 99–104.

25. UGA, J6/25I, Dr. Innes Report 5.

26. Rubaga Cathedral Archives, Kampala, Uganda (RCA), Kumi, Lake Bunyonyi, Nyenga, and Buluba Annual Reports, 1946; UKNA, CO 685/10, Uganda Medical Department Annual Report, 1931, 29.

27. UKNA, CO 685/10, Uganda Medical Department Annual Report, 1931, 8, 17, 92.

28. UKNA, CO 685/30, Uganda Medical Department Annual Report, 1947, 55; UGA, J6/25I, Dr. Innes Report 12.

29. Leprosy Mission, 118/16, Dr. Wiggins, The Proposed Anti-Leprosy Campaign in Teso, 1 June 1928.

30. JDA, Medical Leprosy, Letter from Eastern Provincial Commissioner (PC) to Chief Secretary and Director of Medical and Sanitary Services (DMSS), 23 May 1927; Leprosy Mission, 118/16, Dr. Wiggins, The Proposed Anti-Leprosy Campaign in Teso, 1 June 1928.

31. Clare Aveling Wiggins, 'Ng'ora', *Mission Hospital*, 32.364 (1928): 106.

32. Birmingham, CMS/G3/A10/m1A, Letter from Dr. Wiggins to Hooper, CMS Secretary, 31 March 1929.

33. Leprosy Mission, 118/16, Letter from Dr. Wiggins to Anderson, Secretary, Mission to Lepers, 23 February 1929.

34. Leprosy Mission, 118/16, Letter from J.E.H. Cook to Rev. Syson, 25 April 1929.

35. Leprosy Mission, 118/16, Letter from Dr. Wiggins to Anderson, Secretary, Mission to Lepers, 26 April 1929.
36. Ibid.
37. Ibid.
38. Birmingham, CMS/G3/AL C.A. Wiggins 1930; J. E. H. Cook, 'Editorial Notes', *Mission Hospital*, 33.376 (May 1929): 104.
39. Birmingham, CMS/G3/A10/m1A, Kumi Annual Report, 1941.
40. Bishops House, Jinja, Uganda (BH), Nyenga Leper Camp, Mother Kevin's Proposed Scheme for New Leper Colony, 1933.
41. Kabale District Archives, Kabale, Uganda (KDA), Medical General, District Medical Officer (DMO) Kigezi, Routine Treatment of Leprosy at Sub-Dispensaries, April 1930.
42. KDA, Medical General, Letter from DC Kigezi Philipps to the Western PC, 24 April 1929; KDA, Medical General, DC's Office Diary on Leprosy in Kigezi, 1930.
43. UGA, 4001, Letter from DMS Earl to Chief Secretary, 21 November 1938.
44. JDA, Medical Leprosy, Letter from DMO Mackichan to DC, April 1943; JDA, Medical Leprosy, Letter from DC to Provincial Medical Officer (PMO), April 1943.
45. JDA, Medical Leprosy, Letter from Eastern PMO to DC Busoga, March 1943.
46. UGA, J6/25I, Dr. Innes Report 1.
47. Leonard Sharp, 'Dr. Sharp's Account of the R.G.M.M. and Leprosy', *Ruanda Notes*, 26 (October 1928): 6.
48. KDA, Medical 1930–39, Letter from Dr. Sharp to DC Kigezi Bell, 10 December 1932.
49. Adelaide Kent, 'Leper Children's Home', *Mission Hospital*, 42.486 (July 1938): 162.
50. Sir Leonard Rogers and Edward Muir, *Leprosy* (Bristol: John Wright & Sons), 227.
51. UGA, C1384, Letter from Eastern PC Weatherhead to Chief Secretary, 5 April 1929.
52. Langley, 'Miss Langley's Account', 11–12.
53. Leprosy Mission, 119/4, Letter from A. Downes-Shaw to Anderson, Secretary, Mission to Lepers, 8 June 1934; Margaret Laing, 'Children's Leper Home, Kumi, Teso', *Mission Hospital*, 40.464 (September 1936): 248.
54. Edward Muir, 'Uganda', *Leprosy Review*, 10.1 (1939): 44.
55. Laing, 'Children's Leper Home', 248; KDA, Medical 1930–39, Lake Bunyonyi Annual Report, 1936; BH, Nyenga Annual Report 1933.
56. JDA, Medical Leprosy, Letter from DMO Busoga to DC Busoga, 19 April 1944.
57. JDA, Medical Leprosy, Letter from Eastern PMO to DC Busoga, 23 February 1943; JDA, Medical Leprosy, Letter from DC Busoga Jenkins to Mother Solano, 3 October 1945; JDA, Medical Leprosy, Letter from Mother Solano, 11 June 1946.
58. JDA, Medical Leprosy, Memorandum from DMSS to PCs after BELRA Meeting, 31 July 1943.
59. RCA, Kumi, Lake Bunyonyi, Nyenga, and Buluba Annual Reports, 1946.
60. Rogers and Muir, *Leprosy*, 254.
61. Information gleaned from those annual reports that are available for each settlement.

62. UGA, A46/2374, Report of a Meeting of the Medical Sub-Committee of BELRA, 28 October 1927.
63. Leonard Rogers, *The Foundation of the British Empire Leprosy Relief Association* (Watford: Voss and Michael, 1945), 14.
64. JDA, Medical Leprosy, DMSS Chell, Report on Leprosy, 23 January 1927.
65. UGA, C1384, Letter from DMSS Keane to Chief Secretary, 10 April 1929.
66. KDA, Medical General, Letter from DMSS Keane to DC Kigezi Philipps, 30 March 1929.
67. UGA, C1384, DMSS Keane, 'The Leprosy Problem in Uganda', 10 April 1929.
68. RCA, Letter from Secretary, Uganda Branch BELRA to General Secretary BELRA London, 9 October 1946.
69. UGA, C1384, Letter from Eastern PC Weatherhead to Chief Secretary, 5 April 1929.
70. UGA, 4001, Letter from DMS to Chief Secretary, 18 March 1939.
71. UGA, 4001, Excerpt from record of discussion re Medical Estimates, 1940.
72. UGA, 4001, Excerpts, 28 March 1939.
73. UKNA, CO 685/30, Uganda Medical Department Annual Report, 1951, 5.
74. Directorate of Health, Jinja, Uganda, Leprosy Assistants Annual Reports, 1962–63; Interview with Pat Gilmer, 4 November 2009.
75. Interview with Pat Gilmer, 4 November 2009; Interview with Gabuyeri and Ben Mayanja, 11 August 2011.
76. William Easterly, *The White Man's Burden: Why the West's Efforts to Aid the Rest Have Done so Much Ill and So Little Good* (Oxford: Oxford University Press, 2006), 215–16.
77. Easterly, *The White Man's Burden*, 221–3.
78. De Waal, *AIDS and Power*, 63.
79. Easterly, *The White Man's Burden*, 225–6.
80. Susan Hunter, *Who Cares? AIDS in Africa* (Basingstoke: Palgrave Macmillan, 2003), 9–10.

3
Contraband Charity: German Humanitarianism in Contemporary Kenya

Nina Berman

From its beginning in the late fifteenth century onwards, European and, later, Western economic and political expansion was tied to a presumably humanitarian trajectory. Operating on the premise that colonialism was beneficial to the subjugated populations, this humanitarian trajectory was, at first, carried out under the banner of Christianity, which delivered the ideological framework that legitimized Portuguese, Spanish and then other European efforts to dominate the territories and peoples of the Americas, Africa and Asia. By the eighteenth century, civilizationism, which emerged out of Christian teleology, *Heilsgeschichte* (salvation history) and Enlightenment thought, had become the secular centrepiece of colonial and imperialist ideology.[1] The Christian mission was not replaced but supported by the civilizing mission and both provided the rationale that functioned to justify large-scale destruction and economic exploitation, in spite of, as ought to be acknowledged, often considerable resistance from individual missionaries, especially in Latin America.[2] In today's world, the Christian missionary spirit and civilizationism have found new ways of expressing their age-old tenets in the form of the discourse of humanitarianism. In light of this history it seems neither possible nor meaningful to follow Gary J. Bass who argues for 'keep[ing] a bright line between empire and humanity'.[3] Rather, the history of humanitarianism is one of those complicated entangled histories that are particularly relevant to understanding relations between the global south and the global north.

Humanitarianism is central to modern society's self-image, which is visible in the actions of governments and non-governmental organizations and also in the deeds of ordinary citizens. Thus far, critical inquiry has mostly focused on organized forms of humanitarianism. It has, for example, debated the success of humanitarian interventions, mostly military in nature, into crisis areas, be they led by the United Nations or NATO or various world powers.[4] Scholars have also questioned the success of both governmental and non-governmental economic and political development programmes.[5] But humanitarianism has cast a much wider net. It brings in a vast array of non-governmental actors and structures north–south relations at the micro level in a range of diverse scenarios. One case of humanitarianism that is defined primarily by individuals rather than international non-governmental organizations (INGOs) or political states are the activities of Germans, Swiss and Austrians in contemporary Kenya. Tourism brought a host of visitors to Kenya and these visitors have had a large impact on Kenyan society through a multitude of humanitarian projects. While some of this assistance does occur inside the framework of international and local non-governmental organizations, my discussion centres on the actions of German-speaking individuals who support Kenyans as a result of interpersonal contact – contact that is outside of governmental and INGO structures. This 'contraband charity' has a significant impact on local infrastructures and on the interaction between Kenyans and the (mostly) European visitors and immigrants to the country.

I will begin my discussion of this case of informal charity by briefly reviewing aspects of the history of humanitarianism through one of its central figures, Albert Schweitzer, who plays a crucial role in the German-speaking context. I will then turn to exploring the legacy of Schweitzer, as it emerges in German, Swiss and Austrian humanitarianist activity in contemporary Kenya. My discussion reviews the type of initiatives German-speaking humanitarians engage in, how they set up their work and what effects it has on the Kenyan context. I end my discussion by acknowledging the longue durée of the humanitarianist paradigm through the eyes of some of its critics.

Albert Schweitzer – humanitarianist par excellence

While Henri Dunant, the founder of the International Red Cross, may be seen as representing the beginning of *institutionalized* international humanitarianism, Albert Schweitzer embodies humanitarianism on a more *individualized* and *personalized* level.[6] He is probably the most visible figure of Western humanitarianism in the first half of the twentieth century and, thus, engaging with key tenets of his thought and examples of his actions provides an excellent entry into understanding contemporary forms of humanitarianism.

Schweitzer lived from 1875 to 1965 and worked as a medical doctor in Gabon between 1913 and 1965, with long stretches spent in Europe throughout the years. Salient to understanding the relationship between Christianity and contemporary humanitarianism, originally Schweitzer had wanted to go to Africa as a missionary. In 1904, he had read an article by Alfred Boegner, the director of the Paris Mission Society, concerning the need for personnel in Gabon.[7] For Schweitzer, this request for help became his calling. The revelation resonated with his recent studies on Jesus, so Schweitzer sent a letter to Boegner offering his services as a missionary. But the Paris Mission Society rejected Schweitzer, whose religious views seemed too liberal and thus irreconcilable with the society's missionary goals. Though Schweitzer might have been successful had he applied with another, perhaps Lutheran, missionary society, such as the Allgemeiner Evangelischer Missionsverein, it seems the rejection helped Schweitzer realize that he could reach his goals by pursuing another path. In 1905, though having already been awarded doctorates in philosophy and theology (he was also an expert in organ building and wrote seminal musicological studies for which he received an honorary doctorate in music), he enrolled as a medical student at the University of Strasbourg.

When he had completed his medical studies, Schweitzer contacted the Paris Mission Society again. After some back and forth that was related not only to Schweitzer's controversial theological views but also to political issues and questions of national allegiance in the context of international colonial disputes, he was successful. This success was primarily due to Schweitzer's tremendously effective fundraising efforts, which would allow him to take up his work in Gabon self-funded. He only needed the permission of the Paris Mission Society to stay as a guest at a mission and in 1912, the authorization was finally granted. This nexus of humanitarian aid and personalized fundraising, which Schweitzer pursued throughout his humanitarian career by performing as a pianist and organist and by giving lectures, is noteworthy. It structures the scope and scale of humanitarian work to this day.[8]

As a doctor in Gabon, Schweitzer clearly healed scores of Africans and saved countless limbs and lives in his decades of work in Gabon. But when we take a look at his views of 'Africans' (he rarely speaks about the local Gabonese with any measure of specificity; in spite of being fluent in several European languages, he also never learned any of the local languages) and at his interactions with them, we notice several features that indicate a thoroughly paternalistic approach. Throughout his auto-biographies and also in many of his letters, Schweitzer essentializes the individuals he engages with according to culturalist and civilizationist models of society. The philosophical roots of these views can be found in Schweitzer's theoretical writings, including in his cultural philosophy, published in two volumes in 1923 as *Verfall und Wiederaufbau der Kultur* (Decline and Rebuilding of Culture) and *Kultur und Ethik* (Culture and Ethics). In these works he claims, in Hegelian fashion, that all cultures reflect distinct developmental stages in a presumed evolution of ethics. In a sweeping gesture, Schweitzer divides all civilizations into *non-ethical* and *ethical* cultures.[9] Africa, according to this model, falls into the cate-gory of the non-ethical, while Europe remains the representative of the highest form of ethical culture.

While Schweitzer's philosophical writings present us with an abstract paradigm designed to explain the difference between Africa and Europe, his autobiographical writings provide examples that resonate with his philosophical views. Especially behaviours that conflict with his idea of *reverence for life* (Ehrfurcht vor dem Leben), another key concept in Schweitzer's philosophy that draws on Christianity and Kantian ethics, are seen as indications of an inferior ethical sense. Africans, for example, are unreliable and superstitious (*Zwischen Wasser und Urwald*, GW 1, 344; 350; 363–5; 377; 405). They constantly lie and steal (*GW 1*, 409; 410–12; 459), are wasteful (*GW 1*, 416), irresponsible (*GW 1*, 437) and cruel to animals (*GW 1*, 333). He argues that the African, non-Christian sense of justice precludes empathy (*GW 1*, 385–6). Schweitzer considers the absence of ethics (*Briefe aus Lambarene*, GW 1, 558) a reflection of a peo-ple's state of cultural development: 'As true savages they are still quite far beyond good and evil' (*GW 1*, 555). Christianization remains a central element of the civilizing mission: 'Therefore, the native experiences sal-vation through Jesus as a twofold liberation. He moves from a fearful to a fearless and from a nonethical to an ethical worldview' (*Zwischen Wasser und Urwald, GW 1*, 457). Rationality – the modern Western, scientific view of the world – and Christianity are the cornerstones of Schweitzer's humanitarian philosophy.

An interesting question to ask is why Schweitzer was able to muster significant attention, especially after the Second World War? I suggest that Schweitzer provided an alibi for the Western world at a time when the globe was devastated as a result of the Second World War and the wars of independence that were fought in the colonies. Schweitzer's humanitarianism exculpated the West from its sins and, at the same time, was an integral part of what kept dependency and exploitation alive. Like other internationally known humanitarians he received the Nobel Peace Prize for his work in Gabon (1953, retroactively for 1952). That prize, of course, was tied to humanitarianism from its inception; in 1901, the first prize went to Jean Henri Dunant, the founder of the Red Cross and was shared with peace activist Frédéric Passy. Schweitzer became a global figure who symbolized the blessings of Western civilization. Famous for his medical work more than his occasional work as a missionary, he, more than any other activist of the mid-twentieth century, facilitated and popularized the shift from religiously inspired missionary work to the humanitarianism that we know today. In 1947, *Life* magazine celebrated him as 'the greatest man of the century', and he remained an icon of humanitarianism for many decades.[10]

Particularly in Germany, Switzerland and Austria, the man from Alsace (who had to change citizenship as a result of the First World War) became a vehicle for Germans to restore their shattered self-image after 1945. His legacy is visible to this day in the many societies, hospitals, schools and streets that are named after him in Germany, Austria and Switzerland. His legacy is also visible in the 'Culture of Charity' that has developed since the Second World War, a culture that is primarily directed at Africa and that found expression in countless organizations devoted to helping Africans.[11] This 'Culture of Charity' has roots also in other domestic traditions of voluntary philanthropy, but through the figure of Schweitzer these various traditions merge and provide a direct link to Africa.[12] For the younger generation, Schweitzer has been replaced by Bob Geldof, Bono and Angelina Jolie, to name only a few of the international celebrities who inspire the aid industry. In the German-language context, specifically, actors, musicians and soccer stars, such as Karlheinz Böhm, Herbert Grönemeyer and Philipp Lahm, have played an important role in continuing and further popularizing humanitarian work in Africa.[13] Indeed, I would argue that for the ordinary citizen humanitarian, this genealogy of celebrities, from Schweitzer to Lahm, is more relevant than, for example, the goal of bringing democracy and human rights to crisis areas – the customary argument used to justify military humanitarian interventions and the work of Human Rights INGOs.[14]

Overall, mainstream humanitarianism in the German-speaking world focuses on Africa. A quick search on the Internet will bring up numerous links to humanitarian organizations that seek to raise funds for projects in various locations in Africa. The general interest in helping Africans has increased exponentially over the past 30 years and, I want to suggest, is closely correlated to economic and political policies that have increased African dependency during that same time period. In Germany, Austria and Switzerland, helping Africans has become an integral feature of national culture. Donating to some sort of charity that provides assistance to Africans is a standard ritual during Christmas seasons; special appeals in response to famine or other catastrophes are made throughout the year; and individuals and organizations sponsor orphans or pay school fees. Countless Germany-, Switzerland- and Austria-based networks are tied to specific locations in Africa. These organizations are further complemented by a multitude of individual humanitarians, who are inspired by Schweitzer and his contemporary incarnations and who often hope to emulate these figures in earnest ways.

German humanitarians in Kenya

Direct interpersonal contact is often the first step towards a sustained relationship between humanitarians and the individuals they intend to help and that contact often emerges in the context of tourism. My study focuses on Diani, a community located on the south coast of Mombasa and one of the main centres of beach tourism in Kenya. Germans, Swiss and Austrians were crucial in developing the tourism infrastructure and, over the past 40 years, German-speaking tourists and settlers have contributed to shaping life in the area. In addition to vacationing as tourists, they are active in the area as managers of hotels; owners of boutiques, travel agencies, nightclubs, diving businesses and restaurants; landlords of expensive villas; and employers of Kenyans. Some move to Kenya to retire and some engage in binational romantic relationships. Over time, the activities of these tourists and settlers have had a significant impact on the local community, affecting shifts in landownership, commercial infrastructure, population growth, interpersonal relations and various patterns of social and cultural practices.

In particular, real estate development and those sectors of the economic infrastructure that are related to tourism and owned by white expatriates as well as African, European and Indian Kenyans have often created disadvantages and significant losses for the African Kenyans who are indigenous to the area, namely the Digo people.[15] Particularly consequential were the Structural Adjustment Policies imposed on Kenya by the World Bank and International Monetary Fund in the early 1990s.[16] The negative impact of these policies on populations around the world is, by now, well documented.[17] The policies made it much easier for foreigners to invest and to buy land in Kenya, resulting in substantial changes in landownership and the development of foreign-owned businesses in the area. Some individuals were simply kicked off their land and several lawsuits are still pending. Many title deeds were forged, by various parties and mostly to the disadvantage of less powerful individuals. Other villagers sold their land to German and other developers, but often they were not able to use the profit from the sale in beneficial ways. They were unaccustomed to an investment-oriented economy and in many cases lost the substantial sums received from the sale of land within a short period of time. As a result of these shifts in landownership, some of the individuals who were previously able to sustain themselves because they grew food on their land (and sometimes also for sale) and who owned their own homes now pay rent and work salaried jobs, if they can find any. In addition, the expansion of the tourism industry brought larger numbers of up-country immigrants to the area and intensified the struggle over available resources.

In a way, what has occurred in Diani is an example of gentrification, whereby poorer and less powerful members of a community are forced to give way to profit-based development. Ethnicity, development and economic factors are intricately tied in each case of gentrification. The tremendous changes of the past 20 years have destabilized previously existing social networks and has made the area vulnerable to illegal activities, such as drug trafficking and prostitution.[18] Colonial and postcolonial Kenya has a long and complicated history with regard to landownership and so what we are looking at here adds another chapter to this painful story.[19] What we see happening in Diani is also part of the 'Second Scramble for Africa' that we are currently witnessing throughout the continent and which is generating as of yet unforeseeable consequences.

German tourists and settlers in the Diani area, for the most part, are not aware of the reasons for the poverty and the need they encounter. For the most part, those who engage in humanitarian activity are not aware of the links between the poverty they see and the structural adjustment policies imposed by wealthy Western nations. Rather, they interpret what they see along the lines of deeply ingrained notions about an African need for assistance. Albert Schweitzer, Bono and Karlheinz Böhm have shown the world how to act in Africa and have received worldwide recognition for their actions. Contemporary tourists and settlers are eager to place themselves in this tradition, especially once they realize that even small sums of money can have tremendous impact.

In the late 1990s, I conducted my first study on German, Swiss and Austrian repeat visitors who vacationed on the Diani coast and learnt about the extent and nature of their interaction with the local population.[20] The repeat visitors I interviewed had vacationed in Kenya at least more than once and, in some instances, more than 20 times. In all cases, there was significant contact between the local population and the tourists. The majority (70–80%) of repeat visitors supported Kenyans materially in one way or another. They paid education fees for different types of schools, such as primary and secondary schools, language institutes and driving schools; they bought school supplies and uniforms; they took care of hospital bills and paid for other medical needs; brought clothes, household items and electronic appliances; and even helped people build their own homes.

My present study again explores aspects related to German humanitarian activities in the area, which usually occurs under the rubric of 'charity'. I have widened the scope of my analysis to include the actions of local settlers and to investigate different forms of charity. Some individuals are active as members of INGOs and some have founded locally based organizations that extend support to Kenyan Africans in various forms. The main focus of my discussion here, however, are the actions of repeat visitors who are not tied primarily to an INGO or other form of organizational context, even though some of them may over time have joined an NGO based in Germany, Switzerland or Austria and also decided to support an INGO. Still, their main activity is neither tied to an INGO nor any other organization that is registered in Kenya. This particular form of charity, 'contraband charity', is thus not caught by analyses of humanitarian work that focus on INGOs or official forms of governmental and supra-governmental aid (World Bank, IMF, UN). This omission is significant, as contraband charity is a widespread phenomenon in areas that are tied to a tourism infrastructure, such as the Diani community.

Let us take a look at the actions of one representative couple that, over time, built a support network in Germany and who are increasingly taking on projects of increasing volume and significance. I met Gustav and Bertha Müller in January 2010, sustained email contact with Mr. Müller afterwards, met up with him several times in summer 2011 and once in summer 2012.[21] The Müllers have been travelling to Kenya since 1991 and over time donated time and money to a range of activities. They initially acted quietly or, as Mr. Müller put it, *im Stillen*. While they first pursued their activities alone, eventually they established a support network in Germany that is raising ever-increasing sums of money. While Mr. Müller indicated that his network had raised over €25,000 for 2009, he expected the sum to rise to 100,000 in 2011. As of May 2010, the association, which is also loosely connected to a larger and more visible network, is registered as a non-profit organization in Germany (einge-tragener Verein). The Müllers thus founded what critic Laura Polman calls a 'MONGO', 'My Own NGO', in contrast to more established and professionally organized NGOs or INGOs.[22]

Since 2005 the main focus of the Müllers and their association has been Kijiji village, which is located at a significant distance from Diani. About 12,000 individuals live in the area connected to the village. Among the various projects, including some in locations other than this particular village, are replacing defunct water pumps; building toilets and shower stalls in several areas; sponsoring school children (Germans pay fees and supplies for – in 2011 – 48 children); supporting schools (supplying books and providing water tanks); supporting the Kwale District Eye Centre (through donations, but also by collecting used eyeglasses and buying and reselling items from the Eye Clinic Char-ity Shop); supporting orphans (three children from Kijiji village were brought to an orphanage in another location); building water tanks in various locations (to date, nine water tanks have been built in Kijiji vil-lage alone); providing mosquito nets (in 2008, for example, the initiative distributed over 1000 nets); supporting health dispensaries (the organi-zation provides a significant amount of medications); creating employ-ment (through support of wood carvers and musicians); and supporting an SOS children's village (to date, three children have been sponsored).

The funds are raised in Germany. Initially, the Müllers relied on their private network and over time the association reached a substantial number of supporters in their hometown and the surrounding areas. Various fundraisers are held throughout the year, at birthdays, anniver-sary parties and also more public events. The Müllers have been savvy with regard to the handling of money. Funds for schools and other ini-tiatives are transferred directly into bank accounts in Kenya and the Müllers collaborate with several individuals who keep the books. Mr. Müller, now retired, can draw on his professional experience as a for-mer member of the management team for a company that employed 1000 individuals. Mrs. Müller worked as an administrator in an office. Together they have the know-how pertinent to dealing with various aspects of their humanitarian initiatives.

To give me a sense of the extent of his activities, Mr. Müller invited me in July 2011 to spend a day with him visiting a number of the projects he had sponsored or was in the process of sponsoring. The account of this day-long journey is instructive as it provides insights into the activities of one individual who clearly emulates Schweitzer's model, who has carved out a space and a role for himself that affects the lives of hundreds of Kenyans and whose activities, for the most part, occur without any knowledge or involvement of the Kenyan state or any kind of INGO.

Mr. Müller, who usually stays in one of the most expensive hotels at the coast, had rented a large impressive SUV. To me, it seemed as if he had no problem with this display of wealth, which is something that I also observed in other contraband, as well as sanctioned, charity workers and which does not go unnoticed by locals. As one a local Digo man once said to me, 'At least the missionaries of old used to live with us in the village.' We left Diani at around 8:30 a.m. On our way out, we picked up various people, among them a doctor who works at a dispensary that we would visit later. Others were waiting along the road to hand their requests or contractor quotes to Mr. Müller. One contractor provided Mr. Müller with a quote for a toilet to be built next to another dispensary still under construction.

Just before Kijiji village we stopped at a borehole in the area of Umoja Village. In 2009, Mr. Müller had noticed that the old pump was defunct and decided to replace it and improve the installation and reach of the pump. Materials and labour had cost only about €1000, so with relatively little money Mr. Müller and his organization were able to support the livelihood of the approximately 400 people who benefit from the borehole. Without the functioning pump, villagers would have to walk more than two hours to the next borehole. Closer to Kijiji Village we stopped at another borehole. Here the pump had been replaced in 2010. Mr. Müller also built a trough to catch the dripping water from the pump, which now can be used by thirsty cows. It also nurtures a few banana trees that villagers planted on the moist soil at the end of the trough. Because cows had eaten some of the bananas, the village chairman wanted to build a fence and during our visit he asked Mr. Müller for a kilogram of nails. At this and all other boreholes we visited, locals recognized Mr. Müller and engaged in friendly conversation with him. In a way and visually supported by the impressive vehicle he used, he reminded me of a District Development Officer checking on the facilities of the area.

We then arrived at a private primary school in Kijiji that enrols 160 children, 40 of whom, I was told, are orphans. It includes the three levels of kindergarten and eight classes of primary school. The school, which was founded in 2008, employs 14 teachers, including the headmaster. Mr. Müller came into the picture in 2009. The Müllers and their network donated desks and a cupboard for the office, which they commissioned to local carpenters. Mr. Müller insisted that involving small businesses in the country is much preferred over bringing large machines to existing factories in Kenya: 'That only destroys the local infrastructure', he pointed out to me. He had also commissioned the construction of a water tank for the school. The tank catches the rainwater from a couple of roofs and provides water for cooking and drinking. The government regularly inspects the water quality.

Mr. Müller proudly drew my attention to the cleanliness of the schoolyard. He explained that this was part of the agreement between him and the school, namely that the compound had to be kept in good shape. His organization had also built a new toilet (and here, getting a permit from the Ministry of Health was mandatory) – 1 toilet for 160 students only, but still better than the previous installation. His group also provided a high number of mosquito nets for the children; this time alone they had brought 500. A local doctor helps with the distribution of the mosquito nets and also documents everything for the donors. The headmaster showed us the results of the last state-administered tests and was excited to point out the improvement from the previous year. He was also proud of the fact that 8 out of 11 graduates from 8th grade had continued on to secondary school. 'This would not have been possible without the books you provided', he said to Mr. Müller. Adjacent to the primary school is a vocational school. Here, Mr. Müller was given a 'Request for Assistance', which asked for nine mechanical sewing machines and three boxes. Mr. Müller has supported this school before and accepted the request for consideration.

Our next stop was the Kijiji dispensary. The building, which was originally built in 1990 with funds from several non-Kenyan organizations, consists of five small rooms and serves a community of roughly 1500 individuals each month. The services include outpatient treatment, TB-testing and treatment, HIV-testing and treatment, immunizations, prenatal care, child welfare, laboratory services and family planning. Here, Mr. Müller and his organization supplement the resources provided by the government. The government restocks the dispensary every three months, but, according to a doctor who works at the dispensary, the clinic usually runs out of supplies about halfway through a cycle and the additional supplies are much welcomed. In February of 2011, Mr. Müller funded the installation of solar panels on the roof, which now supply electricity. Apart from the availability of light during, for example, night-time deliveries, the electricity also enables the dispensary to maintain a refrigerator for medications. A staff house was also equipped with solar panels. 'We only bring contemporary technology, nothing outdated', Mr. Müller explained.

During our visit, Mr. Müller received a request for repair and painting of the building, especially the roof. The government had been delayed in allocating funds for building maintenance, although the doctor said that the government just devised a new scheme, called Hospital Services Funds, which may provide some support. The doctor insisted that the fee of 20 KShs collected from each patient (which in some cases is waived) and assistance received by the government do not cover the expenses. Salaries, medical supplies (such as cotton pads and gloves) and medications, let alone building funds exceed the available resources. Other needs exist in addition to the renovation of the building: the existing water tank, for example, is not sufficient and the nearby borehole is not functioning.

Our next stop was another private primary school that was founded in 2005. In the summer of 2011, 187 children were enrolled, including three kindergarten levels and grades 1–8. The school employs 11 teachers, 2 cooks, 1 watchman and 1 guard. Mr. Müller and his organization sponsor 39 children with a scholarship of €150 a year, which covers most of the expenses. They also built two water tanks and a toilet. The school is running in spite of the fact that it is not yet registered. What is missing, according to government guidelines, is a permanent structure, one with a proper foundation. Constructing this permanent building with four classrooms was one of the projects Mr. Müller was supporting in 2011. A building for the administration, including rooms for the headmaster and teachers, is also planned.

Next we visited a public secondary school. It was built about a decade ago on a compound that featured an unfinished school structure that had deteriorated into ruins. Inspired by personal contact with one of the villagers, a German woman had taken on the project and rebuilt the structure. The school opened in 2000 and, when I visited in 2011, it was in excellent shape on well-maintained grounds. The school enrols 800 students, 600 of which are girls who stay on the campus as boarders, while the boys live off campus. Mr. Müller and his organization replaced the existing but defunct water pump. They installed a submersible pump and drilled a very deep hole, after which the pump began to deliver 2500 litres per hour. The water is of drinking-level quality and Mr. Müller was very proud to show me how clear it runs. The pump is running on a generator, as the school has no electricity. For the near future, Mr. Müller was sponsoring the building of a pipe to water tanks located higher up on the school grounds, as well as pipes that will bring the water to other buildings.

Next door is a public primary school. Mr. Müller is planning a project that would also deliver water to that school. The plan is to run a pipe from the secondary school to a 5000-litre capacity water tank that will be built at the primary school. During my visit – and brought on by some of my questions – a discussion occurred about the contribution of villagers to the project. It was agreed upon, after some resistance from the headmaster and only in the vaguest of terms, that villagers will support the building process with their labour, as a kind of matching donation. While we were visiting, Mr. Müller was presented with a handwritten letter of request for assistance, on college-ruled paper, that spelled out the various aspects of the water pipe and water tank project.

On our way back to the Diani area we passed by another borehole where the organization had replaced and enhanced the pump. Our last stop was a large primary school that employs 40 teachers and enrols about 1500 children in kindergarten through eighth grade and that recently added a first level for a secondary school. The headmaster explained that many of the children are orphans and the school also has a unit for mentally challenged children. Mr. Müller's organization installed a 250-meter water pipe, added electricity for a submersed water pump, installed a water tank, built a tower for the new tank, renovated the nursery, bought toys, added an outside veranda and built an indoor kitchen (an improvement over the previous outdoor cooking facility). They also support a feeding programme for the kindergarteners and for the first level of the secondary school; the local representative of the organization delivers food two to three times a month. In addition, the organization was building 20 toilets, in four phases. The first phase had been completed and Mr. Müller proudly presented the five new toilets, a dramatic improvement over the two long-drop toilets that had served the school's children until recently (the teachers had access to another set of two toilets). The headmaster and others call Mr. Müller 'Papa', a clear expression of the role he is playing at this school. He would often pick up one of the children and walk around with a child in his arms. At two of the schools, the children sang for us. Mr. Müller's style of interaction with the various people we encountered was jovial. He picked up the local style of bantering very well and clearly feels comfortable in his role. His English skills are not perfect, so at times he is not able to communicate verbally with quite the politeness he intends, but his gestures and mimicry support the generally warm affect that he exudes.

Why would anyone be critical of the work done by Mr. Müller and his organization? Clearly, the activities of Mr. Müller, his organization and others like it contribute effectively to developing crucial areas of the local infrastructure, such as sanitation, schools, health and water supply. In many ways these activities seem more effective than what results from what Dambisa Moyo calls 'systematic aid – that is, aid payments made directly to governments either through government-to-government transfers (in which case it is termed bilateral aid) or transferred via institutions such as the World Bank (known as multilateral aid)'.[23] As Carol Lancaster has shown, 'aid agencies themselves have often lacked the technical experience, local knowledge, staff and appropriate processes to manage such projects and programs effectively'.[24] In contrast, Mr. Müller and his organization seem more successful than the agents of systematic aid and also those who work for INGOs, which have been criticized for large overhead costs, ineffective management and questionable outcomes.[25] What then are the main objections that can be raised with regard to contraband charity?

1. Contraband charity releases the state from its responsibilities, feeds corruption and impedes the growth of local industries. I asked Mr. Müller about his relationship to the Kenyan state. Clearly, it would be inconceivable for a Kenyan individual to act in Germany or any Western country the way Mr. Müller acts in Kenya, building toilets and schools and distributing medications without permission from the state. Considering Kenya's governmental structures, contraband charity, by definition, occupies an unregulated space. Mr. Müller's organization is not registered in Kenya (and only recently in Germany) and Mr. Müller has never been to Msambweni's or Kwale's District Commissioner, District Education Officer, or District Development Officer. At some point he considered registering as a local organization, but felt this would inevitably lead to conflict with the Germany-based organization: 'Because then we have two organizations with different goals', he explained. In a few cases, Mr. Müller went through official channels – such as when a sanitary unit attached to a dispensary had to be approved – and most of the time these interactions were initiated and carried out by Mr. Müller's local contacts. Mr. Müller admitted to me that, at some point, he had been approached by a representative of the Ministry of Health who had asked him to stop importing and handing out medications free of charge, as this interferes with the local pharmaceutical market. Mr. Müller recounted that on one occasion he had brought in 20,000 tablets for epilepsy, in response, as he insisted, to the absence of a functioning government programme. But it seems that the prohibition to import medications illegally has no effect on Mr. Müller's choices. As he confided to me, this visit alone, he brought

200 kilograms of supplies, including medication, first aid kits, a wheel chair and a bicycle. Interestingly, airlines are complicit in the smuggling in of contraband charity items, as they will transport cargo for various charitable organizations for free.

I interviewed several government officials in Msambweni and Kwale districts about their view on contraband charity.[26] The officials were clearly aware of the phenomenon, but they could not provide any data or quantify the level of activity by any measure. Overall, the agreement was that informal charity interferes with the planning of the respective offices. A tourist might, for example, build a school in an area that already has enough schools, while the biggest need might be in another part of the district. At the same time, government officials did not reject informal charity outright; they granted that the area benefits from the funds, as they do improve the infrastructure. My conversations brought into focus the extent to which government officials have little control over the actions of tourists and other do-gooders in the area. While I have no evidence for corruption that may occur in conjunction with the cases of informal charity I researched, the reputation of Kenyan officials as corrupt may also be a factor influencing donors to act outside of the official channels. With regard to the coastal area, however, the large amount of informal charity may actually buttress the inaction of government officials. Their work is being done by someone else. Thus, there is less pressure on government officials to create a functioning infrastructure. State funds can disappear without anyone noticing their absence; as with other forms of aid, contraband charity 'props up corrupt governments'.[27]

In this regard, contraband charity not only feeds graft and corruption, it is also a dimension of the 'NGOization' of Kenyan society, whereby mostly foreign-based organizations complement, but more often interfere with, the responsibilities of the state and local communities.[28] A health worker who is based in the Diani area stressed that the state at times prohibits the activities of INGOs because they conflict with the work of Kenyan state-run organizations and private industries and thus practically disable the state and impede the growth of the local economy. What emerges then is a fundamental conflict between human rights (which many humanitarian aid organizations and individuals who engage in humanitarian work foreground as a rationale for their actions) and citizenship rights, between the internationalist framework of human rights and the sovereignty of the nation state and national economies. Humanitarians engaging in contraband charity are unlikely to reflect on this dimension and their attitude is reminiscent of dominant features of the colonial period, whereby the laws valid in the colonizer's home country did not apply in the colonized state. Contraband humanitarians put themselves above the Kenyan law, but Kenyan officials and communities enable this behaviour and thus undermine the institutions (which are also weakened by, for example IMF and World Bank structural adjustment policies) that are deemed crucial to sustainable development.[29]

2. Contraband charity encourages illegal activity. Contraband charity may also increase illegal activity in areas other than graft and corruption. Donations of medications have significant consequences here. As medications are delivered to government dispensaries without any official mechanism controlling the volume and nature of the donations, the reselling of donated materials has become a widespread phenomenon.[30] Donors are usually unaware of the black market for drugs and medical supplies. They operate with an image of doctors and other medical personnel that is based on the relative affluence of these professionals in European countries. It may be inconceivable to these donors to think that a doctor they befriended would choose to sell donated medications under the table.

Humanitarians are dependent on their local confidantes and usually do not suspect them to be complicit in illegal schemes or to simply betray their trust. I came across cases where the local contacts of a donor or donor organization were clearly taking advantage of their role by managing to put 20–50 per cent of the costs associated with projects into their own pockets. One organization claimed that they had a foolproof system of reconciling expenses, which entailed bringing all of the involved parties to the table to compare the figures. 'One hundred percent of our money goes to Kenyans!' the representative of the donor organization proudly assured me. It is certainly true that a much higher percentage of these aid funds arrive in Kenya than is the case with, for example, systematic development aid, where much of the aid remains in the donor country and large sums disappear into the pockets of government officials. With contraband charity, yes, all of the money arrives in Kenya, but not all of it necessarily reaches the aid projects humanitarians are supporting. What this particular donor did not know was that everyone but him had already agreed on the figures in advance of the meeting and he was thus cheated collectively by the whole lot of contractors and collaborators. My background research clearly showed that Müller's organization pays significantly more to contractors and other contacts than the various projects call for. Another organization did not suspect that it had collaborated with individuals, such as the principal of a school, who were known to be corrupt. In addition, there are questions around the practice of donating funds to schools that are not registered. Is this wise? Who checks on the qualifications of teachers? What are the indicators that the children receive a proper education? What is the mechanism for establishing that a child is indeed an orphan? Often based on whim and without a system of checks and balances, all in all, contraband charity encourages a culture of betrayal and graft.

3. Communities are not held accountable. Most tourists and others who engage in contraband charity make no attempt to ask for a contribution from the communities or individuals they support. At times villagers may be asked to do some of the manual labour needed to dig a well or build a school. But most of the time, donors will simply also pay for the labour and consider these payments support of the local labour force through the creation of job opportunities. This approach is contrary to approaches common in the more professional sectors of the aid industry, whereby mechanisms are devised so that communities can be self-empowering, instead of even more dependent on outside assistance.[31]

The dominant model of charity in Diani assumes, creates and perpetuates a lack of agency in individuals and the community as a whole. Historical forms of solidarity, such as the *mweria* or *utsi* (helping each other) system of the local Digo and Duruma peoples, are replaced by appeals to charitable organizations to, for instance, build toilets and dig wells.[32] The older generation of villagers born in the Diani area remembers the days of *mweria* and *utsi* events, such as communal fishing, harvesting and building activities. Humanitarians have never even heard about these practices. But even the younger generation of local Digos, for example, has never participated in these activities; they have come to rely heavily on outside assistance. Especially the younger African Kenyans I interviewed insisted that they were glad for the support they received from international donors; they complained that the government was not helping them and that it was better to receive aid from German and other individuals and organizations. These attitudes point to the generational conflicts that plague Kenyan society, whereby younger men and women feel immobilized by the gerontocratic power structures of the society. In addition, the often repressive and corrupt nature of post-independence African governments has led to disenchantment with state institutions.[33] Avoiding or diverting the conflict with their elders, the younger generation often turns to outside assistance.[34]

Another factor enabling the culture of charity are indigenous social structures, by which older and more powerful members of a community are expected to help others. These patterns of support were rooted in reciprocity but also in other forms of philanthropic forms of support. As Steven Feierman explains,

> [s]ub-Saharan Africa, in the centuries, before colonial conquest, was a region where voluntary giving was, in a majority of cases, grounded in reciprocity and yet where inequalities existed, where kindly help was as double-edged as it is in the philanthropic West – a peculiar combination of caring and dominance, of generosity and property, of tangled rights in things and in people, all in a time and place where the strong would not let weak go under, except sometimes.[35]

After reviewing various forms of philanthropy in pre-colonial Africa, he stresses that 'After colonial conquest, every one of the philanthropic institutions described in this essay was transformed.'[36] Developments in the Diani area indicate that the age-old structures of communal support and philanthropy are indeed no longer in place and I suggest that they are, in part, being transferred onto the relationships involving humanitarians. The number of registered contemporary community-based organizations is quite low; as of summer 2012, for example, 29 organizations were registered in Kwale District, one of the main areas close to Diani and their activities range from a focus on poultry-keeping to poverty eradication.[37] Certainly, a significant disconnect exists between local community-based organizations and the international aid industry.

Charity, in this regard, mirrors aspects of the colonial paradigm by assuming a lack of initiative and a high degree of helplessness in the local population and by misinterpreting local conditions. Historical predecessors for the activities of today's humanitarians include the anti-slavery campaigns which generalized African servitude, masked the reasons for it and suppressed awareness of the fact that, for example, large sectors of the pre-colonial East African economy drew on salaried labour.[38] The paternalist model of charity disempowers Kenyan Africans and shifts responsibility for a wide range of social concerns to non-Kenyans. It encourages Kenyans to manipulate and exploit the aid industry, seemingly pursuing opportunity, but clearly not considering the long-term detrimental effects.

4. Informal charity, like most forms of contemporary humanitarian aid, compensates for the effects of disempowering international economic and political policies and actions. What emerges in this analysis

of German, Swiss and Austrian activities in present-day Kenya are a number of unintended and poorly understood consequences of humanitarian work. On a larger scale, charity compensates for the inequalities exacerbated by globalization. Yet, those involved in charitable action usually have no knowledge of World Bank and IMF structural adjustment policies; they lack historical knowledge; and they are unaware of the connection between, for example, debt politics, currency politics and privatization and the poverty levels that have increased as a result of some of these policies.[39]

While scholarship has amassed considerable evidence about the various failures of aid, the general public in, for example, Germany, Switzerland and Austria, has not been sufficiently exposed to these arguments. In fact, they tend to *culturalize* the situation they intend to address, identifying culture and pre-modern lifestyles as the root causes of Kenya's economic and political challenges. While contraband humanitarians are quick to talk about sustainability and insist that 'Africa must help itself', they are neither aware of the overall structural impact of their actions, nor of the relationship between humanitarian aid and the economic and political dimensions of the current phase of globalization. Also, they do not at all see their actions and attitudes as part of a continuum that includes the colonial period; rather, they emulate historical models of charity as part of what Nicholas Stockton, a former executive director of Oxfam, calls the 'moral economy'.[40]

5. Contraband charity, like other forms of aid, does not address systemic issues. In spite of the tremendous influx of money provided by contraband humanitarians, INGOs and systematic aid, the coastal province remains one of the least developed in Kenya. Kwale and Msambweni, the two districts in Kenya's Coast Province that receive most of the humanitarian aid, show alarming rates of poverty and illness:

- over 70 per cent of the population in Kwale District lives below the poverty line,[41]
- the area lags behind in terms of education, in particular 'enrollment of girls in primary and secondary schools is one of the lowest in Kenya at 63.8 per cent and 10 per cent respectively, compared to 76.3 per cent and 21 per cent nationally',
- the infant mortality rate is above the national average, at 9 per cent,
- malnutrition in children under five is 13 per cent,[42]
- people living in the rural areas have no electricity,[43]

- access to health care facilities is limited, 'with some people having to walk more than 20–30 kilometres to reach the nearest health facility'.[44]

These figures confirm findings discussed by, among others, William Easterly, who has shown that, in most cases, aid does not lead to an increase in growth and development.[45] While the reasons for the lack of development in Kwale and Msambweni are more complex than what can be addressed here, it seems that the various forms of aid that have been initiated by Europeans and that have poured into the districts over the past 40 years has had only little effect on improving the overall situation of people living in the area.

From tutelage to coevalness

From the beginning of Europe's expansionism, critical voices condemned Christianization by force and questioned civilizationism. Dominican friars Antonio de Montesinos (died 1545) and Bartolomé de las Casas (1484–1566) were among the first to expose the abuses of the colonial regimes. Specifically, Las Casas's *A Short Account of the Destruction of the Indies* (written in 1542, published 1552) and *Apologetic History of the Indies* (written in the 1550s, first published completely in 1909) stand out as testimonials chastising the genocide of the indigenous Americans.[46] Another early critique was articulated by Michel de Montaigne in his essay 'Of Cannibals' (1580), in which he exposes the hypocrisy of the civilizationist argument.[47] By the nineteenth century, the contradictions inherent in the Christian mission and civilizationism were quite apparent to individuals living under colonial rule. Edward Wilmot Blyden (1832–1912), for example, who hailed from the Caribbean and was born to slaves with Igbo background, is a case in point.[48] Blyden became an important political figure in the newly founded Liberia (he served as Liberian Secretary of State, Minister of the Interior and ambassador to Britain and France) and produced a significant corpus of philosophical and political writings. He was also a key figure in the development of Pan-Africanism. In what is probably his most widely known work, *Christianity, Islam and the Negro Race* (1887), he outlines the differences between Muslim and Christian approaches to conversion in Africa. Islam, he says, did not destroy local culture and institutions, but rather produced a 'healthy amalgamation and not an absorption or an undue repression'.[49] Most importantly, 'Mohammedanism and learning to the Muslim Negro were coeval. No sooner was he converted than he was taught to read and the importance of knowledge was impressed upon him.'[50] As a result, 'the Mohammedan Negro is a much better Mohammedan than the Christian Negro is a Christian, because the Muslim Negro, as a learner, is a disciple, not an imitator. A disciple, when freed from leading-strings, may become a producer; an imitator never rises above a mere copyist'.[51]

In Blyden's view, the Christian approach towards Africans was thus fundamentally different from the Islamic approach. Blyden describes the basic relationship between Islamic missionary and African convert as one of sympathy.[52] In contrast, 'The Negro, under Protestant rule, is kept in a state of such tutelage and irresponsibility as can scarcely fail to make him constantly dependent and useless whenever, thrown upon himself, he has to meet an emergency.'[53] He further states that, 'the African Christian, who from the pressure of circumstances has been forced into European customs, presents very often to the foreign observer, in contrast with his native brethren, an artificial and absurd appearance. And the missionary, looking from a comfortable social distance, surveys the Europeanised native, sometimes with pity, sometimes with dismay, seldom with thorough sympathy'.[54]

I invoke Blyden here to emphasize the fact that Western humanitarianism, which came to Africa first in the form of Christianity and civilizationism, was inspired primarily not by a sense of shared humanity but rather based on premises of incommensurable difference. The *inclusive* gesture of Christianity as a community of believers was cancelled out by the *exclusive* effects of civilizationism and racism. Overall, the culture of charity in Diani and elsewhere does not indicate a significant break from the colonial models of tutelage and dependency chastised by Edward Blyden and practiced by the likes of Albert Schweitzer. Schweitzer's approach to Africa remains a central source of inspiration, especially for today's contraband humanitarians. Their humanitarianism has religious roots and often continues to operate quite openly under the banner of religious humanitarianism. In addition, the notion of human rights along with naïve ideas about sustainability, self-empowerment and modern civilization provide the ideological framework that inspires informal humanitarians. Much of today's humanitarian work retains the exculpatory function that was observable in the work of Schweitzer and other earlier humanitarianists, especially the anti-slavery activists. The step from tutelage to coevalness still remains to be taken.[55]

Notes

1. For studies on the connection between colonialism and the civilizing mission, see Kavita Philip, *Civilizing Natures: Race, Resources, and Modernity in Colonial South India* (New Brunswick: Rutgers University Press, 2004); Alice L. Conklin, *A Mission to Civilize: The Republican Idea of Empire in France and West Africa, 1895–1930* (Stanford, CA: Stanford University Press, 1997); Lewis Pyenson, *Civilizing Mission: Exact Sciences and French Overseas Expansion, 1830–1940* (Baltimore, MD: Johns Hopkins University Press, 1993); Michael Adas, *Machines as the Measure of Men: Science, Technology, and Ideologies of Western Dominance* (Ithaca, NY: Cornell University Press, 1989).

2. Enrique Dussel, *A History of the Church in Latin America: Colonialism to Liberation (1492–1979)*, trans. Alan Neely (Grand Rapids, MI: Eerdmans, 1981). For a general critique of Christian missionaries, see Gert von Paczensky, *Verbrechen im Namen Christi: Mission und Kolonialismus* (München: Knaus, 1991). On the role of Christian missions in the German context, see Horst Gründer, *Christliche Mission und deutscher Imperialismus: Eine politische Geschichte ihrer Beziehungen während der deutschen Kolonialzeit (1884–1914) unter besonderer Berücksichtigung Afrikas und Chinas* (Paderborn: Schöningh, 1982); Klaus J. Bade, ed., *Imperialismus und Kolonialmission: Kaiserliches Deutschland und koloniales Imperium* (Wiesbaden: Steiner, 1982); Bernhard Mirtschink, *Zur Rolle christlicher Mission in kolonialen Gesellschaften: Katholische Missionserziehung in 'Deutsch-Ostafrika'* (Frankfurt: Haag & Herchen, 1980).

3. Gary J. Bass, *Freedom's Battle: The Origins of Humanitarian Intervention* (New York: Alfred A. Knopf, 2008), 5.

4. See, for example, Linda Polman, *The Crisis Caravan: What's Wrong with Humanitarian Aid?*, trans. Liz Waters (New York: Picador, 2010); Sandra Whitworth, *Men, Militarism, and UN Peacekeeping: A Gendered Analysis* (Boulder, CO: Lynne Rienner, 2004); Anne Orford, *Reading Humanitarian Intervention: Human Rights and the Use of Force in International Law* (Cambridge: Cambridge University Press, 2003).

5. Dambisa Moyo, *Dead Aid: Why Aid is not Working and How there is a Better Way for Africa* (New York: Farrar, Straus and Giroux, 2009); William Easterly, *The White Man's Burden: Why the West's Efforts to Aid the Rest Have Done So Much Ill and So Little Good* (New York: Penguin, 2006); Carol Lancaster, *Aid to Africa: So Much to Do, So Little Done* (Chicago, IL: University of Chicago Press, 1999); Axelle Kabou, *Et si l'Afrique refusait le développement?* (Paris: L'Harmattan, 1991); Brigitte Erler, *Tödliche Hilfe: Bericht von meiner letzten Dienstreise in Sachen Entwicklungshilfe* (Freiburg: Dreisam, 1985).

6. See Linda Polman's critique of Dunant, whom she juxtaposes with Florence Nightingale who argued that 'voluntary efforts, which reduced the expense faced by war ministries, merely made it easier for governments to engage in wars more often and for longer'. *The Crisis Caravan*, 5; see also 2–7. See also John F. Hutchinson who demonstrates that the Red Cross often supported militarism. *Champions of Charity: War and the Rise of the Red Cross* (Boulder, CO: Westview Press, 1996).

7. For an extended discussion of Schweitzer's humanitarianism, see my study *Impossible Missions? German Economic, Military, and Humanitarian Efforts in Africa* (Lincoln, NE: University of Nebraska Press, 2004), 61–97.

8. The literature on fundraising is too vast to cover here in appropriate terms; note, however, that most of the publications are self-help books and other types of supportive literature. Critical studies exist in particular with regard to its connection to upper-class wealth and the corporate world; see, for example, Diana Elizabeth Kendall, *The Power of Good Deeds: Privileged Women and the Social Reproduction of the Upper Class* (Lanham, MD: Roman & Littlefield Publishers, 2002); Reynold Levy, *Give and Take: A Candid Account of Corporate Philanthropy* (Boston, MA: Harvard Business School Press, 1999). For a study on the history of giving in West Germany, see Gabriele Lingelbach, *Spenden und Sammeln: Der westdeutsche Spendenmarkt bis in die frühen 1980er Jahre* (Göttingen: Wallstein, 2009).

9. *Verfall und Wiederaufbau der Kultur, Gesammelte Werke in fünf Bänden*, v. 2, Rudolf Grabs, ed. (München: Beck: 1973), 48. This German edition of Schweitzer's works, which I will quote in the following (*GW 1, GW 2*), was first published by the East German Union-Verlag in 1971. All translations from the German are mine.

10. 'Greatest Man in the World: Albert Schweitzer', *Life*, 6 October 1947: 95.

11. The US has a comparable history of 'good intentions' that focuses on improving the situation of, among others, African Americans. Susan M. Ryan, *The Grammar of Good Intentions: Race and the Antebellum Culture of Benevolence* (Ithaca, NY: Cornell University Press, 2003).

12. For studies on historical forms of philanthropy in the German context, see, among others, Jean H. Quataert, *Staging Philanthropy: Patriotic Women and the National Imagination in Dynastic Germany, 1813–1916* (Ann Arbor, MI: University of Michigan Press, 2001); contributions to Jonathan Barry and Colin Jones, eds, *Medicine and Charity Before the Welfare State* (London: Routledge, 1991); and Catherine M. Prelinger, *Charity, Challenge, and Change: Religious Dimensions of the Mid-Nineteenth-Century Women's Movement in Germany* (New York: Greenwood Press, 1987).

13. In late 1981, Böhm founded 'Menschen für Menschen', an organization dedicated to providing humanitarian assistance to Ethiopia. See http://www.menschenfuermenschen.de/ (accessed 12 October 2012). A German version of Bob Geldof's *Band-Aid* concert was organized by Herbert Grönemeyer in 1985; Band für Afrika produced a single, 'Nackt im Wind', and gave a concert in July 1985. Currently, the Bavarian soccer organization, in conjunction with the Philipp Lahm Foundation, is promoting a fundraiser in support of projects in Africa, 'Tore für Afrika', accessed 12 October 2012, http://www.philipp-lahm-stiftung.de/projekte-aktuelles/tore-fuer-afrika.html.

14. Anne Orford, for example, writes that 'some of the appeal of the idea of humanitarian intervention lies in the moral authority of the notion of democracy'. See *Reading Humanitarian Intervention*, 18.

15. The terms African, Indian and European (or African Kenyan, Indian Kenyan and European Kenyan) are used by Kenyans to describe themselves and others. Only rarely are 'black' and 'white' used as descriptors.

16. Gurushri Swamy, 'Kenya: Patchy, Intermittent Commitment', *Adjustment in Africa: Lessons from Country Case Studies*, Ishrat Husain and Rashid Faruqee, eds (Brookfield, WI: Ashgate, 1996), 193–237; World Bank, *Kenya: Re-Investing in Stabilization and Growth through Public Sector Adjustment* (Washington, DC: The World Bank, 1992).

17. Howard Stein, *Beyond the World Bank Agenda: An Institutional Approach to Development* (Chicago, IL: University of Chicago Press, 2008); Moyo, *Dead Aid*, 19–22; Joseph Kipkemboi Rono, 'The Impact of the Structural Adjustment Programmes on Kenyan Society', *Journal of Social Development in Africa*, 17.1 (2002): 81–98; Natalie Avery, 'Stealing from the State (Mexico, Hungary & Kenya)', in Kevin Danaher, ed., *50 Years is Enough: The Case Against the World Bank and the International Monetary Fund* (Boston, MA: South End Press, 1994), 95–101; Gloria Thomas-Emeagwali, ed., *Women Pay the Price: Structural Adjustment in Africa and the Caribbean* (Trenton, NJ: Africa World Press, 1995); Pamela Sparr, *Mortgaging Women's Lives: Feminist Critiques of Structural Adjustment* (London: Zed Books, 1994).

18. Wanjohi Kibicho, *Sex Tourism in Africa: Kenya's Booming Industry* (Farnham: Ashgate, 2009).

19. Roger Southall, 'The Ndungu Report: Land & Graft in Kenya', *Review of African Political Economy*, 103 (2005): 142–51; Christopher Leo, *Land and Class in Kenya* (Toronto, ON: University of Toronto Press, 1984); John W. Harbeson, *Nation-Building in Kenya: The Role of Land Reform* (Evanston, IL: Northwestern University Press, 1973).

20. For an extended discussion of repeat visitors in Kenya, see 'Tourism: Repeat Visitors Turned Aid Workers in Kenya', in my study *Impossible Missions?* pp. 175–212; an appendix with statistics regarding the interaction between repeat visitors and Kenyans can be found on pages 221–33.

21. The names of the individuals have been changed and I also altered other aspects of their story to ensure anonymity.

22. Polman, *The Crisis Caravan*, 50. Polman argues that nobody knows how many MONGOs exist (53).

23. Moyo, *Dear Aid*, 7. For a brief overview of the recent history of aid to Africa, see Moyo, *Dead Aid*, 10–28.

24. Lancaster, *Aid to Africa*, 4.

25. See, for example, Keith Horton and Chris Roche, *Ethical Questions and International NGOs: An Exchange between Philosophers and NGOs* (Dordrecht: Springer, 2010); for an exemplary critique of human rights INGOs, see Amanda Murdie and Tavishi Bhasin, 'Aiding and Abetting: Human Rights INGOs and Domestic Protest', *Journal of Conflict Resolution*, 55.2 (2011): 163–91.

26. The interviewees chose to remain anonymous.

27. Moyo, *Dead Aid*, 49. The argument is also made at length by George B. N. Ayittey in *Africa in Chaos* (New York: St. Martin's Press, 1998). See also Michaela Wrong's account of the story of John Githongo. While her narrative is often sensationalist and conceptually flawed, Githongo's descriptions of Kenyan graft and corruption are chilling. *It's Our Turn to East: The Story of a Kenyan Whistle-Blower* (New York: HarperCollins, 2009).

28. Makau Matua, ed., *Human Rights NGOs in East Africa: Political and Normative Tensions* (Kampala, Uganda: Fountain Publishers, 2009); Maurice Nyamanga Amutabi, *The NGO Factor in Africa: The Case of Arrested Development in Kenya* (New York: Routledge, 2006); Julie Hearn, 'The "NGO-isation" of Kenyan Society: USAID and the Restructuring of Health Care', *Review of African Political Economy*, 25.75 (1998): 89–100.

29. Ayittey, in his analysis of why structural adjustment programmes failed, insists that 'economic reform without a concomitant political reforms is meaningless'. See *Africa in Chaos*, 247.

30. See Roger Bate, Kimberly Hess, Lorraine Mooney, 'Antimalarial Medicine Diversion: Stock-Outs and Other Public Health Problems', *Research and Reports in Tropical Medicine*, 2010.1 (2010): 19–24; Samuel Siringi, 'AIDS Drugs Being Sold Illegally on Market Stalls in Kenya', *The Lancet*, 363 (31 January 2004): 377.

31. See, for example, Rotary International's publication, 'Communities in Action: A Guide to Effective Projects', which stresses the need to involve communities at any level of project planning and execution (accessed 12 October 2012, http://www.rotary.org/ridocuments/en_pdf/605a_en.pdf). Christoffel-Blindenmission is another organization that emphasizes work with local partners and communities and explicitly states that it 'does not support the "charity model" of disability and of rehabilitation'. *CBM Disability and Development Policy* (Bensheim: cbm, n.d.), 6.

32. On this socio-cultural practice of the Digo and Duruma, see Ministry of Gender, Sports, Culture and Social Services, Department of Culture, Kenya, *Socio-Cultural Profile of the Digo and Duruma Communities, Kwale District: Implications for Development* (Nairobi: Ministry of Gender, Sports, Culture and Social Services, Department of Culture, 2004), 9.

33. Achille Mbembe provides an account of the continuities of colonial structures in postcolonial African states in *On the Postcolony* (Berkeley, CA: University of California Press, 2001).

34. See essays on the situation of youth and youth culture in Kimani Njogu and G. Oluoch-Olunya, eds, *Cultural Production and Social Change in Kenya: Building Bridges* (Nairobi: Twaweza Communications, 2007); Kimani Njogu, ed. *Culture, Performance and Identity: Paths of Communication in Kenya* (Nairobi: Twaweza Communications, 2008).

35. Steven Feierman, 'Reciprocity and Assistance in Precolonial Africa', in Warren F. Ilchman, Stanley N. Katz and Edward L. Queen II, eds, *Philanthropy in the World's Traditions* (Bloomington, IL: Indiana University Press, 1998), 4.

36. Feierman, 'Reciprocity and Assistance', 21.

37. According to Fredrick O. Wanyama, data on successful community-based initiatives in Kenya, remains scarce. 'Grass-Roots Organization for Sustainable Development: The Case of Community-Based Organizations in Western Kenya', *Regional Development Studies*, 7 (2001): 56.

38. See Jan-Georg Deutsch, *Emancipation without Abolition in German East Africa, c. 1884–1914* (Oxford: James Currrey, 2006); Stephen J. Rockel, *Carriers of Culture: Labor on the Road in Nineteenth-Century East Africa* (Portsmouth: Heinemann, 2006); Michael Pesek, *Koloniale Herrschaft in Deutsch-Ostafrika: Expeditionen, Militär und Verwaltung seit 1880* (Frankfurt: Campus, 2005).

39. These policies have been criticized for a long time and recently it seems that, for example, the World Bank is reversing some of its devastating policy decision. Convinced, for example, by the success of Malawi's agricultural subsidy programme, something it had outlawed in the early 1990s, it has begun to provide loans for agricultural subsidy programmes. Roger Thurow and Scott Kilman, *Enough: Why the World's Poorest Starve in an Age of Plenty* (New York: PublicAffairs, 2009), 169.

40. Polman, *The Crisis Caravan*, 39.
41. Kwale Health Forum, 'Strategic Plan' (Diani Beach, Kwale Health Forum, 2004), 5.
42. Ministry of Gender, Sports, Culture and Social Services, *Socio-Cultural Profile*, 1.
43. Ibid., 11.
44. Kwale Health Forum, 'Strategic Plan', 11.
45. Easterly, *The White Man's Burden*, 44–51.
46. Bartolomé de las Casas, *A Short Account of the Destruction of the Indies*, trans. Nigel Griffin (New York: Penguin Books, 1992); Fray Bartolomé de Las Casa, *Apologética historia sumaria*, Vidal Abril Castelló, Jesús A. Barreda, Berta Ares Queija and Miguel J. Abril Stoffels, eds, *Obras Completas*, v. 6–8 (Madrid: Alianza Editorial, 1992). A complete English translation of the text does not seem to exist.
47. Michel de Montaigne, ed., 'Of Cannibals', in *The Complete Works: Essays, Travel Journal, Letters*, trans. Donald M. Frame (New York: Knopf, 2003), 182–93.
48. For a discussion of Blyden in the context of African intellectual history, see Kwaku Larbi Korang, *Writing Ghana, Imagining Africa: Nation and African Modernity* (Rochester, NY: Rochester University Press, 2003), especially pp. 70–89.
49. Edward Wilmot Blyden, *Christianity, Islam and the Negro Race* (Baltimore, MD: Black Classic Press, 1994), 14.
50. Ibid., 15.
51. Ibid., 44.
52. Ibid., 22.
53. Ibid., 47.
54. Ibid., 24.
55. Johannes Fabian identifies the 'denial of coevalness' as one of the central tropes of anthropological discourse on Africa and other non-European cultures. See *Time and the Other: How Anthropology Makes its Object* (New York: Columbia University Press, 2002; 1983), especially pp. 25–69.

4
'Reading' British Armed Humanitarian Intervention in Sierra Leone, 2000–2

Josiah Kaplan

Introduction

Few modern efforts by the international community to resolve complex emergencies through military force have been as widely celebrated in scholarship and the popular imagination as the UK's military deployment to Sierra Leone between 2000 and 2002. In both academic and policy circles, it is almost universally agreed that the UK mission was a resounding success. A small but elite element of British troops is credited with stabilizing the Government of Sierra Leone (GoSL) and the United Nations Mission in Sierra Leone (UNAMSIL), a 17,000-strong peacekeeping force on the verge of collapse at the hands of the insurgent Revolutionary United Front (RUF). Only months after Britain's arrival, the RUF found itself turned back from a position of strength to one of country-wide retreat before GoSL and UNAMSIL counter-offensives coordinated under the direction of the newly arrived UK Army. Shortly thereafter, the country's 11-year old civil war came to a close, with the main rebel ranks surrendering wholesale to the UN's disarmament, demobilization and reintegration (DDR) process a year later. Today, more than decade on, Sierra Leone remains a stable post-conflict state, the beneficiary of sustained British foreign development and advisory assistance.[1]

As such, the British intervention in Sierra Leone has become enshrined as an influential model for future operations throughout the international peace operations policy community. Connaughton argues that the mission 'is probably as good as it gets' in terms of force structure for a rapid-reaction armed humanitarian intervention.[2] For the British public and Western audiences *writ large*, the mission also represents a reassuring confirmation of both the potency and moral authority of the international community. Here, the sound professionalism and leadership of a NATO member-state succeeded in vanquishing a personification, in the RUF, of the kind of African anarchic brutality most often associated with Robert Kaplan and his influential piece 'The Coming Anarchy'.[3]

Sierra Leone also remains a high-water mark in Tony Blair's controversial legacy of interventionist foreign policy, one articulated by Blair in his 'New Doctrine of International Community'.[4] Particularly after the challenges and disappointments of his other troubled experiments in armed humanitarian intervention in Kosovo, Iraq and Afghanistan, Sierra Leone remains to date a personal victory for Blair's legacy – 'at least one place in the world', he joked recently to the BBC, 'where [I] remain wildly popular'.[5]

Indeed, so widely accepted is the British triumph in Sierra Leone that very little academic scholarship in IR and the subfields of peace operations and armed humanitarian intervention studies has bothered engaging it with a critical eye. Within a surprisingly small body of work actually dedicated to examining the operation in depth, Dorman notes that an 'official line' has emerged around this accepted narrative of British success.[6]

This critical silence, however, obscures what I suggest are several problematic issues inherent in the case of Britain's Sierra Leonean intervention. First, I contend that an alternative analysis of Britain's military operations in and around Freetown between 2000 and 2002 suggests a mission far more fragile, prone to risk and idiosyncratic in nature than the literature searching for best practice lessons typically acknowledged – and thus one which, while successful in its own right, should be viewed with greater caution when used as a foundation for modelling future missions. Second, I argue that the very narrative of Britain's experience in Sierra Leone – the accepted 'story' told and retold in both academic and policy circles to lend to these events symbolic meaning – holds explicit parallels to classic 'heroic' intervention narratives of the colonial era, which relied on disempowering racial constructs and the presentation of a totalitizing moral universe for meaning and which, I contend, still find manifestations in contemporary discourse. Following a brief review of the history of Sierra Leonean intervention, I address each critique in turn below.

British intervention in Sierra Leone, 2000–2: History and operational critique

Britain's arrival to Sierra Leone in spring of 2000 was at a late point in the country's complex civil war, a conflict which had been ongoing since the early 1990s and rooted, earlier still, in a post-independence history fraught with instability and political violence.[7] Fighting had first began in March 1991, when Foday Sankoh and his small band of paramilitaries – the self-styled RUF – entered Sierra Leone from Liberia under the guidance and support of Charles Taylor, who sought to destabilize the GoSL by proxy.[8] Sankoh quickly attracted local volunteers with legitimate grievances against the corrupt central state, but just as quickly squandered this base of nascent popular support as RUF fighters began to inflict horrifying abuses on rural Sierra Leoneans – most notoriously through mutilation and child conscription.[9] For the next eight years, the successive efforts of the Sierra Leonean Army (SLA), the private South African security company Executive Outcomes and ECOMOG, a military intervention launched by the Economic Community of West African States and lead by Nigeria to evict the brief but brutal AFRC/RUF junta from Freetown, all failed to halt the RUF's advance permanently.[10] By 1999, a stalemate had arisen, the RUF controlling much of the countryside and well supplied from sales of diamonds from the mineral-rich Eastern and Southern provinces, while the GoSL and ECOMOG troops held Freetown.[11]

A temporary ceasefire in May 1999 led, six weeks later, to a formal peace agreement signed in Lomé, Togo between the GoSL and the RUF, which mandated a ceasefire and ambitious DDR plan for the combatants.[12] To oversee these processes, the UN Security Council deployed UNAMSIL under robust Chapter VII authorization.[13]

From the start, however, the mission proved ineffectual, unable and unwilling, even under its permissive mandate and a subsequent expansion, to force compliance from a defiant RUF.[14] Following a campaign of harassment which culminated in the humiliating capture of 500 Zimbabwean troops and their equipment to an RUF ambush in April 2000, UNAMSIL appeared on the verge of collapse and with it, the GoSL.[15] There thus rose the immediate danger that the capital's civilian population left would be left defenceless against mass violence on the scale of the last RUF occupation of Freetown as part of the AFRC/RUF junta.[16]

Internationally, UNAMSIL's failure also threatened to prove yet another symbolic failure for UN peacekeeping, one that UN Secretary

General Kofi Annan feared might be fatal for its credibility after a trau-
matizing decade of past failures from Rwanda to the Balkans. Against
this tense backdrop, the security council called an emergency meeting in May, pleading for 'all States in a position to do so to assist the
Mission'.[17] Privately, Britain – Sierra Leone's former colonial ruler – had
become the Annan's last hope following firm refusals by France and the
US to commit forces.[18]

Annan's pleas fell on receptive ears within the Blair Administration, for several reasons. Most immediate was the sizeable British
and Commonwealth expat community in Freetown, who demanded
immediate evacuation.[19] Second, Blair had by 2000 identified 'ethical
interventionism' as a defining pillar of his administration's foreign policy in his 'Doctrine of International Community'.[20] A credible UN peace
operations capacity was integral to this doctrine – Britain thus had a
clear strategic incentive in preventing the potential bankruptcy of UN
peace operations legitimacy.[21]

To this end, Foreign Secretary Robin Cook announced Britain's intent
to deploy an evacuation mission to Sierra Leone on 5 May. The following day, a 15-officer Observational Readiness Team (ORT) was deployed
by MoD to Freetown to assess the situation in advance of a larger evacuation force. In conjunction with the British High Commissioner on
the ground, Alan Jones, the ORT sent an urgent – but, ultimately, erro-
neous – report back to Whitehall claiming that RUF troops were within
days of assaulting the city.[22]

On this intelligence, the decision was made to immediately deploy a
650-strong spearhead element from the first Battalion Parachute Regi-
ment Paratroopers (1 PARA) via Senegal, to secure Lungi International
Airport so that British civilians could be evacuated.[23] Here, MoD and
Whitehall, sceptical of the UN's ability to manage the situation on the
ground, were explicit in their desire to deploy unilaterally – all British
forces were to be kept strictly separate from a UN command.[24] This mission, termed 'Operation Palliser', was placed under the command of
Brigadier Sir David Richards and restricted to a limited role of civilian
evacuation.[25]

Once on the ground, however, Brigadier Richards, decided – amidst
confusion from Whitehall and, it appears, largely on his own initiative – to stop what he perceived to be an impending humanitarian
emergency, by escalating Palliser's objective from evacuation to one of
peace enforcement.[26] To this end, armed British patrols were quickly
established around Freetown's perimeter, where they soon clashed with
and twice rebuffed an RUF assault on the airport that left an estimated

20 rebels dead.[27] Meanwhile, rafts of proactive efforts were taken to stabilize the government's threatened lines. British military advisors were
assigned to key positions within the GoSL, the SLA and UNAMSIL HQs
to provide guidance and planning support, while British helicopters and
a newly arrived off-shore naval element offered logistical support to
the overstretched UN contingents.[28] These advisors also began a process of training and equipping local groups opposed to the RUF – such
as the Civilian Defence Force (CDF), a loose coalition of paramilitary
groups and the indigenous militia known as the *Kamajors* – who began
assisting the SLA in a push back on RUF positions outside the city.[29]
In a fortuitous circumstance, Sankoh was captured by local Freetown
paramilitaries and jailed amidst anti-RUF protests.[30] And at the UN, the
Blair Administration spearheaded diplomatic and intelligence-sharing
efforts to curb the international sale of conflict diamonds, effectively
curtailing Taylor's ability to finance the rebel force.[31]

Britain's dramatic and timely arrival had an immediate and unmis-
takeable impact on the morale of both the GoSL and UNAMSIL, with
UN and SLA troops soon resuming patrols into the interior with a
new-found assertiveness as MoD transitioned from Operation Palliser to
Operation Basilica. Momentum, however, was threatened in early 2001
by the capture of 11 British troops and one SLA officer on patrol to
a local bandit group known as the 'West Side Boys' (WSB). This debacle represented a potential disaster for the British, who were presented
with a direct challenge to their legitimacy similar to what had precip-
itated UNAMSIL's crisis of legitimacy the previous year.[32] In response,
MoD authorized Operation Barras, an extremely high-risk airborne rescue operation conducted by SAS operators, which culminated in a
violent raid freeing the British hostages and killing an estimated 26
bandits.[33]

Following Operation Barras, UK forces resumed their scaled-down role
of supporting UNAMSIL and the GoSL, focusing on the tasks of instituting training and security sector reform (SSR) within the SLA under
Operation Silkman.[34] Denied Freetown, weakened by its loss of diamond
revenue, increasingly pushed back by UN/SLA patrols and a new, aggressive Guinean offensive and riven by internal dissent, the RUF finally
surrendered to a new peace treaty and disbanded, its forces entering
the UN-administered DDR process.[35] On 14 January 2002, the Sierra
Leonean Civil War was officially declared over.[36] British military advisors, however, remained in Sierra Leone to oversee continuing SSR
efforts while UK advisors began instituting an ambitious and innovative
development agenda focusing on economic, security governance and

transitional justice reform which continues to this day.[37] Significantly, in 2007 Sierra Leone celebrated its first transparent and peaceful election since 1996, a fitting coda to the accomplishments of the international community in bringing the Sierra Leonean Civil War to a halt.[38]

Operational analysis

Given the events described above, it is hardly surprising that the British military is so widely celebrated for its role in Sierra Leone. Indeed, its performance strongly conforms to the popular image of what Western peace enforcement *should* look like: it is the story of a the potent military capacity of a first-tier NATO member state, deployed rapidly and with a light footprint and unfettered by cumbersome and restrictive UN bureaucracy. Upon arrival, it used the clinical application of force to quickly impose order and stability on the kinds of modern Africa conflicts otherwise beyond the capabilities of weak Southern governments or under-resourced, overly constrained UN peacekeepers to resolve. For influential scholars like Collier, Britain's intervention in Sierra Leone represents, in short, the ideal model for future missions, one which suggests that 'we needed less than a thousand proper soldiers' – Western, professional and well equipped – 'to achieve decisive military change' in armed humanitarian interventions.[39]

Behind the very real accomplishments of Britain in Sierra Leone, however, I suggest that a series of important observations, too often excluded from the literature, problematize the prevailingly optimistic assessment of the mission's performance. These points in no way diminish the laudable achievements of Britain's central role in helping to restore peace and stability to Sierra Leone. They do, however, suggest a note of caution against drawing overly confident conclusions about the ease of reproducing such results in future operations.

First, Britain's success in Sierra Leone was far more contingent on the idiosyncrasies of good fortune that is commonly acknowledged – Connaughton cites 'luck and the process not being tested to the extreme' as a key factor in its impact.[40] Operation Palliser's initial airhead in Lungi, for instance, was tenuous at best and it would have been difficult for Richards to maintain or scale-up to a more ambitious stabilization role had not the naval assets of the Amphibious Readiness Group (ARG) happened to be in region on an exercise and available to reinforce at the time of deployment.[41]

Similarly, the success of Operation Barras' dramatic hostage rescue was by no means a forgone conclusion – tactical details of the operation reveal a raid which could easily have resulted, given on a few differing factors of chance, in the same sort of disaster as befell the equally elite US Delta operators in the disastrous 'Battle of Mogadishu' in 1993.[42] Given the tenuous support for the operation among the British public at the time, it is reasonable to conjecture that the Blair Administration would have faced similarly severe political ramifications as those which forced an American withdrawal from Somalia.[43] Such points underscore just how little leeway even the world's most powerful militaries have in complex, unconventional combat environments – to downplay such risks in drawing best practice lessons for future intervention operations is a potentially dangerous exercise in optimism. Dorman is, to this end, explicit in his warning that, 'in many ways Sierra Leone was too easy for the British and thus provided an artificial example' of the dangers of peace enforcement. He concluded that, while a success, the campaign 'represented an ideal rather than normal mode from which to take lessons' is critical.[44]

Second, the literature tends to focus on Britain's role in halting violence in the Sierra Leonean Civil War at the exclusion of other critical peace enforcement contributing actors on the ground. SLA and UNAMSIL troops, for example, were largely responsible for the bulk of ground combat operations against the RUF, while the UN clearly demonstrated its capacity to conduct robust operations in aggressive actions such as Operation Khukri and its subsequent patrols in RUF territory.[45] ECOMOG's long campaign against Sankoh's forces, notably problematic, nonetheless represented a significant commitment of resources and manpower which achieved several victories, most notably the eviction of the brutal AFRC/RUF junta from Freetown in 1998. The *Kamajor*, an indigenous militia denied the rebels unchallenged control of the countryside for years.[46] Finally, after the RUF leadership opened a late second front on Guinea's border, it was the Guinean Army's devastating counter-offensive which contributed strongly to breaking the RUF's back.[47]

By comparison, although the literature emphasizes British military pressure, UK troops shouldered very little of the burden of combat operations, clashing with the main RUF forces in only one major engagement near Lungi, but otherwise remained restricted to patrols around the Freetown 'horseshoe'. Again, Britain's role in improving morale, stabilizing Freetown and coordinating subsequent efforts against the RUF were instrumental in ending the war – but the RUF's defeat was not accomplished by British troops alone. Anecdotally, interviews with former UNAMSIL and ECOMOG officers routinely highlight resentment at the perceived marginalization of their accomplishments by international media coverage of British accomplishments.[48]

Furthermore, non-coercive efforts were often equally – if not more – effective than military force in subduing the RUF. Olonisakin, for instance, demonstrates the critical impact of the 'Kambia Formula', a diplomatic initiative pushed by UN SRSG in Sierra Leone, Oluyemi Adeniji to reach out to a cornered RUF in May 2001, which ultimately 'opened the floodgate to all sorts of compliance by the RUF'.[49] This effort, integral in revitalizing the UN's stalled DDR process, was initially opposed by the British, who advocated a new push on RUF positions with military force.[50] Yet Britain's own diplomatic and intelligence efforts in interdicting Taylor's diamond trade likewise proved a tremendously influential, and non-violent, component in the RUF's defeat.[51]

These observations are emphatically not intended to diminish the tremendous successes achieved by the British military in Sierra Leone, whose accomplishments speak for themselves. They do, however, suggest that the uncritical promotion of the mission within peace operations literature as a reproducible model of best practice should be avoided. Furthermore, as a basis for suggesting that powerful Western militaries represent a panacea for the operational challenges of peace enforcement, the successful legacy of Britain in Sierra Leone must be considered within the sobering context of a dubious 20-year track record of modern Western experimentation with models of humanitarian intervention, peace enforcement and stabilization involving the use of force. The fact that these endeavours have routinely proven deeply flawed in their implementation – including the recent challenges of US, UK and NATO forces in Iraq and Afghanistan – raises further questions as to whether such unconventional military operations can be reliably conducted with similar success in the future.

'Reading' Sierra Leone: The postcolonial narrative of British intervention

Beyond such technical debates, however, lies a deeper issue for exploration: namely, how the Western imagination has constructed Britain's experience in Sierra Leone within a narrative premised upon normative assumptions regarding international development, Northern and Southern identity. Closer deconstruction of this narrative below helps illustrate, in turn, several important points about the power relations embedded in the conventional wisdom on contemporary humanitarian intervention, particularly from the lens of postcolonial critical theory.

A narrative of any form represents, to begin, a story – a description of events which invest them with an overt or hidden subtext of symbolic meaning that turns subjects of description into signifiers of something else.[52] Cultures continually share and reproduce narratives through a range of popular texts – whether in the form of political rhetoric, media coverage, creative productions such as literature, film and music, or academic scholarship. All narratives carry meanings which are codified and reproduced through their telling and retelling and all contain structural devices used to bring the subject – the reader – 'into' the story, where they can engage with its plot, characters and symbolism on a personal as well as intellectual level. Due to their power to define, reinforce and reproduce specific subjectivities among audiences, narratives in any form of text are thus tremendously influential in shaping individual's understanding of the world around them.

Critical theorists, who seek to identify and challenge hegemonic knowledge, are especially interested in the study of narratives, because it is through this very form of engagement with and subordination to a dominant ideology that individuals are incorporated into pre-existing systems of power. This process of the individual's subordination to prevailing norms via narrative engagement was given the term 'interpellation' by Althusser, a concept later developed in greater depth by Marxist critical theorists such as Ranciere.[53] According to Althusser, a subject is 'interpellated' into a specific ideological *status quo* through the recycling of familiar tropes and narrative structures in a particular text which serve to absorb him or her, as Gauntlett writes, 'into a certain set of assumption' which, as a result, 'cause[s] us to tacitly accept a particular approach to the world'.[54] This process, which Althusser describes as the 'hailing' of a subject, is effective because of how compelling and comforting, the reader finds it – narratives contain familiar characters and plots which reaffirm conventional wisdom. Ultimately, the act of engaging with dominant narratives provides the audience member with a 'sense of self and a way of understanding his or her relation to the world'.[55]

The phenomenon of contemporary armed humanitarian intervention, like any other aspect of international affairs, possesses its own set of cultural narratives which directly shape and inform popular conventional wisdom about the legitimacy and conduct of such operations. As a number of scholars writing in the critical theory tradition argue, these stories possess a legacy born out of the Western colonialism and rely on entrenched racial constructs alongside rigid juxtapositions of Northern and Southern identity to provide meaning to the intervention it describes.[56] Such stories of humanitarian intervention, Orford writes, have long 'governed encountered between Europe, later the "West" or the "international community" and those colonized or enslaved by Europeans'.[57] Yet postcolonial critical theory remains somewhat of a rarity in IR scholarship; as a result attempts to deconstruct these stories are few and far between.[58] Instead, Gordon notes, 'have become so ubiquitous that [the premises of such narratives] appears almost natural' in the conventional wisdom.[59]

Just as with any narrative, however, the story of armed humanitarian intervention can also be deconstructed. Orford offers a particularly useful identification of several core juxtapositions and framing structures which associates a particular contemporary intervention narrative with the tradition of the colonial-era 'heroic' intervention story.[60] Each of these features is well represented in the 'story' of Britain's intervention in Sierra Leone, as it appears in academic scholarship, policy discourse, media and popular imagination. Together, they point to a narrative which is decidedly neo-colonial and one which raises several troubling conceptual issues. Below, several of these devices are briefly examined.

A 'call to arms' in defence of the ideological status quo

First, Orford observes that the classic 'heroic intervention' story opens by confronting the reader with a ringing and urgent 'call to arms' in defence of a particular ideological *status quo* – one which it expects and demands, said reader to associate closely with. This 'call to arms' represents 'a crisis to the international order, whether that be an armed conflict or civil war that requires military intervention, or an economic crisis that requires monetary intervention'.[61] Here, the 'international order' in question almost always refers to the neo-liberal world system which the 'international community' – the institutions, governments and power structures of the Global North – have collectively instituted as the dominant post-Cold War structure of international geopolitics, one revolving around core universalist norms and values of economic liberalization, stability and human rights.[62]

Such crises are presented as geographically external to the West, arising – in the problematic post-Cold War narrative of international security, 'new wars' and internecine, substate conflict – from the anarchic and violent periphery of the Global South, where the entrenchment of neo-liberal values remains most contested. Here, neo-liberal values are at their weakest, while the alterative power structures ruling in their absence intrinsically challenge the progressive agenda of international development. It is within this ostensibly 'anarchic' global space which has deviated from Western paradigms of development and modernization that humanitarian threats originate. The South, in short, is presumed by the narrative to represent, as Chinua Achebe writes, a 'metaphysical battlefield devoid of all recognizable humanity into which the wandering European enters at his only peril'.[63]

Specific threats arising from this Southern space are, in turn, featured as 'Other'-ed constructions, aberrations of Western order. Arrayed against the peace of the Global North are exclusively Southern 'problems of racist and ruthless dictators, tribalism, ethnic tension, civil war and religious fundamentalism thrown up in the post-Cold War era', of 'the horrors of genocide or ethnic cleansing' and the impact of 'internal armed conflict on civilians'.[64] More broadly still are endemic poverty, underdevelopment and weak political institutions, rotted by corruption, which are presumed to give rise to such cycles of violence.

The reader of the intervention story is therefore invited – and expected – to identify with the ideological *status quo* being threatened and to be disturbed by the implied disruption to their 'ideals of coherence and fullness' which this symbolic order provides.[65] The story's hero, however, exists to vanquish the threat in question and restores the symbolic world order at the end of the story, reaffirming the reader's faith in the durability and righteousness of the prevailing norms of the international community.[66] Thus the narrative offers both 'crisis and redemption' as functional tools 'to reassert the viewers into a discourse or symbolic order which heals the crisis revealed at the start of the narrative', in this way re-interpolating them into the ideological orthodoxy at the end.[67]

Such 'calls to arms' can manifest themselves in responses to a perceived physical threat to the Western reader's person – national security crises such as terrorist attacks originating in the South. More common in armed humanitarian intervention narratives, however, is the *symbolic* threat posed to humanitarian values by Southern violence. Actors who actively oppose or threaten these values and agendas of the international community, in turn, are offered little space by the narrative to become other than 'enemies' of human progress and development.

As a result of this narrative structure, the international community is called to defend its own core values – 'such as peace, security, human rights, justice and freedom' – wherever they are challenged.[68] Here, international institutions – including the IMF, World Bank, UN Security Council, NATO and others – are, as Gordon writes, unerringly 'depicted as the purveyors of freedom', liberating Southern states and populations 'from the grip of a lawless tyranny and then assist[ing] in rebuilding their communities in the image of the civilized West'.[69] They are entreated by media, advocates, citizens and, at times, foreign policy doctrines, as Razack writes, 'to do something about the chaos, the descent into tribalism and the massive human rights violations that accompany these conflicts'.[70]

This binary, totalitizing 'call to arms' provides fertile ground for the narrative's justification of military humanitarian intervention as the only tool robust enough to respond to such crises in defence of the 'established liberal international order'.[71] 'From this perspective', explains Gordon, 'humanitarian crises result from a dearth of law and the absence of the international community, prompting grave situations that must be remedied through armed humanitarian intervention'.[72] Here, throughout the 1990s, armed humanitarian intervention – and the range of concurrent peace operations (peacekeeping, peace enforcement, peacebuilding, transitional administration) – gained increasing legitimacy and prevalence as 'a means for the liberal alliance of democratic states to bring human rights, democracy and humanitarian principles to those in undemocratic, authoritarian or failed states' and today 'collective humanitarian intervention has become necessary to address the problems of local dictators, tribalism, ethnic tension and religious fundamentalism thrown up in the post-Cold War era'.[73]

These points are, again, all too rarely acknowledged in security studies and international legal scholarship – which as a rule tends to offer predominantly technical, 'problem-solving' analysis of armed humanitarian intervention as '[a]n exercise of rationalized positivism'.[74] Here, writes George, intervention literature takes for granted the fact that 'the international community only lays claim to peace, democracy, security and liberty. Development and economic liberalization are assumed to such an extent they are almost considered instinctive'.[75] The danger in allowing such stories to remain unchallenged is the threat of 'preserve[ing] an unjust and exploitative status quo' which 'promotes paternalism, dependence [and] colonial fantasies' in every retelling.[76]

Indeed, this 'calls to arms' in defence of the international community's project of international development deeply mirrors aspects of the colonial-era 'civilizing mission'.[77] Peacekeeping operations, writes Razack, are presented routinely to Northern audiences as a call to go forth 'as members of a family of civilized nations, nations that understand themselves to be carrying the traditional white man's burden of instructing and civilising the natives'.[78] Here, Razack references Said's concept of imperialism as representing not simply the accumulation of territory but rather an 'idea of empire' – 'a structure of feeling, a deeply held belief in the need to and the right to dominate others *for their own good*, others who are expected to be grateful' and that 'certain territories beseech and require domination' for noble ends.[79] In accepting the humanitarian intervention's call to arms uncritically, Razack argues, the reader's interpellation into the story of armed humanitarian intervention 'depends on consigning whole groups of people in the category of those awaiting assistance into modernity' – a disempowering exercise which 'appeals to a deeply racially inflected memory [of] African and Asian colonial adventures'.[80]

These are all themes well represented in the structure of the British 'story' of intervention in Sierra Leone. This Sierra Leone intervention narrative began with an unambiguous 'call to arms' in defence of the international Western order from the 'anarchic' South, battle-lines which any reader engaging with the operation is demanded to sympathetically associate with. At the most basic level, the threat was to British civilians and business interests caught up in the fighting of a former colony, which necessitated the initial deployment. At a broader level, it was a challenge to the tenets of the Blair Doctrine and, through it, to the very foundations of Western decency. As a result, the threat faced by Kabbah's government from the RUF became a symbolic front on the broader, continent-wide agenda of the Blair Doctrine. As Foreign Secretary Robin Cook stated, 'I don't see how we could maintain our self-respect if we turned away from this kind of savagery.'[81]

Here, the Blair Administration was explicit in justifying the intervention as a clear defence of British foreign policy's core neo-liberal agenda in Africa, one explicitly set out in Blair's 'Doctrine of International Community'. As Kampfner writes, Blair – along with Robin Cook and Claire Short, Secretary of State for International Development – identified an agenda of governance reform in African states, which focuses on anti-corruption initiatives, support for increased democratization and liberalization of markets as the defining feature of New Labour's African foreign policy.[82] This agenda was formalized by Blair's New Partnership for Africa's Development (NEPAD), which he inaugurated at the July 2001 G8 Summit Genoa. NEPAD's core concept, to this end, was to tie 'debt relief and development firmly to political and economic reform' – an arraignment Kampfner describes as a 'deal between Africa and the developed world in which the latter agreed to provide more aid for infrastructure projects, debt relief and education and to ease access for African goods to international markets', in return for Africans' acceptance of 'the post-Cold War neo-liberal economic orthodoxies – in other words, globalization – and …the principles of good governance'.[83]

This was not an agenda which permitted equivocation. Those African leaders who agreed to further this modernizing agenda Blair 'regarded as "modernisers" ' – those who questioned it, on the other hand, were dismissed as enemies of progress, 'cynics', Blair noted dismissively, under whose overly cautious direction 'we would still be in the dark ages'.[84]

Sierra Leone was, for the Blair Administration, a frontline of his struggle to 'modernize' Africa. The country itself was poverty-stricken and its institutions of governance exceptionally weak. The RUF, in turn, represented everything opposed to Western conceptions of progress and the *status quo* of the international order. While there is notable debate on this point, the RUF, by 2000, arguably lacked a coherent ideology or political agenda, motivated instead by base greed and economic exploitation – an agenda antithetical to the Blair Doctrine's goals of good governance, transparency and liberalization. Moreover, their horrific human rights abuses and – to a Western perspective – inexplicable battle practices (such as the use of drugs and odd costumes) denied them any remaining legitimacy.[85]

Conversely, Kampfner notes how Blair was 'advised by the FCO that Kabbah was just his kind of modernizer' – as such, Blair actively aligned himself early in the Sierra Leonean Civil War with the Kabbah administration, through policies as aggressive as circumventing the UN Security Councils' ban on arms shipments to Sierra Leone (an embargo Britain itself pushed to impose) in order to provide armaments to the Kabbah government in what came to be known as the 'Arms-for-Africa' scandal.[86]

Furthermore, the narrative of British intervention in Sierra Leone imbues the intervention with an aspect of satisfying closure few humanitarian interventions to date have achieved, concluding with a resounding reaffirmation of the existing order under firm British guidance in everything from governance to SSR and a resumption of the 'civilizing project' of international development. It is this ending which allows the story of British intervention the positive symmetry of the 'heroic' narrative so typically denied, throughout the last 20 years, to other stories of humanitarian intervention – in Rwanda, the Balkans and Iraq/Afghanistan – and which in turn provides it with a unique interpolative strength in reaffirming the reader's faith in international order.

The story of British intervention in Sierra Leone thus began with an unambiguous 'call to arms' in defence of the international Western order from the 'anarchic' South, battle-lines which any reader engaging with the operation is demanded to sympathetically associate with.

'White Knights' of the international community

Another key component of the 'heroic intervention' story is the characterization of the military force deployed to restore the international community's normative *status quo*, who are imbued with 'heroic' traits denied to both their villainous rivals and to their 'helpless' subjects of emancipation. As Orford explains, these heroic figures, as protagonists 'with whom the spectator is invited to identify [with]', serve as a reader's point of entry into the armed humanitarian intervention story.[87] Orford co-opts Bellamy's term 'White Knights' to describe these 'largely interchangeable characters' – UN peacekeepers, NATO coalitions, or unilateral state militaries – who function as 'heroic agents of progress, democratic values, peace and security' in such narratives.[88]

The empowering traits such 'White Knights' are granted by the traditional armed humanitarian intervention narrative include *potency*, *agency* and *authority*.[89] 'Potency' here is most explicitly demonstrated in the form of military capacity – Western militaries in particular are presumed by conventional wisdom (and the majority of strategic studies) as possessing nearly unrivalled military power predicated on professionalism, institutional expertise and technical equipment which can, in certain cases, border on the mythical.[90] Compounding their potency is the tremendous diplomatic influence and financial power Western governments are able to leverage in order to advance their political agendas on the international stage. Southern peacekeepers, while afforded nowhere near this level of capacity, are at least typically afforded greater potency than the belligerents they confront and their association with the international *status quo* allows them collective political potency through international and regional organizations such as the UN, AU and ECOMOG.

A sense of *agency*, Orford also notes, again holds important similarities to the 'enormous freedom to act and to create ideal worlds' with which the hero of colonial narratives is imbued – both rely on an 'imperialist character ... associated with attributes including freedom, creativity, authority, civilisation, power, democracy, sovereignty and wealth'.[91] In contemporary Western imagination, interventionist heroes, in deploying into the Global South, still enter 'the world of the colonies... a space in which the white man is imagined as having an enormous freedom to act and to create ideal worlds'.[92]

In Sierra Leone, the portrayal of the British military provides a striking fulfilment of 'White Knight' archetype. Britain is clearly presented by the narrative as uniquely potent military presence, particularly in comparison to the much larger, but operationally weak, UNAMSIL forces, the non-existent GoSL security apparatus and the ostensibly shambolic, poorly organized and ill-disciplined RUF.

Perhaps most importantly, as defenders of the moral/normative order which has been disrupted, the intervening forces are invested by the narrative not only with the potency to exercise their agency but the moral *authority* to do so. They are not only *able* to act, but ethnically justified – often beyond reproach – in said actions due to the unimpeachable moral grounding of their agendas. Laffey and Barkawi strongly tie this to another colonial parallel: as they write, this authority to act with force manifests itself in the conceptualizing of 'civilizing mission of one kind or another'. Whether 'white man's burden', humanitarian intervention in the 1990s, or the post-9/11 invasions of Afghanistan and Iraq, the assumption is that it is the right of the West to bear arms to liberate the 'natives'. This is and has always been the primary justification of imperialism in all its forms; it is about civilizing the barbarians.[93]

Here, owing to the uncompromisingly totalizing worldview offered by the Blair Doctrine, with its clean division between 'modernizers' and enemies of human progress, British forces were deployed with the clear presumption of moral authority – made even clearer in the face of the RUF's ostensibly nihilistic campaign of human rights abuses. In Sierra Leone, the countries' legacy as a former colony of the UK added a paternalistic dimension to this authority – a sense of moral responsibility alongside moral authority. A *Guardian* op-ed by Young made this point explicitly, noting that Britain was justified in expanding Operation Palliser's initial remit from civilian evacuation to peace enforcement because '[t]the place is, after all, our legacy', imposing 'special post-imperial duties...to a former European power'.[94]

At the same time, however, this *prime face* association with moral agency is deeply predicated on a narrative which is decontexualized and ahistorical: the hero is rarely considered complicit, or even tangentially involved, in the conflict it seeks to resolve.[95] Indeed, a particularly troubling feature of the portrayal of 'White Knights' in 'heroic stories' is that Western states, governments and populations are presented, Razack writes, as 'disembodied liberal subjects who have no prior history',[96] while Western humanitarian intervention 'is everywhere depicted as the engagement of the compassionate but uninvolved observer' with the global South.[97] In short, the narrator of the heroic 'story' speaks from the 'objective and disembodied space of the universalist standpoint', in which Western action is spontaneous, unexpected and warranted.[98]

Removed in this discourse are any references to Northern complicity in the roots of the violence in the first place, past or present. In this narrative, Razack writes, 'warlords and ethnic nationalism, indisputable scourges of our age, are often pictured as though they have risen up from the landscape itself' – rather than contested 'histories in which the West has featured as a colonizing power'. Pieterse identifies three prime assumptions underlying this positivist perception of Western actors: '(1) the perpetrators are mad, (2) the West and onlookers are sane and (3) humanitarian intervention under these crazy circumstances, although messy, is the best we can do.'[99]

This perception, however, denies culpability and responsibility for the West's detrimental post-Cold War impact on Africa, including a 'legacy of authoritarianism, the supremacy of security in politics, surplus armaments and a tradition of politics of polarisation – one often laid upon the earlier authoritarian legacy of colonialism'.[100] Indeed, Kaldor's 'new wars' are often anything but 'new' – the explosion of post-Cold War insecurity in the Global South owes much to the impact of European colonialism and hasty decolonization practices.[101]

The Sierra Leonean narrative's unquestioning assignment of moral agency to British forces illustrates this point with its blatant disregard for the legacy of the country's former colonial rule. Kargbo, for example, persuasively shows how the Sierra Leonean Civil War was intimately tied to British colonial and immediate postcolonial governance.[102] Specifically, he lays blame partially at the feet of Britain's hasty decolonization, which led Siaka Stevens, Sierra Leone's first president to 'lose faith in the democratic process, leading him to dismantle the democratic institutions bequeathed to Sierra Leone at independence' and usher in decades of cyclical autocratic rule and political instability.[103]

One hardly needs to adopt a strict dependency-theory argument laying blame on the feet of colonialism for Sierra Leone's contemporary problems to acknowledge Britain's colonial complicity in the contemporary security challenges faced by Sierra Leone. Yet rarely is the point brought up in literature on the intervention – conforming to Razack's observation that in the common intervention narrative, the notion that 'the histories of colonialism might have anything to do with how it comes to be that white men are in Africa teaching Africans about democracy (a lesson taught with guns) is resolutely struck from the story'.[104]

Furthermore, to the reader of heroic intervention narrative, the international community appears as a compassionate but detached agent, motivated solely by humanitarian incentives – a position which leaves little room for acknowledgement of the hard *realpolitik* motivations Western states follow in their decisions to intervene. As Orford notes, such construction of the narrative in effect 'ignores the ways in which domination and exploitation are maintained through military and economic intervention' as ongoing drivers of the conflict.[105]

Indeed, Kargbo shows, again, how the very collapse of the Sierra Leonean state itself presented Britain a unique opportunity 'in terms of investment and trade opportunities' to maintain its privileged position as a controlling force in Sierra Leonean foreign direct investment, particularly the country's vast mineral wealth – an opportunity which it did not hesitate to secure in its 'rush to sign an Investment Promotion and Protection Agreement (IPPA) with the Sierra Leonean government in January 2000'.[106] In particular, Richards writes of 'the huge kimberlite mining concession an Anglo-South African business consortium (managed in Sierra Leone by a former British military intelligence agent) had negotiated with the National Provisional Ruling Council and renegotiated with the incoming elected government', an asset the RUF eyed with suspicion and which thus encouraged British support for Executive Outcomes' attempt to challenge the rebellion in the lead-up to the Abidjan peace treaty.[107]

Nor did British foreign policy objectives always align with the broader conflict resolution effort in Sierra Leone. For instance, British reticence to show active support for Abuja's poor domestic democratic rights record – for which it had suffered sanctions imposed by the Commonwealth – led it to lend only minimal logistical support for ECOMOG's counter-RUF campaign, 'instead of substantial lethal support in the forms of arms and ammunition', which it could otherwise have done.[108]

Most dramatically, the 'Arms-to-Africa' scandal mentioned above underscores elements of hypocrisy in British foreign policy. It is telling that Blair was relatively unrepentant about circumventing the UN arms embargo – to the press, he defended the arms shipments as a sincere effort by the UK 'to help the democratic regime restore its position from an illegal military coup. [The civil servants involved] were quite right in trying to do it'.[109]

In light of such observations, argues George, the heroic narrative is thus 'especially pernicious because it obscures the causes of local violence and the full purpose of the international community's intervention'.[110] He points out that, '[f]or the international community to then embrace the role of savoir in the wake of local violence, assigning guilt to local populations and implying its own innocence, is the height of hypocrisy'.[111]

To go even further and imply that the notable popularity of Britain's military intervention among many Sierra Leoneans today represents a justification for 'reviving' colonial rule in post-African societies through neo-trusteeship, while in the same breath excluding reference the historical and contemporary factors involved in the origins and continuation of such violence, is thus especially troubling and deserving of extreme scepticism. Such calls have been surprisingly explicit – Brigadier Richards, for example, generalized of the Sierra Leonean people as a whole that 'I've never been to a country where so many people genuinely ask us if we could recolonise. They really mean it.'[112] BBC's Alan Little likewise concludes that Sierra Leoneans have simply 'had enough' of the 'familiar post-colonial African narrative that blamed all the country's ills on the legacy of European Imperialism'. Instead, '[t]he British are back, trying anew to plant the seeds of progress'.[113]

Razack writes that similar calls 'for a revival of colonialism has been a feature of the New World Order for most of the post-cold war period' under a different garb of a 'new civilizing mission'.[114] In this new civilizing mission, she explains, 'History is evacuated and the simplest of storylines remain: more civilised states have to keep less civilised states in line. In this sense, the story of the New World Order continues a much older theme.'[115]

'Symbols of helplessness', emancipation and gratitude

A third and final feature of the 'heroic intervention' story considered here is the tendency to limit the identity of Southern actors facing armed humanitarian emergency as 'symbols of helplessness', awaiting rescue by the heroic 'White Knights' of the international community. These actors may be on the same 'side' of the international community's norms and agenda, but are denied the potency and agency of their rescuers – indeed, their own helplessness has necessitated humanitarian intervention in the first place. In this regard, Orford explains, they are confined to the status of 'secondary, passive character[s] ... who serve as a background and foil to the action of the heroes'.[116] Here, '[i]nternational organizations and major powers are imagined as the bearers of human rights and democracy, while local peoples are presented as victims of abuses conducted by agents of local interests'.[117]

This construction serves a distinct interpolative function: by being reduced to victimhood, Southern actors ultimately serve to validate the hero of the story, who is provided a platform for their emancipation and salvation.[118] The *disempowerment* of the Southern 'Other' – is, indeed, absolutely essential for the construction of the Western hero's identity, whose own heroic traits of potency, authority and agency are largely reliant on the corresponding *absence* of those traits among the people and institutions the intervention is deployed to save. As such, these narratives 'involve detailed descriptions of powerless, victimized states and peoples'.[119]

The people of Sierra Leone were, in this fashion, described by British politicians and the Western press as disempowered victims of war crimes, which neglected the important role of indigenous resistance in the form of the *Kamajor* fighters and CDF in both opposing the RUF and, indeed, in committing humanitarian violence of their own.[120] As Alie demonstrates, the complex evolution and operational history of these groups' struggles against the RUF demonstrate a degree of agency and potency which challenge the conventional narrative's prescribed identity.[121]

The heroic narrative does admittedly allow space for such 'symbols of helplessness' to become beneficiaries of institutional reform and capacity building/empowerment, although 'the aim is not to make further heroes, of equal statues to the hero', but rather objects which reflect the hero's 'desires and ambitions but do not quite achieve them'.[122] In colonial narratives, Orford observes, 'the hero's journey is about the civilisation, progress or development of that colonised subject' – an agenda which she argues remains the dominant paradigm of conventional humanitarian intervention narratives.[123] Today, as in the colonial era, the Southern recipient of Western guidance can aspire to become reformed, but always 'a recognisable Other, *as a subject of a difference that is almost the same, but not quite*'.[124] This sentiment is well reflected in both technical development policy and scholarship in IR and extends to the hierarchical relationship of British military advisors to both UNAMSIL and the SLA.[125]

The story tells us that, following the arrival of the UK Army forces in Freetown, these 'symbols of helplessness' were empowered by British advisors and military consultants, raising their potency and agency but remaining subservient to the hierarchical arrangement of capacity building instituted by the hero. 'Thanks to Britain's arrival', wrote Richards, '[t]he UN have a much stronger resolve now and are clearer about their mandate and have the resolve to fight [...] When we arrived here about six weeks ago, [UNAMSIL] did appear on the verge of collapse. Today they have been transformed'.[126] In this way, local empowerment became another aspect of the international community's mission of 'emancipation' and 'salvation'.

Finally, the narrative of heroic intervention places a particular demand on displays of gratitude by local populations in recognition of the international community's work – the reward, in essence, for Western selflessness in pursuit of humanitarian aims. Receiving such 'images of grateful natives', George writes, produces an important inter-pellative effect in the mind of Western readers, 'confirm[ing] Westerner's sense of superiority, discoursing critique and mobilizing support for peacekeeping activities'.[127]

In this regard, Sierra Leone represents a rare exception in the troubled historical record of post-Cold War armed humanitarian intervention operations. For once, British government, military and public enjoyed – so the story goes – clear articulations of local appreciation among the 'liberated' Sierra Leoneans. It is a place where, as Little assures us, '[t]he people of Sierra Leone saw the British as their saviours' and where Tony Blair, architect of the interneuron, 'is more than a folk hero… He has become some kind of talisman, a protective force' for the grateful local subjects of modern-day emancipation from conflict and civil war.[128]

The tremendous reaffirmation of Western moral authority and com-passion afforded by these public expressions of gratitude further heighten the appeal of this narrative. It is this very interpellative effect which manifests itself, for instance, in a speech made to a crowd of appreciative villagers outside Freetown, Blair responded by noting, 'with utter seriousness', that their appreciative enthusiasm 'made him feel he was single-handedly responsible for their freedom'.[129]

In closing, I contend that the triumphant narrative of British inter-vention in Sierra Leone, one widely and uncritically reproduced in both academic and popular discourse, can be problematized on several grounds. I argue first that an over-optimistic reading of British success in Sierra Leone presents a problematic precedent for the expectation of similar missions in the future. Secondly, the observations I raise above regarding the 'story' of Britain's experience suggest that, at the least, it shares several notable traits in common with the classic 'heroic' inter-vention stories, long used to sensitize Western audiences to the norms of the colonial 'civilizing mission'. I again stress, strongly, that through these preceding points I in no way intend to diminish the very real accomplishments of Britain intervention in Sierra Leone – accomplish-ments which have maintained the country's stability under continuing British support and, in particular, earned the gratitude with which so many Sierra Leoneans view the UK. Nonetheless, troubling parallels exist within this narrative which, as Orford concludes, harkens back to colonial racial constructs and divisions which ultimately 'limits the extent to which we can even begin to think about the humanity of Others'.[130]

It is for this very reason that there exists a greater need for the study of contemporary armed humanitarian intervention to engage with postcolonial critical theory, in order to identify and challenge such constructions of the other embedded in the conventional wisdom and replicated through the retelling of unexamined 'heroic' narratives. It is my hope that this chapter will similarly contribute in a modest way to the encouragement of greater such critical discourse within the field of peacekeeping studies and broader IR – an agenda which I hope will benefit from the perspectives of an interdisciplinary audience.

Notes

1. See Adeniji Ebo, 'The Challenges and Lessons of Security Sector Reform in Post-Conflict Sierra Leone', *Conflict, Security & Development* 6.4 (2006): 481–501.
2. Richard Connaughton, 'Organizing British Joint Rapid Reaction Forces', *Joint Forces Quarterly* (Autumn, 2000): 77.
3. Robert Kaplan, 'The Coming Anarchy', *The Atlantic Monthly* (February, 1994): 44–65.
4. See Tony Blair, 'Doctrine of the International Community, 24 April 1999', *The National Archives*, http://webarchive.nationalarchives.gov.uk/+/http://www.number10.gov.uk/Page1297.
5. Alan Little, 'Sierra Leone: A British Colony Again?', *BBC News*, 10 January 2010.
6. Andrew Dorman, *Transforming to Effects-Based Operations: Lessons from the Sierra Leone Experience* (Carlisle, PA: Strategic Studies Institute, 2008), 17.
7. Michael Kargbo, *British Foreign Policy and the Conflict in Sierra Leone, 1991–2000* (Oxford: Peter Lang, 2006), 89.
8. Taylor patronage of Sankoh and the RUF was motivated both by a desire to secure Sierra Leone's mineral assets and to open a second front to distract the Economic Community of West Africa States, which were at this time sponsoring a military intervention which threatened his own position in Liberia.
9. See, for instance, Human Rights Watch. 'Coercion and Intimidation of Child Soldiers to Participate in Violence – Sierra Leone', *Human Rights Watch* (16 April 2008), http://www.hrw.org/en/news/2008/04/16/coercion-and-intimidation-child-soldiers-participate-violence#_Sierra_Leone.
10. The origins of the RUF movement and the Sierra Leonean Civil War are covered by the historical literature in greater depth. A brief review includes Paul Richards, *Fighting for the Rainforest: War, Youth and Resources in Sierra Leone* (Portsmouth, NH: Heinemann, 1996); John Hirsch, *Sierra Leone: Diamonds and the Struggle for Democracy* (Boulder, CO: Lynne Reinner, 2001); David Keen, *Conflict and Collusion in Sierra Leone* (Oxford: Currey, 2005);

and J. Peter Pham, *The Sierra Leonean Tragedy: History and Global Dimensions* (Hauppauge, NY: Nova Science, 2006).

11. See Greg Campbell, *Blood Diamonds: Tracing the Deadly Paths of the World's Most Precious Stones* (Boulder, CO: Westview Press, 2002), for an in-depth examination of Taylor's diamond-laundering networks.

12. Government of Sierra Leone, 'Peace Agreement Between the Government of Sierra Leone and the Revolutionary United Front of Sierra Leone (Lomé Accord)', Lomé, Togo, 19 May 1999, http://www.sierra-leone.org/lomeaccord.html.

13. Ibid., Article VXI.

14. See Funmi Olonisakin, *Peacekeeping in Sierra Leone: The Story of UNAMSIL* (London: Lynne Rainer, 2008).

15. Trevor Findlay, *The Use of Force in UN Peace Operations* (Oxford: Oxford University Press, 2002), 299–300.

16. For more on the humanitarian impact of the AFRC/RUF junta, see M. P. David Pratt, 'Sierra Leone: The Forgotten Crisis', *Report to Canadian Minister of Foreign Affairs*, 23 April 1999, http://www.globalsecurity.org/military/library/report/1999/crisis-e.htm; and William Fowler, *Operation Barass* (London: Cassell, 2004) 39.

17. United Nations Security Council President Statement, 4 May 2000 (S/PRST/2000/14); and Stuart Griffen, *Joint Operations: A Short History* (United Kingdom Ministry of Defence: Joint Doctrine Command Centre, 2005), 203.

18. Richard Connaughton, 'The Mechanics and Nature of British Interventions into Sierra Leone (2000) and Afghanistan (2001–2002)', *Civil Wars*, 7.1 (Spring, 2004): 83.

19. Ibid.

20. Lansana Gberie, *A Dirty War in West Africa: The RUF and the Destruction of Sierra Leone* (London: Hurst, 2005), 2.

21. Connaughton, 'The Mechanics and Nature', 84.

22. Maj.Gen David Richards, 'Expeditionary Operations: Sierra Leone – Lessons for the Future', *World Defence Systems*, 3.2 (July, 2001): 135.

23. Tim Butcher, 'Paras Dig in As Rebels Head for the Airport', *Daily Telegraph*, 12 May 2000. See also Connaughton, 'Organizing British', 93; and John Kampfner, *Blair's Wars* (London: Free Press, 2004), 70.

24. Connaughton, 'The Mechanics and Nature', 83.

25. Ibid.

26. Richards, 'Expeditionary Operaitons', 135.

27. Gberie, *A Dirty War*, 173.

28. BBC News, 'UK Extends Sierra Leone Mission', *BBC News*, 12 May 2000. http://news.bbc.co.uk/1/hi/uk/745502.stm.

29. Dorman, *Transforming to Effects*, 93.

30. BBC News, 'The Strange Tail of Sankoh's Capture', *BBC News*, 18 May 2000. http://news.bbc.co.uk/1/hi/world/africa/752036.stm.

31. Alain Lallemand, 'Drugs, Diamonds and Deadly Cargoes', *The Center for Public Integrity* (28 November 2002), http://www.publicintegrity.org/2002/11/18/5697/drugs-diamonds-and-deadly-cargoes.

32. Ibid.

33. Ibid., 117.

34. Keen, *Conflict and Collusion*, 273.
35. Ibid., 268.
36. Government of Sierra Leone, 'Speech by the President of Sierra Leone, His Excellency, Alhaji Dr. Ahmad Tejan Kabbah, at the Ceremony Marking the Conclusion of Disarmament and the Destruction of Weapons', Lungi, Sierra Leone, 18 January 2002, http://www.sierra-leone.org/Speeches/kabbah-011802.html.
37. For more on the British IMATT training teams, see Ebo, 'The Challenges and Lessons', 481–501; and Osman Gbla, 'Security Sector Reform Under International Tutelage in Sierra Leone', *International Peacekeeping*, 13.1 (March, 2006): 78–93.
38. BBC World Service, 'Sierra Leone's Election', *BBC World Service*, 18 September 2007, http://www.bbc.co.uk/worldservice/focusonafrica/news/cluster/2007/08/070806_sleone_elections.shtml.
39. See Paul Collier, *The Bottom Billion* (Oxford: Oxford University Press, 2008), 129.
40. Connaughton, 'The Mechanics and Nature', 93.
41. Dorman, *Transforming to Effects*, 14.
42. Connaughton, 'The Mechanics and Nature', 84.
43. Peter Beaumont and Jason Burke, 'Close Call in the Battle of Rokel Creek', *The Guardian*, 17 September 2000: 19.
44. Dorman, *Transforming to Effects*, 144.
45. For a detailed tactical account of Operation see Anil Raman, 'Operation Khukri: Joint Excellence', *United Services Institute Journal*, 227 (October–December, 2002): 515–31.
46. Sierra Leone Truth and Reconciliation Commission, *Witness to Truth: Report of the Sierra Leone Truth & Reconciliation Commission*, vol. 3A (Accra: GPL Press, 2004), 213–19. (Referred hereafter as *TRC*.)
47. Keen, *Conflict and Collusion*, 268; and Gberie, *A Dirty War*, 172. As the TRC noted, the effectiveness of GAF's military operation 'was so crushing that the RUF [...] suffered untold destruction to its internal infrastructure and organization on the ground', leading to the deaths 'of some of the RUF's most influential field commanders'. In *TRC*, 460.
48. These perspectives were encountered during my doctoral research with former UNAMSIL and ECOMOG in Sierra Leone and Nigeria. Olonisakin likewise recorded complaints of former UNAMSIL staff towards what they described as 'the trend in the British press to downgrade what the UN has done and play up the British role'. See Olonisakin, *Peacekeeping in Sierra Leone*, 9.
49. Ibid., 103–4.
50. Ibid.
51. Lallemand, 'Drugs, Diamonds and Deadly Cargoes'.
52. Kali Tal, *Worlds of Hurt: Reading the Literatures of Trauma* (Cambridge: Cambridge University Press, 1996), 6.
53. Louis Althusser, *Lenin and Philosophy and Other Essays* (London: Ben Brewster, 1971), 127, 162; Jaques Ranciere, 'Politics, Identification and Subjectivization', *October* (Summer, 1992): 58–64.
54. David Gauntlett, *Media, Gender and Identity* (London: Routledge, 2002), 27.

55. Anne Orford, *Reading Humanitarian Intervention* (Cambridge: Cambridge University Press, 2003), 161.

56. Two key theorists relied on in this essay are Orford, *Reading Humanitarian*; and Sherene Razack, *Dark Threats and White Knights: The Somalia Affair, Peacekeeping and the New Imperialism* (Toronto, ON: University of Toronto Press, 2004).

57. Orford, *Reading Humanitarian*, 161.

58. This critique is echoed in the similar arguments of several prominent peace operations scholars – including Paris, Pugh and Bellamy – all of whom have stressed the need for greater application of critical theory to the field of peace operations studies in order to balance this predominance of 'problem-solving' research. See Roland Paris, 'Broadening the Study of Peace Operations', *International Studies Review*, 2.3 (Fall, 2000): 27; Michael Pugh, 'Peacekeeping and International Relations Theory: Phantom of the Opera?', *International Peacekeeping*, 10.4 (Winter 2003): 104–12; and Alex Bellamy, 'The "Next Stage" in Peace Operations Theory?', *International Peacekeeping*, 11.1 (April, 2007): 17.

59. Ruth Gordon, 'Review: Deconstructing Armed Humanitarian Intervention', *The George Washington International Law Review*, 36.4 (2004): 952.

60. Orford, *Reading Humanitarian*, 158–80.

61. Ibid., 182.

62. Broadly speaking, neo-liberalism's core policies are articulated in Williamson's ten-point deconstruction of what he famously termed the 'Washington Consensus'. See John Williamson, ed., 'What Washington Means by Policy Reform', in *Latin American Adjustment: How Much Has Happened?* (Washington, DC: Institute for International Economics, 1990).

63. Chinua Achebe, *Hope and Impediments: Selected Essays, 1965–1987* (London: Heinemann, 1988), 8.

64. Orford, *Reading Humanitarian*, 164.

65. Kaja Silverman, *The Subject of Semiotics* (Oxford: Oxford University Press, 1983), 221.

66. Orford, *Reading Humanitarian*, 162.

67. Silverman, *The Subject of Semiotics*, 221.

68. Orford, *Reading Humanitarian*, 165.

69. Gordon, 'Review', 949.

70. Razack, *Dark Threats and White Knights*, 41.

71. Orford, *Reading Humanitarian*, 164.

72. Gordon, 'Review', 949.

73. Orford, *Reading Humanitarian*, 4, 164.

74. Heike Härting and Smaro Kamboureli, 'Discourses of Security, Peacekeeping Operations and the Cultural Imagination in Canada', *University of Toronto Quarterly*, 78.2 (Spring, 2009): 662.

75. Gordon, 'Review', 951.

76. Stephen George, 'Review: Reading Humanitarian Intervention: Human Rights and the Use of Force in International Law', *Harvard Human Rights Journal*, 17 (Spring, 2004), http://www.law.harvard.edu/students/orgs/hrj/iss17/booknotes-Reading.shtml.

77. Razack, *Dark Threats and White Knights*, 9–10.

78. Ibid., 156.

79. Ibid., 10.
80. Ibid., 17.
81. Quoted in Daily Telegraph, 'Cook's Double Trouble', *Daily Telegraph*, 15 May 2000, http://www.telegraph.co.uk/comment/4251306/Cooks-double-trouble.html.
82. Kampfner, *Blair's Wars*, 75–7.
83. Ibid., 75.
84. Ibid., 76–7.
85. Paul Richards, *Fighting for the Rain Forest: War, Youth and Resources in Sierra Leone* (Portsmouth, NH: Heinemann, 1996), in his exploration of the ethnography and ideology of the RUF cadre, offers an important rebuttal to such perceptions.
86. Kampfner, *Blair's Wars*, 76–7.
87. Orford, *Reading Humanitarian*, 165.
88. Ibid.
89. Orford, *Reading Humanitarian*, 165–71.
90. See, for instance, Cassidy's analysis of US military culture and the fetishization of military technology. In Robert Cassidy, *Peacekeeping in the Abyss* (Westport, CT: Praeger, 2004), Chapter 3.
91. Ibid., 166.
92. Ibid.
93. Tarak Barkawi and Mark Laffey, 'The Postcolonial Moment in Security Studies', *Review of International Studies*, 32.4 (2006): 351.
94. Hugo Young, 'We are Good at Getting in, not so Good at Getting out', *Guardian*, 18 May 2000, http://www.guardian.co.uk/world/2000/may/18/sierraleone.comment.
95. Razack, *Dark Threats and White Knights*, 157.
96. Ibid., 49.
97. Ibid., 26.
98. Dana Nelson, *National Manhood: Capitalist Citizenship and the Imagined Fraternity of White Men* (Durham, NC: Duke University Press, 1998), 10.
99. Jan Pieterse, *World Orders in the Making: Humanitarian Intervention and Beyond* (Basingstoke: Macmillan, 1998), 244.
100. Ibid., 236.
101. Mary Kaldor, *New and Old Wars: Organised Violence in a Global Era*, 2nd edn (Cambridge: Polity Press, 2006). For criticism of 'New War' theory, see among others, Mats Berdal, 'How "New" Are "New Wars"'? *Global Governance*, 9 (2003): 477–502; and Edward Newman, 'The "New Wars" Debate: A Historical Perspective is Needed', *Security Dialogue*, 35.2 (June, 2004): 173–89.
102. Kargbo, *British Foreign Policy*, 89.
103. Ibid., 89, 315.
104. Razack, *Dark Threats and White Knights*, 49.
105. Orford, *Reading Humanitarian*, 16.
106. Here, mineral companies such as Branch Energy 'were actively involved in shoring up President Kabbah's government', placing pressure on the Blair Government 'to pursue a more proactive policy in Sierra Leone so as to secure their investments and regain influence' threatened by the possibility of its ouster. See Kargbo, *British Foreign Policy*, 319–20.

107. Paul Richards, 'Review: Rebels and Intellectuals in Sierra Leone's Civil War', *African Studies Review*, 49.1 (April, 2006): 119–23.
108. Ibid.
109. Quoted in Kampfner, *Blair's Wars*, 68.
110. George, 'Review'.
111. Ibid.
112. Chris McGreal, 'Whitehall Launches Second Colonisation', *The Guardian*, 19 May 2000: 4.
113. Little, 'Sierra Leone'.
114. Razack, *Dark Threats and White Knights*, 49.
115. Ibid., 48.
116. Orford, *Reading Humanitarian*, 171.
117. Ibid., 170.
118. Ibid., 171.
119. Ibid., 172.
120. See *TRC*, 213–19.
121. Joe Alie, 'The Kamajor Militia in Sierra Leone: Liberators or Nihilists?' in David Francis, ed., *Civil Militia: Africa's Intractable Security Menace?* (Aldershot: Ashgate, 2005).
122. Orford, *Reading Humanitarian*, 171–2.
123. Ibid.
124. Homi Bhabha, *The Location of Culture* (London: Routledge, 1994), 86, emphasis in original.
125. Indeed, as Laffey and Barakawi write, 'to the extent that it addresses them at all, a Eurocentric security studies regards the weak and the powerless as marginal or derivative elements of a world politics, as at best the site of liberal good intentions or at worst a potential source of threats'. Therein, the traits of 'agency, rationality, power and morality' granted to heroes from the Global North are denied Southern partners – 'these various others are assumed to be just like us, only weaker' (Tarak Barkawi and Mark Leffey, 'The Postcolonial Moment in Security Studies,' *Reivew of International Studies* 32 (2006), 332). For more on hierarchies of development and capacity-building in international partnerships, see Norman Girvan, 'Power Imbalances and Development Knowledge', paper prepared for North-South Institute Project in Reform of the International Development Architecture, September, 2007, http://www.oecd.org/site/oecdgfd/39447872.pdf.
126. BBC News, 'On This Day: 2000: British Marines Leave Sierra Leone', *BBC On-line*. http://news.bbc.co.uk/onthisday/hi/dates/stories/june/15/newsid_2512000/2512669.stm.
127. Razack, *Dark Threats and White Knights*, 43.
128. Little, 'Sierra Leone'.
129. Kampfner, *Blair's Wars*, 77.
130. George, 'Review'.

5

Humanitarian Intervention in the Horn of Africa

Christopher Clapham

Introduction

The Horn of Africa – the region comprising Dijbouti, Eritrea, Ethiopia, Somalia and Somaliland – figures in Western discourse overwhelmingly (and with some justice) as a zone of intense human suffering, notably as a result of famine, which has historically figured in the Western imagination as one of the great biblical scourges and as a focus for the obligations of human charity indicated by the names of such prominent non-governmental organizations as Oxfam and War on Want. Closely associated with famine, and contributing heavily to it, have been a very high incidence of armed conflict, both between states and within them, a large population of refugees and internally displaced persons and, in Somalia, the most prominent case of state collapse anywhere in the world. The region has accordingly provided a privileged site for the articulation of Western conceptions of humanitarianism and for numerous programmes, operating at many different levels, intended on the one hand to relieve suffering in the area and on the other to express a sense of global moral obligation, which itself exemplifies ideas of how the world *ought* to be constructed, and what roles the wealthier and more powerful parts of the planet can and should play in bringing this ideal into being.

At the centre of this enterprise lie two iconic episodes, each of which did much to define the parameters and limitations of the Western humanitarian engagement, not only with Africa but with the world as a whole, in the late twentieth century. The first was the great Ethiopian famine of 1984–5, which projected onto the Western consciousness the idea of famine as an essentially natural disaster, calling for a response at the most basic level of humanity and exemplified by Band Aid, a famine relief fundraising operation launched by two prominent popular musicians, which linked humanitarianism into popular culture in a way that would previously have been difficult to conceive. The second was Operation Restore Hope, the intervention in Somalia undertaken by the US from 1992 onwards and intended to create through military means the conditions required to deliver famine relief to large numbers of starving Somalis. The spectacular failure of this mission not only has much to tell us about the extremely problematic nature of humanitarian intervention itself, but also had a powerful impact on the attempt to create a new and morally justified global order in the aftermath of the Cold War. It is however only part of a much broader external engagement with the region, stretching back to the nineteenth century and expressed in more recent times in terms of famine relief, conflict management and state-building, to which have lately been added the demands of the 'global war on terror' and the protection of major shipping lanes against piracy.

This chapter seeks to place this experience in the context on the one hand of the changing politics of the Horn and on the other of the construction of a global order predicated on the establishment of 'states', and increasingly of states of a particular kind, as a critical means through which a structure of governance dedicated to human welfare could be established. These two elements have fitted together in an extremely uneven fashion, given the peculiar social and political structure of the region and the correspondingly discriminatory impact of external intervention on different actors within it. The underlying theme of the chapter is therefore that local actors have not been mere passive subjects or victims of external projects supposedly undertaken on their behalf, but have instead actively appropriated interventions in order to serve their own interests within the structures and agendas of regional and domestic politics. The resources provided by outside engagement have provided ample opportunities for 'extraversion' on the part of local elites,[1] which have often had the effect of negating or even reversing the objectives that the interveners sought to achieve.

The historical antecedents of humanitarian engagement in the Horn

The origins of external engagement in the Horn of Africa, predicated not on mere conquest but on the realization of ideals related to the construction of a just and sustainable global order, derive from a peculiar incident in 1867–8, which nonetheless continues to carry a resonance in the modern world. The then Ethiopian emperor, Tewodros – a towering figure in Ethiopian history, who set in motion the restoration of a state that was eventually, uniquely in Africa, to retain its independence through the period of colonial conquest – was angered by the failure of the British government to respond in an appropriate manner to a letter that he had sent, and retaliated by imprisoning the British consular officials sent to negotiate with him. This was a slight, not only on the UK but on the acceptable means of conducting business between states, and a military mission was despatched from India at great expense, with the objective of rescuing the consuls. Tewodros (who could, obviously, have killed them had he wished to do so) released his hostages unharmed and after the defeat of his army committed suicide rather than submit to the humiliation of capture. The British, who had no intention of colonizing Ethiopia, then withdrew and left the country to its own devices.[2]

This episode already carries resonances that were to recur over the following century and a half. First of all, the sending to Ethiopia of British diplomats indicates at least a quasi-recognition of the country as a legitimate participant in the global system, implicitly enjoying a status superior to that of mere 'chiefs' in other parts of Africa. Second, this quasi-recognition was predicated on the Ethiopian government's adherence to diplomatic norms, a lesson that was well learnt on the Ethiopian side and was to enable successive regimes to enjoy a privileged status in their dealings with the outside world. Third and perhaps most basically of all, the British intervention was to have a significant and quite unintended impact on the country's domestic power structure and its relations with neighbouring groups. As it withdrew, the intervening force left behind it significant quantities of firearms that were then appropriated by the local governor on its line of march, Kassa Mercha, who was able to use them to establish his own claim to the throne as Tewodros' successor and assume the imperial title of Yohannes IV. This relatively early introduction to the critical importance of modern weapons helped Yohannes to defeat invasions by Egypt in the mid-1870s and the Mahdists in 1889, and eventually enabled his successor Menilek to crush Italy's attempted colonization of Ethiopia in 1895–6. Equally significantly, the powerfully armed Ethiopian state was able to expand its territory massively by the conquest and incorporation of neighbouring peoples who lacked its military technology. The lesson was clear: external engagement was not *only* a threat to be resisted (though it certainly had important elements of that), but also provided great opportunities to those who were able to appropriate the resources that it offered.

The independent Ethiopian state was then able to construct its relations with the rest of the region in ways that differed significantly from the colonial norms imposed elsewhere in Africa. Though peripheral coastal areas – Eritrea (Italy), the French Somali Coast (now Djibouti), British Somaliland and Somalia (Italy) – fell to colonial rule, these were effectively appendages to the great African state at the region's core. Ethiopia failed to recognize (save when it suited it) the sacrosanct nature of colonial frontiers, pressed with eventual (and disastrous) success for the 'reunion' of Eritrea with the motherland, and readily intervened in the affairs of its neighbours. Since the core of the Horn fell outside direct colonial control, it evaded the standard models of state-building and regional order imposed by colonialism in other parts of Africa. This led both to the creation of highly discriminatory domestic power structures and to the perception of the region as 'problematic' from the perspective of colonial and indeed postcolonial conceptions of order. External powers, nonetheless, had to recognize the key role of Ethiopia in maintaining 'stability' in the region, albeit often stability of a highly discriminatory kind, and construct their relations with the regional hegemon as the central element in their regional diplomacy – a pattern that was to recur through the reign of Haile-Selassie in the mid-twentieth century, the military Marxist regime of Mengistu Haile-Maryam between 1977 and 1991, and the EPRDF government under Meles Zenawi that assumed power in 1991.

When the League of Nations was established after the First World War, the Ethiopian government under Ras Tafari – later to be better known as Haile-Selassie – joined it, in the belief that this would guarantee the country's independence, abolishing domestic slavery in a move designed to demonstrate its adherence to global humanitarian norms. Membership of the league proved tragically incapable of preventing Ethiopia's conquest and colonization by fascist Italy in 1935–6, but this episode did at least have the consequence of raising the country to the summit of international moral concern, and at a time when anti-colonial nationalism was already stirring in other parts of the continent, establishing both the country and notably emperor Haile-Selassie as symbols of pan-African heroism on the one hand and colonial turpitude on the other.[3] When Italy entered the Second World War on the side of Nazi Germany in 1940, the British-led campaign to defeat the Italians in north-east Africa (regardless of its strategic role in the context of the war as a whole) could plausibly be presented by the British as a war of liberation. Despite the colonialist mentalities and aspirations of some of the British officials involved in the campaign, there was no alternative to the restoration of Ethiopian independence under Haile-Selassie.

Post-war administration in the two recognized Italian colonies of Eritrea and Somalia also provided cases of 'humanitarian intervention', and the pamphlet produced by the British government to commemorate its enlightened administration of the former fascist territories was entitled *The First to be Freed*.[4] Their disposal by the United Nations was likewise intended to guarantee the welfare of their inhabitants, though with extremely mixed results. Somalia was turned into a UN Trust Territory, controversially administered by Italy – albeit a very different Italy from that of Mussolini. Still more controversially, Eritrea was 'federated' with Ethiopia in 1952, a move that essentially amounted to annexation, reflecting in part Ethiopia's legitimate security interests, access to the Red Sea and some support within Eritrea itself, but in part also Western guilt at Ethiopia's abandonment in 1935–6 and the support of the US as it started to establish its post-war global security structure; the *quid pro quo* was a US base in Eritrea that provided a vital military communications link until the advent of satellite technology.[5] The peculiar interaction of humanitarian and security considerations was to prove another enduring theme in the politics of the region.

Revolution, famine and the humanitarian impulse

During the two decades that ended in 1974, the Horn of Africa came as close to 'normality' as at any time in its recent history. To be sure, the union of British Somaliland and Somalia at independence in 1960 created a single Somali state that sought to annex the large Somali-inhabited area of south-east Ethiopia, but Ethiopia's alliance with the US, coupled with its striking diplomatic success in establishing the Organisation of African Unity with its headquarters in Addis Ababa, kept this threat well within manageable bounds, even when Somalia after the military takeover of 1969 established a rival strategic partnership with the Soviet Union. An armed Eritrean independence movement made its presence felt from the mid-1960s, but was generally contained within the peripheral areas of the territory. The dangers of famine and state collapse aroused, at that time, no significant concern.

All this changed dramatically in the mid-1970s. An outbreak of famine in the historically vulnerable Wallo region in 1973–4 brought the issue to the attention of the outside world, largely through a British television programme which sharply contrasted emperor Haile-Selassie's luxurious lifestyle with the suffering of his subjects.[6] This was skilfully exploited in the Ethiopian revolution of 1974 – the one true revolution that Africa has yet experienced – which not only overthrew the imperial regime and replaced it by a Marxist military dictatorship, but reversed the existing pattern of external alliances in the region and set in train a massive expansion of armed conflicts. The collapse of Ethiopia's strategic alliance with the US prompted the Somali government to take advantage of what looked to be a historic opportunity to annex the Somali-inhabited areas of Ethiopia, which however succeeded only in confirming the adage, 'never invade a revolution'. The initially successful Somali attack late in 1977 resulted not only in a mobilization campaign on the part of the revolutionary government, but in a reversal of alliances by the Soviet Union, which recognized in the Ethiopian regime – known as the Derg – both a far more valuable strategic partner and a much closer ideological soulmate. The defeat of the Somalis, with the aid of Soviet weapons and a Cuban strike force, set in train the collapse of the Somali state, examined in the next section, that was to have major repercussions for the tangled humanitarian politics of the Horn.[7]

More immediate problems arose in northern Ethiopia, where the Eritrean insurgencies fighting to reverse the 1952 federation and create an independent Eritrean state, likewise received a major boost from the collapse of the imperial regime and the diversion of Ethiopian forces to counter the Somali threat in the south-east. At much the same time, the internal struggle for 'movement hegemony' in Eritrea, which pitted the original Eritrean Liberation Front (ELF), formed in the Moslem areas of the territory and supported by a number of radical Arab states, against the Eritrean People's Liberation Front (EPLF), which drew its core support from Christian highland Eritreans, was decisively won by the latter.[8] At one moment in 1978, the EPLF overran almost the whole of Eritrea, and although it had to retreat once victory over the Somalis enabled the regime to move its army to the north, it was still able – in a saga of extraordinary heroism and highly effective guerrilla organization – to retain control of at least some 'liberated areas' within the territory. Meanwhile in the Tigray region immediately to the south of Eritrea, a distinct but tactically allied movement, the Tigray People's Liberation Front (TPLF), started operations against the Derg.[9]

This was the complex political situation when the 1984 Ethiopian famine made its dramatic appearance on the television screens of the West, replete with what were soon to become the familiar pictures of dying people and animals, barren landscapes and vast crowds of destitute and desperate individuals huddled in the relief camps where they hoped to find food, which were to define the external image of the Horn.

The celebrated opening words of Michael Buerk's October 1984 BBC television report, undoubtedly the most famous such report in media history – 'Dawn and as the sun breaks through the piercing chill of night on the plain outside Korem, it lights up a biblical famine, now, in the twentieth century'[10] – were also to open a new dawn in global humanitarianism. The very use of the word 'biblical' linked the horrors of Wallo to the most basic source of Western Christian morality and aroused a very high level of publicity within donor states, that was predicated on an entirely apolitical or indeed anti-political response, best captured by the rise of celebrity humanitarianism, in the form especially of the Band Aid phenomenon promoted by two well-known popular musicians, Bob Geldof and Bono. The activities of Geldof and Bono, who rapidly acquired the status of secular saints, greatly increased the amount of money collected for famine relief, and at the same time placed political pressure on donor governments to respond to the public pressure that they aroused. The conception of famine that this effort promoted was however one that placed all its emphasis on the 'human' level, notably on the benevolent Western donor on the one hand and the starving African victim on the other, that completely bypassed the very important political dimensions of the famine and – still more insidiously – reinforced an image of Africa as a helpless and suffering continent that was to resonate long after the immediate emergency had passed.[11]

As with most famines, this one had multiple causes. In much of northern Ethiopia, famine was a recurrent hazard, resulting from thin soils and uncertain rainfall, combined with a relatively dense population at risk. There was undoubtedly a major rainfall failure, which led the Ethiopian government – eager to present the situation as simply a 'natural disaster' – to describe it as a 'drought emergency', thus playing to the external perception of famine as a straightforward natural phenomenon, which in turn facilitated the raising of resources to aid the relief operation, while evading awkward questions about the role of government policy. The upheavals resulting from the revolutionary land reform – which while ostensibly delivering 'land to the tiller', actually brought agriculture under far closer state control than before – made at least some contribution to the conditions that led to famine. And even though some of the worst affected areas, notably Wallo, fell outside the war zones, the ongoing insurgencies and counter-insurgency campaigns both contributed directly to famine in some parts of the country and massively disrupted the delivery of relief food.

The scale of suffering induced the Ethiopian government, which over the previous seven or eight years had effectively closed the country to the West, to open its doors to famine relief aid, for which the West, in the then state of the global agricultural economy, was the only possible supplier. The Western response was in turn heavily affected not only by official government aid schemes, but by popular reaction and concern. Though governments were induced by public pressure to provide assistance – the British government then under Margaret Thatcher, for example, made Royal Air Force transport aircraft available to deliver food to inaccessible areas of Ethiopia – both the funding and the political agendas of the Western aid programmes were to a large extent directed through non-governmental organizations. This in turn placed these organizations in an extremely difficult political position, given that the government of the state involved was not only closely allied with the Soviet Union (a problem to which NGOs were generally less sensitive than national governments) but was also guilty of appalling human rights violations. In a territory simultaneously wracked by famine and by civil war, food presented a means not only to save the lives of millions of human beings, but also to assure the control by those who delivered the food over those who desperately needed it: indeed, the sack of relief grain (which required the affected populations to come to those who possessed it) was far more effective than the barrel of a gun (which the affected populations understandably tended to run away from) as a technology of control.

Respect for the conventions of sovereign statehood, historically initiated in Europe and enthusiastically adopted by African states after their independence from colonial rule, dictated that this aid should be delivered to the internationally recognized government of Ethiopia and distributed through channels under its control. This was the only course of action available for official relief and was likewise adopted for the larger part of the food aid supplied by NGOs. There were good practical reasons for this. Most of the affected population, notably in Wallo, were in government-controlled areas and the Ethiopian government itself set up a generally effective and respected organization, the Relief and Rehabilitation Commission (RRC), to liaise with donors, raise external aid and coordinate the delivery of relief food.[12] Logistically, by far the quickest and most effective way to get food to the famine areas was through lines of communication that were likewise overwhelmingly under government control. Though this left agencies in the uncomfortable position of tacitly supporting a government with which they had very little in common, the overriding priority was simply to get food into mouths, and in the agencies' view, guided by the humanitarian *raison d'être* of their own organizations and perfectly expressed in the maxim that 'a starving child knows no politics', this took precedence over all other considerations. These official channels became known in the jargon of the time as the 'front door'.

The alternative was to deliver famine relief through the 'back door', or in other words to send it through Sudan (where it could be packaged as aid for Sudan itself, which had its own troubles), into territories controlled by the armed insurgencies (or liberation movements) fighting the Ethiopian regime, where it served precisely the same function on behalf of the opposite side.[13] Both the EPLF and the TPLF formed their own equivalents to the Ethiopian government's RRC, the Eritrean Relief Association (ERA) on the one hand and the Relief Society of Tigray (REST) on the other, which were closely controlled by their parent fronts and for the most part staffed by disabled ex-fighters and other non-combatants. While each of these insisted, every bit as vociferously as the RRC, that they were solely humanitarian organizations and that the food under their control was destined only for famine victims, there can be no doubt that some of it found its way to the fighters. In any event, if the starving could be fed from external sources, this released such domestic supplies as were available for military purposes: 'humanitarianism' and war were simply inseparable. A small number of NGOs, most prominently War on Want, a British organization with a pronounced left-wing ethos that strongly sympathized with the EPLF and TPLF, publicly delivered their aid only through the 'back door'; others, while officially operating only through the 'front door', since they could not otherwise send relief to government areas at all, tacitly allowed some of their aid to be diverted from stocks ostensibly delivered to Sudan.

The famine thus represented a loss of innocence on the part of many relief agencies, which were forced to confront their naive assumption that they could in some way operate on a solely 'humanitarian' plane, distinct from and infinitely superior to the grubby world of 'politics', whether domestic or international. While there can be little doubt that famine relief, however distributed, saved the lives of millions of people who would otherwise have succumbed to starvation, it also played a significant role in sustaining the very conflicts that had helped to create the famine in the first place. The lesson of earlier episodes, that external intervention provides resources for internal actors that can in turn enable these to pursue their domestic political agendas was sharply reinforced. Though the victory of the two principal insurgent movements in 1991 enabled donors of every persuasion to deal with a single effective regime in both Ethiopia and (now independent) Eritrea, the fundamental ambiguity in the aid relationship could not go away.

Operation Restore Hope and the climax of humanitarian intervention

While in Ethiopia, the politics of famine relief turned on the role of a brutal but generally effective regime, in Somalia the problem was quite the opposite. Following the failure of its attempt to annex the large Somali-inhabited part of Ethiopia, the Somali government progressively lost control over the recognized territory of Somalia itself. Somalia has always been an extremely difficult area to govern, because its sparse and largely pastoralist populations owed their primary allegiance to their various individual clans and sub-clans (themselves liable to almost limitless fissiparation), and governance largely turned on the management and manipulation of constantly shifting clan alliances. After 1978, the whole system progressively fell apart, and the attempts of the national government of Mohamed Siyad Barre (itself a military dictatorship formerly backed by the Soviet Union) to impose its control by force led only to an escalating process of state collapse, which culminated in January 1991 when the president fled the capital, Mogadishu, in his last remaining operational tank. But whereas in Ethiopia, the overthrow of the old regime led to its replacement by a disciplined and effective successor, in Somalia it led to anarchy, with shifting territories controlled by militias loosely associated with different clans and sub-clans.

In this situation, the distribution of famine relief to the increasingly large affected population became impossible, as each militia tried to appropriate whatever food was available and deny it to its rivals. The viciously competitive struggles of these clan factions, themselves derived from the harsh environment of Somali pastoralism, carried little, if any, ethos of common humanitarianism and operated at a level of ruthlessness shocking to the moral sensibilities of Western agencies seeking to deliver famine relief, which turned to the then dominant states of the international system to supply both the physical and moral order that the successful management of the resulting humanitarian crisis evidently required. Implicit in the humanitarian agenda is the expectation that its objects must behave like the victims as which they are constructed in the minds of its benevolent promoters. In Ethiopia, both the government and the insurgents were adept at constructing an appropriate façade, which they could use to attract resources and at the same time they could use to promote their own political objectives; in Somalia, even the façade was lacking.

The resulting Operation Restore Hope, which more than any other incident would define the idea of humanitarian intervention in the aftermath of the end of the Cold War, derived from peculiar junctures both in the global system and in domestic US politics. At the global level, the sudden collapse of the Soviet Union and its allies had left the Western powers, led by the US, in a position of apparently unchallengeable global dominance, providing in turn a historic opportunity to refashion the world in accordance with the ideals of democracy, good governance and capitalist development on the basis of which it had fought and won the Cold War. At the domestic level, the outgoing US administration of President George H. W. Bush had lost the 1992 presidential election to the Democratic Party candidate, Bill Clinton, but remained in office during the period of two months before the inauguration of his successor. Far from acting as the 'lame duck' president characteristic of such periods, Bush sought to make a striking intervention which, as well as assuring a legacy for the outgoing administration, was clearly also intended to provide the model for a new structure of global order, in which a right of intervention or *droit d'ingérence* would be assumed by the now dominant states in the post-Cold War international system, in the case of humanitarian catastrophes that the normal diplomatic processes could not resolve. He accordingly sought to resolve the problem of the Somali famine by a spectacular demarche, through which food would be delivered to the starving under the security umbrella provided by a large US military force.[14]

Whatever the suspicions of ulterior strategic motive often aroused by US engagement in the 'third world', there is no plausible reason to regard this intervention as having been undertaken for any other purposes than those publicly ascribed to it. As Bush himself put it, in a New Year 1992–3 visit to the troops on the ground, the US army was 'doing God's work'. Though the occasion was orchestrated for maximum publicity effect – television camera crews were already installed on a beach outside Mogadishu to film the US marines storming ashore into a supposedly hostile environment – its initial impact was all that could have been wished. The Somali factions were indeed shocked and awed by the massive display of firepower and the distribution of food was rapidly assured. For a moment, at least, the operation looked like a complete success. The central weakness of the mission was, however, that, orchestrated as it was on the plane of a high humanitarian endeavour concerned to bring succour to the suffering, it had absolutely no political agenda, designed first of all to guide the relations between the US forces and the numerous, fractious, confusing and often heavily armed Somali militias already in place, or secondly to assure some more lasting order under which Somalis would be able to govern themselves in a manner that assured adherence to the basic norms of the new global system, without the need for a large foreign military presence. The initial US assumption was that the force was there simply to assure the delivery of aid, without intervening in domestic Somali politics or, notably, attempting the extremely difficult task of disarming the different factions; Bush even offered the astonishingly naive aspiration that it would be withdrawn before the end of his term of office on 20 January 1993.

The problem was, in its way, the precise counterpart to the very different situation in Ethiopia: the failure to recognize the impact of intervention on domestic political forces, some of which were affected negatively and others positively, by the US presence. The ineluctable logic of such situations is that those factions that are, at the moment of intervention, in a relatively weak position will welcome external intervention, since this protects them against their rivals, and these will constitute themselves as the supporters of the outside forces and as needed intermediaries between them and the domestic population – with which, at the most basic social and cultural level, the US forces had absolutely nothing in common. Those who feel themselves to be in a relatively strong position are correspondingly likely to resent the presence of the intervention force, which they will see as cheating them of victory. In this way, the intervenors can readily become associated, not only with one of the competing factions in the civil war that led to their intervention, but with the weaker one. In Mogadishu in December 1992, the first or weaker group consisted of factions linked to Ali Mahdi Mohamed, who enjoyed the entirely titular position of interim president, the second and stronger group of those linked to Mohamed Farah Aidid, who consequently came before long to be identified as the principal 'bad guy', to use the simplistic binary classification that almost inevitably comes into being on such occasions.

It likewise became evident that the apparently overwhelming advantages enjoyed by the intervention force were actually far less imposing than had been assumed. Asked in advance about the likely attitudes of Somalis towards the sudden presence of the US military in their midst, policymakers in Washington would undoubtedly have taken the view that these would be highly positive: the intervention was intended to (and indeed initially did) bring peace to a city embroiled in apparently endless conflict and at the same time rescue large numbers of Somalis from imminent death by starvation. It would thus create highly visible public goods which would assure it public support and provide a moral and political basis for its continued presence. The problem with this analysis was at one level that, in the highly factionalized environment of wartime Mogadishu, public goods in the sense that it took for granted could scarcely be said to exist, assuming as they did that there were common human benefits overriding the interests of individual factions. The military domination supposedly conferred by the presence of some 28,000 heavily armed US troops – a number vastly in excess of the forces that any Somali faction leader could muster – was likewise extremely fragile. The moment one asked how and under what circumstances the available firepower could actually be used, its limitations became clear. Civilian casualties, inevitable in any sustained use of force within a densely populated city, were to be avoided at all costs. Distinguishing between the 'good guys' and the 'bad guys', a difficult enough task even for those intricately involved in following the constantly changing alliances of Somali clan politics, was impossible for the US soldier on the ground, unless he was able to return fire directly against someone who fired at him. All Somali fighters looked the same from an American point of view: a US soldier was instantly identifiable from a Somali one. The very weaponry used by Somali fighters – characteristically hand-held AK47 assault rifles, supplemented by heavy machine-guns mounted on the back of pick-up trucks and known as 'technicals' – was better suited to the terrain than that at the disposal of the US military, which was technically more powerful and sophisticated, but designed for very different circumstances. Somalis could find their way around back streets and alleyways and find refuge behind the blank walls of Moslem compounds in a way that Americans could not match.

As a result, the US (and a number of other states which associated themselves with it) became sucked into domestic conflicts that it was entirely unequipped to manage and from which it could eventually only withdraw, as happened under the Clinton administration as mounting casualties (which were especially unacceptable when they occurred within the context a 'humanitarian' operation in which no strategic interests were involved and US troops were supposedly 'doing good' to the very people who then killed them), culminating in the 'Black Hawk Down' incident when a US helicopter was shot down, destroyed domestic political support for the mission. A face-saving formula was devised, under which the US-led force handed over to a multinational United Nations mission, which itself withdrew a year or so later and

Mogadishu was effectively left to the mercy of its own factions. In the process, a lethal blow was dealt to the doctrine that Operation Restore Hope had been designed to establish, in which basic standards of acceptable humanitarian behaviour would, if necessary, be assured worldwide under the aegis of the dominant states of the post-Cold War international order. This order itself, of course, proved to be short-lived. It was the product of the extraordinary vacuum created by the sudden collapse of the Soviet Union and its global alliance, a vacuum that would before long be filled by the emergence of alternative countervailing forces to Western domination, in the form notably of radicalized Islam and of the rising Asian economic powers led by China. It is nonetheless important to recognize that the project failed as the result of its own internal inadequacies, not simply as a result of changes in the global system.

Islam, piracy and Somali state-building

The resounding failure of Operation Restore Hope led, for a while at least, to the disappearance of humanitarian intervention from the political agendas of the Horn. On the one hand, the political impetus in Western states that had sustained it was destroyed: given the absence of substantial Western interests in the region, the evident costs that it involved and the lack of public support, it was simply not worth pursuing. Even a government as devoted to global humanitarian agendas as the Blair administration in the UK and as willing to put military resources behind them, found little to do in the region and devoted itself instead to broader concerns for African aid and governance expressed notably through its Commission for Africa, to other areas of the continent such as Sierra Leone where it could make a more immediate impact, and eventually and destructively to intervention in Iraq and Afghanistan. Another important factor was the emergence in Ethiopia after 1991 of the Ethiopian Peoples' Revolutionary Democratic Front (EPRDF) regime under Meles Zenawi, which made it possible to convert the core state of the region into a 'normal' country broadly aligned with Western donors, subject indeed to potentially worrying concerns over the relationship between aid (of which it was a major recipient) and defective levels of domestic democracy and human rights observance that figured much more prominently than before, but not involving the level of exceptionalism that humanitarianism in the Horn had previously aroused. The country in the region in which humanitarian issues might most plausibly have been raised was Eritrea, which after independence in 1993 rapidly degenerated into an intensely authoritarian state, in which however there was no effective source of leverage that external powers could use: the regime maintained close and effective control over the whole of its national territory and spurned any aid that might expose it to external constraints.

The form in which humanitarian politics of a kind resurfaced in the Horn was one that drew much more specifically than before on Western security considerations and in which intervention was closely geared to the establishment of a global order acceptable to powerful outside states, rather than to the welfare of individuals within the region itself. Whether such intervention can be characterized as 'humanitarian' at all, of course, is a questionable issue, but it aroused such similar constructions of the relationships between the dominant states of the international order and its peripheries, of a kind indeed that stretched back to Tewodros and the mid-nineteenth century British intervention in Ethiopia, that it is well worth considering in this context. The most important trigger for renewed engagement was the '9/11' Islamist attacks in September 2001 on New York and Washington, half a world away from the Horn itself but following events much closer to the region, notably the US embassy bombings in Nairobi and Dar-es-Salaam in August 1998 and the attack on the USS Cole in Aden harbour in October 2000. As well as drawing attention to the role of radicalized Islam, these raised in acute form the 'threat' posed by ungoverned spaces to the international order, as potential hiding and organizing places for 'terrorists' and hence as a legitimate concern for the 'global war on terror'. This dictated that such spaces could no longer be left to their own devices, but had to be brought within some structure of control.

Somalia, as the world's most prominent 'collapsed state', bordering on areas of strategic significance not only to eastern Africa but much more sensitively to the Middle East, thus came to be reconstructed within the new security framework. Nor was this difficult. As an entirely Muslim society, Somalis drew heavily on Islam both at a broad moral and cultural level and more specifically as a structure of law. With the collapse of the state as an alternative provider of security and essential public services, Islamic institutions inevitably came to fill the gap in important respects: for education, for legal redress and also for the transmission of remittances from the huge Somali diaspora on which Somalis remaining within the national territory heavily relied. Inevitably, too, radical Islamists fleeing especially from Afghanistan identified Somalia as an area where they could be at least relatively safe, while Salafists originating largely from Saudi Arabia and seeking to institute a pure form of Islam saw it as providing a target for proselytization, not least since much Somali Islam – over matters such as women's dress, for instance – had been extremely lax.

These developments came to a head in 2005-6, as the Sharia courts which had dispensed justice, especially in Mogadishu, within the limited zones controlled by the particular clans and sub-clans to which their judges belonged, started to group together within an umbrella 'Union of Islamic Courts' (UIC) that aspired to transcend clan boundaries and establish a structure of order within the city as a whole. The movement proved extremely successful, as long-established roadblocks were removed and people were able to move freely around the city for the first time in many years. Almost inevitably, however, any structure capable of exercising such powers both rested on, and came to attract the attention of, specific interest groups within the wider Somali setting and in turn defined the UIC in ways that aroused opposition, both domestic and external. For one thing, the UIC came to be associated with a particular sub-clan (or indeed sub-sub-clan) within the perennially factionalized world of Somali clan politics and sought to escape from this limitation by articulating wider Somali nationalist goals that threatened regional order: in particular, it threatened the self-proclaimed but unrecognized 'Republic of Somaliland', established in 1991 in the former British Somaliland, which had succeeded in establishing generally effective and consensual government within its own territory;[15] and it revived historic claims on the Somali-inhabited areas of Ethiopia. More dangerous still, from a global perspective, the UIC came under the control of Salafist elements who for instance, in one of the more bizarre expressions of religious purity, forbade Somalis from watching the 2006 football World Cup on television, despite the fact that both the Iranian and the Saudi national teams were playing in it. If Somalia were to be reconstituted as an effective state, which external powers ardently desired, it looked likely to be reconstituted as an Islamist and expansionist one, which they equally did not.

In the short term, this possibility was prevented by an Ethiopian invasion, a thoroughly non-humanitarian exercise in national realpolitik, with tacit support from the US, in which the Ethiopian military destroyed the Somali and Islamist forces opposed to them and proceeded to occupy Mogadishu. The US, which had in the meantime established a military base, Camp Lemonnier, in Djibouti, took advantage of the opportunity to pursue fleeing Islamists into south-western Somalia. In the longer term, the Islamist movement inevitably revived, under the banner of an organization called al-Ittihad, and the Ethiopians were replaced by an African Union force, which succeeded in maintaining enough control over Mogadishu to enable a token government, the Transitional Federal Government (TFG) to maintain a nominal presence, with the help of Western aid, which did nothing to resolve the underlying problems of Somali statehood. These were indeed exacerbated by the emergence of Somali-centred piracy as a threat to the major global trading routes through the Indian Ocean and the Gulf of Aden, Red Sea and Suez Canal. Funded and organized by businessmen in the huge Somali diaspora, but employing seamen in the small ports especially in eastern Somalia, pirates operated from lightly armed speedboats that served much the same function at sea as the 'technicals' had by land, and captured ships and their crews that were released only by paying large ransoms. They proved astonishingly resilient, in the face of lumbering attempts by largely Western navies to control them, and reinforced the status of the Horn as a source of global disorder that the most powerful states in the international system were unable to control.[16]

Conclusion: The problematic legacies of humanitarianism in the Horn

The humanitarian agenda and the politics of aid within which it is set embodies profound conceptions of global inequality, moral every bit as much as military or economic. It conveys the sense of an ordered international system, conceived and organized by the dominant states within that system and dispensed originally within the framework of straightforward imperialism, but in modern times by the articulation of global norms that subordinate states and other actors are obliged to respect and that dominant states are correspondingly both empowered and obliged to promote. Though the sense of moral obligation is most strongly conveyed by humanitarian responses to disaster such as Band Aid and famine relief more generally, and the empowerment of leading actors is most convincingly demonstrated by military activities ranging from the British expedition against emperor Tewodros in the 1860s to Operation Restore Hope in the 2000s, they may best be seen as complementary aspects of a much wider project: the creation of a global order, guided fundamentally by the values of the successful Western states, which seeks to establish a stable framework of governance conducive to peace and human welfare. The promotion of liberal democracy and the protection of human rights, neither of them particularly salient in the Horn of Africa (and therefore not considered here), are further elements in the same agenda.[17]

Given the premise of inequality on which the whole project rests, and the very evident disparities in almost every respect between those who have devised it and those on whom it has been imposed, it is easy to assume that we are indeed seeing the creation of such a global order in the image of the West – an assumption that readily ties in with a conception of human history in terms of 'progress' that itself resonates very firmly in Western thought, not least indeed in Marxism. The experience of the Horn, nonetheless, gives us at the very least some reason to pause. Here is one of the poorest regions in the entire planet, replete with all the problems that the humanitarian agenda has been expected to resolve, and which might have been expected likewise to display the crudest power disparities between the intervening forces on the one hand – whether in the shape of relief agencies bringing in desperately needed food, or of the US military creating the conditions of order in which this food could be made available to the starving – and the suffering victims on the other. Suffering victims there were indeed aplenty, and millions of human lives have been lost in the Horn over the last 40 years, as a result not only of famine, but of the political conflicts which helped to intensify it. Yet between these victims and the external agencies which sought to assist them – the great majority with entirely genuine charitable impulses which it would be quite wrong to disparage – lay an intermediary group of political entrepreneurs who came to exercise a remarkable level of leverage over the entire 'humanitarian' enterprise and in the process shape it to their own agendas. Again, these should not be crudely pigeonholed as the 'bad guys', operating to thwart the admirable aspirations of the 'good guys' drawn from the charitable West. Some of them – notably both the Ethiopian central government in the mid-1980s and the insurgencies in Eritrea and Tigray against which it was fighting – had clearly articulated (though opposed) political agendas geared to their own conceptions of what their territories should become, into which the activities of external relief agencies were readily incorporated. Others – notably the 'warlords', as they came to be called, in Somalia in the 1990s – were operating within the parameters of Somali clan politics, in a way that was incomprehensible and indeed evil to external actors guided by other motivations, but which constituted an enduring frame of reference not only to the 'warlords', but to virtually the whole of the very distinctive society within which they lived. Essentially, we are looking at the juxtaposition of alternative mentalities, driven in part by culture and ideology, in part by considerations of survival and self-interest, that were brought into sharp contrast by the exigencies of humanitarian relief. And in this clash of culture and interest, the indigenous political entrepreneurs enjoyed a very considerable level of leverage.

In terms of the broader themes explored in this volume, the experience of the Horn is in some degree distinctive. On the one hand, it provides some of the most extreme examples, anywhere in Africa, of the international politics of victimhood. The terms in which the moral obligation to aid Ethiopian victims of famine was articulated, for example, resonate with the motto of the anti-slavery movement on the other side of the continent, 'Am I not a Man and a Brother?'. On the other, it likewise exemplifies, to a striking degree, the underlying failings of the entire humanitarian project. Critical here is that this is the region of Africa that, more than any other, escaped or evaded the imposition of not only the structures but the ideologies of governance associated with colonial rule. Ethiopian conceptions of statehood, skilfully adapted though they were to the need to operate within the modern international system, remained at heart indigenous; and though the Somali territories came for the most part under formal colonial rule, the depth and intensity of Somali culture, allied to the unproductive and sparsely inhabited terrain, meant that the imprint of colonialism was relatively light. This is why the region came to be seen as 'problematic', from the viewpoint not only of dominant Western powers, but also of postcolonial African states, most of which enthusiastically adopted European conceptions of statehood as the means through which to manage their own relations with the international system. In the process, it came to be seen as – and remains – a 'challenge' to those conceptions of statehood and the normative ideals of universal humanitarian obligation associated with them.

Notes

1. For the concept of 'extraversion', see Jean-François Bayart, *The State in Africa: The Politics of the Belly* (London: Longman, 1993), esp. 20–32, 196–200.
2. See Sven Rubenson, *The Survival of Ethiopian Independence* (London: Heinemann, 1976), 239–87; Bahru Zewde, *A History of Modern Ethiopia 1855–1974* (London: James Currey, 1991), 25–32.
3. Haile-Selassie's appeal to the League of Nations in June 1936, 'I, Haile Selassie I, Emperor of Ethiopia, am here today to claim that justice which is due to my people', remains the most poignant affirmation before that undistinguished organization of the principles of international law and security for which it was ostensibly founded; see *Selected Speeches of His Imperial Majesty Haile Selassie I* (Addis Ababa: Imperial Ethiopian Ministry of Information, 1967), 305–16.

4. K.C. Gandar Dower, *The First to be Freed: The Record of British Military Administration in Eritrea and Somalia, 1941–1943* (London: Ministry of Information, 1944).
5. See Harold G. Marcus, *A History of Ethiopia* (Berkeley, CA: University of California Press, 2002), 158–9.
6. Peter Gill, *A Year in the Death of Africa: Politics, Bureaucracy and the Famine* (London: Paladin, 1986), 4–5.
7. See Gebru Tareke, *The Ethiopian Revolution: War in the Horn of Africa* (New Haven, CT: Yale University Press, 2009), Chapter 6.
8. See David Pool, *From Guerrillas to Government: the Eritrean People's Liberation Front* (Oxford: James Currey, 2001).
9. See John Young, *Peasant Revolution in Ethiopia: The Tigray People's Liberation Front, 1975–1991* (Cambridge: Cambridge University Press, 1997).
10. Cited from Alex De Waal, *Famine Crimes: Politics and the Disaster Relief Industry in Africa* (London: James Currey, 1997), 122; the film can be watched on http://www.youtube.com/watch?v=eLLsTdaVgsc; see also Michael Buerk, *The Road Taken: An Autobiography* (London: Arrow, 2005).
11. For a powerful critique of this apolitical approach to famine, see De Waal, *Famine Crimes*.
12. For an account by the head of the commission, see Dawit Wolde Giorgis, *Red Tears: War, Famine and Revolution in Ethiopia* (Trenton, NJ: Red Sea Press, 1989).
13. See Gill, *A Year in the Death of Africa*, Chapters 11, 12.
14. See Walter S. Clarke and Jeffrey Herbst, eds, *Learning from Somalia: The Lessons of Armed Humanitarian Intervention* (Boulder, CO: Westview, 1997); and John L. Hirsch and Robert B. Oakley, *Somalia and Operation Restore Hope: Reflections on Peacemaking and Peacekeeping* (Washington, DC: US Institute of Peace, 1995).
15. See Stig Jarle Hansen with Mark Bradbury, 'Somaliland: a new democracy in the Horn of Africa?', *Review of African Political Economy*, 34.113 (2007): 461–76.
16. See Ken Menkhaus, 'Dangerous Waters', *Survival*, 51.1 (2009): 21–5; Roger Middleton, *Piracy in Somalia: Threatening Global Trade, Feeding Local Wars* (London: Chatham House Briefing Paper, 2008).
17. See James Mayall and Ricardo Soares de Oliveira, eds, *The New Protectorates: International Tutelage and the Making of Liberal States* (London: Hurst, 2011).

6
The Democratic Republic of Congo: The Land of Humanitarian Interventions

Claude Kabemba

Introduction

This chapter revisits the different humanitarian interventions since the Berlin Conference of 1885. Throughout the past century, the Congo has continually been the subject of 'humanitarian' intervention by various Western powers. First, Leopold II of Belgium intervened to end the slave trade; then the Belgian government intervened to end Leopold's atrocities; then the UN intervened to promote a certain kind of 'self-determination'; and finally the UN intervened again to end a civil war. In all of these cases, the fundamental reality behind the interventions was always an economic one. Control of the Congo's mineral and natural resource wealth has been the primary role of intervention. Because humanitarianism has always been the mask for economic intervention, true humanitarian efforts in the country are continually fruitless. INGOs, governments and local people have vastly different priorities in the provision of humanitarian assistance and the conflicting goals lead to stagnation, corruption and ineffectiveness of intervention.

This chapter argues that what has driven all engagements in the Congo – now DRC – has been directed by an imperial/colonial mindset that sees the Congolese as backwards and 'other' and therefore as inferior and needing intervention. The chapter draws on the theories of Jean-Paul Sartre, Aimé Césaire and other theorists of empire to support this idea. While true *humanitarian* intervention is required in the DRC, what has long been called humanitarian intervention by Western powers and the UN has been anything but humanitarian, with economic concerns predominating and imperial superiority undermining any real efforts to provide relief and assistance.

Humanitarianism under King Leopold II and the Belgian government

King Leopold II of Belgium set the stage for the West humanitarian interventions in Africa in general and the Democratic Republic of Congo (DRC) in particular. Pre-empting potential confrontations over the territory of the Congo, the King of Belgium, in 1876, summoned a conference in Brussels to which he invited representatives from Europe and America to launch the International African Association (IAA). He used this platform to put his diplomacy in motion for the control of the Congo for humanitarian reasons. He set himself above those who had pretensions to the Congo's resources. He convinced the other powers – Britain, France, Germany, Portugal and the US – to give him control of the vast DRC territory using humanitarian concerns for the natives who had been displaced and decimated by slavery. His intervention, he argued, was to go and end the 'savage' and 'barbarous' rule in the colonies.[1]

Leopold presented himself before the other countries as a man not interested in profit but in serving others. The king convincingly used the notion of a failed state which needed to be rebuilt to justify his argument for humanitarian intervention. He went further in his argument in an effort to convince the other powers that his intention was to open 'civilisation to the only area of the globe to which it has not yet penetrated, to pierce the gloom which hangs over entire races, constitute a crusade worthy of this century of progress'.[2]

Belgium was too small to pose a threat to the interests of big and powerful nations. The other powers saw in Leopold II a compromise, to avoid going to war over the Congo, which at the time was known to possess important strategic resources. The European powers decided to give the king the authority to oversee the Congo on behalf of all powers. The conference defined the trade rules. From this time, the Congo Free State was looked upon as free for exploitation by the capitalist world.[3] From this time forth, the DRC has not known peace and has received international humanitarian actions more than any other country on the African continent.

In most African countries, imperialism and colonialism were embedded into the notion of humanitarianism. As Michael Doyle puts it, 'Empire is a relationship, formal or informal, in which one state controls the effective political sovereignty of another political society.'[4] This control can be achieved by force, by political collaboration, by economic, social, or cultural dependence. The King of Belgium's humanitarian intervention turned out to be simply domination and subjugation of the Congolese people. Humanitarian intervention became the politics of power of Western civilizations over non-Western civilizations, which occurred through the discourse and dynamics of economic domination, deemed necessary not only for the colonizer, but also and especially for the colonized. The imperialist humanitarian is well elaborated by D. K. Fieldhouse when he suggests that 'the basis of imperial authority was the mental attitude of the colonist; his acceptance of subordination, whether through a positive sense of common interest with the parent state, or through inability to conceive of any alternative'.[5]

It was this social relationship that made the king's 'humanitarian' intervention in 1885 and the Belgians' in 1908 durable. Instead of taking the Congolese out of slavery, the Belgians reinforced the concept of 'others' or the idea of 'otherness' in the DRC. Leopold II and the Belgians' humanitarian intervention in the Congo was based on identification of the Congolese as inferior and savage who needed to be educated and civilized. In this system the humanists monopolized power to psychologically and physically enforce the identity of the 'other'. In this form of humanitarianism, as Sartre explains, 'other human beings (Congolese) are perceived as objects, as tools or as obstacles and because "I am not them, I only know them as object"'.[6] This attribute was so entrenched that colonized people became unable to define themselves. To ensure the sustainability of the project there was the need for a constant circulation and recirculation of Europeans, which allowed decent men and women (Europeans) to accept the notion that distant territories and their native people should be subjugated.

Despite the rhetoric in Europe, there was nothing humanitarian in the Belgian intervention. Instead of improving the organizational capacity of the Congolese, Leopold's 'humanitarian' intervention was transformed into forced labour and criminalized Congolese socio-economic and political structures. Captain Vallier wrote in 1900 from the depths of the Congo rainforest 'We find here nothing but anarchy and ill-will, in other words, a society in its infancy, without any organisation, a scattering of humanity, who escape from contact with us and paralyse our most generous efforts with inertia.'[7] Leopold presented the pre-colonial history of the Congolese as backward and uncivilized, operating without any agreed system and values and freely trading their neighbours as slaves. It is this representation which necessitated a humanitarian intervention.

In the 1890s, periodic reports of abuses from the Congo started to be received through the international press, particularly in Britain and America, where a strong movement to overthrow Leopold's rule was undertaken. In the Belgian parliament voices began to be raised in protest against their king. These Belgian voices were raised not so much against the abuses as against the selfishness of the king. Finally, the British government asked the powers which signed the Berlin Act of 1885 to work out a solution to the Congo question. The solution seemed to be to remove power from Leopold and transfer it to the elected government of Belgium.

When the Belgian government took over from Leopold in 1908, the Congo became once again forgotten until the Second World War, when it played a modest (although very important) role with its copper, diamonds, rubber, cotton and its uranium which were of great strategic value to the Allied forces.[8] During that time, Belgian colonialism was unparalleled in the continent in its control and penetration of African society, organized by the trinity of bureaucracy, capital and church.[9] The breadth and depth of the Belgian colonial penetration in the Congo was probably second to none in sub-Saharan Africa. One historian labelled the colonial state in Congo 'totalitarian'.[10] Although this designation might be debated, there can be little doubt that the entire humanitarian intervention was extractive, oppressive and authoritarian. Like all imperialists, the Belgians justified colonialism on cultural, religious and economic grounds. They argued that colonialism was a solution to the problems of underdeveloped people. As such they equated colonialism to humanitarianism.

Post-independence humanitarian interventions

In 1960 just few months after its independence, Congo degenerated into political instability. The period of global institutions had begun in the wake of the decline of global empires and the United Nations was created to deal with global issues, especially conflict. The newly independent Congo was one of the first to experience the UN's humanitarian interventions. While the conflict on the surface seemed to be a conflict among the Congolese, underneath it was a conflict within the Western bloc and between the Western bloc and the Eastern bloc for the control of the Congo and its abundant mineral resources. The Belgian decision to give independence to the Congolese before they had the necessary preliminary managerial skill was strategic. By granting independence, the Belgians hoped to create a pseudo-independent state, or what Ghana's president, Kwame Nkrumah (1961) called 'clientele-sovereignty', a practice of granting a sort of independence, with the concealed intention of making the liberated country a client-state and controlling it effectively by means other than political ones. For Belgium, Congolese independence was supposed to be a transfer of partial political power to a group of local bourgeoisie who could be trusted to preserve and extend some of the colonial relationships of domination and exploitation. Independence, in reality, was about creating neo-colonial relationships which, if closely analysed, simply meant a continuation of pre-colonial control. Thomas Pakenham, speaking of the state within which Belgium left its colonies – Rwanda, Burundi and the Congo – says: 'Belgium scuttled out leaving these countries ready for civil war.'[11]

Although the Belgians gave the colony an ostensibly democratic constitution which was a copy of the Belgian constitution, it did not prepare the Congolese to run the state. After losing direct political control, the Belgians were hoping to control the Congo economically. Post-independence Congolese foreign policy (under the leadership of Patrice Lumumba) became a product of the fear of continued exploitation of its resources and political control by Belgium. Not only had Lumumba been physically eliminated, his life and work were not to become a source of inspiration for the people of Congo and Africa. His vision of creating a unified nation-state and an economy serving the needs of the people were to be wiped out. The killing of Lumumba was a clear expression that the entire Western essence in the DRC had nothing humanitarian in it.

The nationalist movements of the early 1960s, which called for national unity and economic independence, were a threat to Western interests. Three strategies were used to weaken the nationalist movements: assassination of national leaders, disinformation against national leaders, and ethnic divisions. The capitalist bloc, though united in its willingness to see the Congo stay under its control, was also divided regarding access to resources. There were competing interests over the control of Katanga's mineral resources. The US was in competition with Belgium, France and Britain. They competed fiercely for the control of Congolese minerals in the early years of the country's independence. This competition sustained and prolonged the Congolese conflict. It was clear from the start that the independence granted by Belgium was political and not economic. In fact, Mario Cardoso, the

Congo's representative at the UN put it very clearly, saying 'Western capitalism (had) provoked Katanga's secession... It is not the Congolese that are divided, it is the world that is divided. Therefore, leave the Congo alone.'[12]

Western competition in the new state was mostly over the control of Katanga's minerals. During colonization, Congo's resources were exploited for many decades by British and Belgian capital. Before 1967, 14.47 per cent of the share capital of the Belgian company *Union Minière du Katanga (UMK)* belonged to the British Tanganyika Concessions.[13] The diamond industry was the monopoly of De Beers Consolidated Mines. But since the 1940s, the US also wanted to penetrate and control some part of the Katanga mining sector. Decolonization and self-determination, although regularly associated with humanitarianism in the 1990s interventions, was not a humanitarian act in the 1960s; it was intended to create space for American businesses. After independence, the progressive Congolese leaders had a double challenge; to control the imperialists on one hand and to deal with stooges in their own ranks on the other. These stooges included Tshombe, Kasavubu and Mobutu. All three worked for the Western powers to undermine the Lumumba programme. In fact Mobutu's dictatorship was erected on the heritage of colonial conquest and the exigencies of the Cold War, which portrayed Mobutu as an anti-communist leader and friend of the West. This aggressive move by the US pushed Belgium and Britain to put in place some defensive mechanisms.

It is important to understand that the Belgian military intervention was not part of the UN operation which was already in the country since 14 July 1960. The UN was not in favour of Belgian troops in Katanga, but the UN Secretary General, Dag Hammarskjold, was killed in a mysterious plane crash on his way to meet Tshombe in Ndola, Zambia. The objective of the meeting was to try and persuade Tshombe of the need to have UN troops stationed in Katanga in place of the Belgians. Tshombe's agreement to Hammarskjold's proposal would have been tantamount to siding with the US against Belgian and Britain interests in Katanga. When Western powers were acting against each other, the Congolese elite did not understand the strategic battle that these powers were engaged in. The divisions among the Western powers also played themselves out in the UN Security Council. On 14 July 1960 the US voted for a resolution calling for the withdrawal of Belgian troops from Congo. France voted against and Britain abstained. When in November 1961 the African and Asian representatives to the Security Council (United Arab Republic, Liberia and Ceylon) tabled a resolution calling for the removal of the chief cause of the Congolese crisis (the colonial powers' military intervention in Katanga) Britain, Belgium and France opposed it. However, with US diplomatic manoeuvring, the resolution was adopted after amendments, with both France and Britain abstaining. It is clear that the struggle within the Western bloc, linked to control and extraction of minerals in Katanga, was the main factor that divided Congolese post-independence leaders in the conflict which was at the time attributed to lack of political maturity of the Congolese.

In 1961, the US, under President John F. Kennedy, was now backing the government of Adoula in Kinshasa, a government that it helped to win the election. Adoula won in a contest that, according to Gleijeses, could easily have been won by a Lumumbist if elections had been free and fair.[14] The Adoula government was the first imposition of a government over the Congolese people by the US. The imposition was resisted by two groups from vastly different backgrounds. The first was Moise Tshombe, who had the support of Belgium. The US pushed for reconciliation between Adoula and Tshombe but the latter rejected this move. Belgium, Britain and France were not in favour of Katanga being under the central government, now controlled by a pro-US leadership. As Walter Lippmann puts it, 'Behind Adoula the main power was the United States government. Behind Tshombe the main power consisted of large private interests of Great Britain and Belgium.'[15] Things only changed in December 1962 when President Kennedy approved the use of the UN force to put down the Katanga rebellion. The Anglo-Belgium coalition compromised under UN pressure. By late January 1963, the rebellion in Katanga had been crushed and the province had been reintegrated into US controlled Congo-Kinshasa. The UN was used by the US not for humanitarian purposes but to advance neo-colonialist ambitions. The fact that the UN refused to give support to a legitimate government (of Lumumba) meant that, instead of being a humanitarian mission, it became an added cause of the crisis.

The UN troops left Congo on 30 June 1964. Immediately fierce fighting between Simba guerrillas and government troops broke in the east of the country. After the victory in Katanga, the US also dealt with the rebellion in the Kivu province. In the meantime, there was change of government in the US following the assassination of President Kennedy. Lyndon Johnson became the president. Like his predecessors, Johnson viewed Congo-Kinshasa as strategic and was determined to crush the Simba rebellion. But his administration was confronted with two problems: first, the unpopularity of the Adoula government in Kinshasa; and second, the US army was stretched with the war in

Vietnam and could not send troops to the Congo. Two things happened. First, Tshombe came back from exile in Spain and replaced
Adoula; second, the US asked the European powers and South Africa
for military support in the Congo. The US promised to provide hard-
ware and CIA instructors. The ground offensive against the Simba was
done mostly by mercenaries brought in from South Africa and the air
attacks by Belgian pilots. By 24 November 1964 the mercenaries had
recaptured all the towns in Kivu Province. The US victory in Congo-
Kinshasa was sealed when Joseph Mobutu staged a coup in 1965 with
the backing of the CIA. With this victory, the American monopolies
were able to share in the profit of the *Union Minière*, which continued to
exploit Katanga up to January 1967 when Mubutu nationalized companies and *Union Minière* became *Société générale Congolaise des Minerais*
(GECOMIN). In this new company, 40 per cent of the share capital
continued to belong to Belgian, British and US companies.

The post independence instability was caused more by Western posi-
tioning to control Congo's minerals than by ethnic conflict. Had it not
been for the imperialist contradictions, the problem of Katanga would
not have arisen and even if it had, it would not have been so acute
and would not have undermined the life of the young state the way it
did. Progressive forces in the Congo might have resolved the conflict
quicker if there had been no foreign interests fuelling the conflict under
the pretext of humanitarian intervention.

Once in power, Mobutu declared war against communism and became
the darling of the West. Mobutu presided over the DRC during the
time of the Cold War. Throughout the Cold War period the US and
its allies (especially France and Belgium) were quick to shore up the
central government's political control whenever that became necessary.
In March 1977 France and Morocco intervened to save Mobutu's regime
from secessionists in the Shaba (Katanga) province. A year later France
and Belgium intervened after armed groups seized the major mining
town of Kolwezi in Shaba province. Clearly, Mobutu was dependent on
the support he received from outside. Mobutu played the communist
card, citing Zaire's strategic importance to justify the need for Western
humanitarian military interventions. In an effort to justify their support
to a regime that was suppressing the rights of its own people, Richard
Moose (the US assistant secretary of state for African affairs) argued:

> We are not simply trying to maintain a static situation [into] main-
> taining an individual in power. We are trying to support, to help,
> to reform, to strengthen an economy that is very important in the

functioning of the western industrial system, a large economy with large resources which we would like to stay within the western economic system and in friendly political relationship to us.[16]

The 1998 Congo war and United Nations humanitarian interventions

In 1996 the DRC was invaded by its neighbours – Rwanda and Uganda – in an effort to eliminate members of the Rwandan armed forces who fled the country after committing genocide in Rwanda in the face of an advancing Tutsi rebel movement led by the current President Paul Kagame. The international community, on humanitarian grounds, forced President Mobutu to allow passage of Rwanda Hutu refugees, some with arms, to enter the DRC.

The invasion later turned into a revolutionary movement led by Laurent Kabila to overthrow President Mobutu. One year after the overthrow of Mobutu, the conflict started again between Rwanda, Uganda and the new Congolese government they helped to put in place. SADC countries – Angola, Namibia and Zimbabwe – sent in troops in support of the DRC government. The war was termed 'Africa's Great War'. The 1996 and 1998 wars have displaced and killed millions of Congolese, especially in the east of the country. The war has also attracted multiple forms of humanitarian interventions in the DRC to reflect the evolution of humanitarian assistance. Humanitarian assistance has expanded to include categories of victims produced by political crises.[17] These crises include interstate conflicts with gross human rights violations resulting in huge numbers of refugees and the displacement of people within the state. According to a survey conducted by the International Rescue Committee (IRC), between August 1998 (when the second Congo war began) and January 2008, an estimated 5.4 million died of the war-related causes, including hunger and disease. Approximately half of the dead were children under the age of five. On average 45,000 people die each month in the Congo because of the crisis.

The United National Security Council sent troops to keep peace in the DRC soon after the Lusaka peace accord was signed in 1999. One element of the peace accord was that a peacekeeping force under Chapter 7 of the UN Charter be established to ensure implementation of the agreement. UN troops were increased incrementally to reach the number of 20,000 today. MONUC has played a critical role throughout the years but it has not succeeded in ending conflict.

The humanitarian intervention in the DRC has brought to the fore controversies and disputes that exist on the definition of humanitarianism (humanitarian intervention). MONUC has been a source of security for the population in the eastern provinces and an instrument that supports operational capacity of the Congolese armed forces (FARDC). It has also played a role of providing information to the international community on the humanitarian and security conditions in these provinces.[18] Keeping the transition on track has required a continuous reinforcement of the UN mission military presence throughout the country, mainly in the east. At critical times, MONUC has received back-up by the EU (ARTEMIS and EUFOR RDC). The massive presence of MONUC remains fundamental considering that the DRC government has no control on the entire territory. The 20,000-strong UN Mission in the DRC has been credited with a range of achievements that include: restoring peace to more than two-thirds of the country, following a conflict that erupted in 1997, involving seven regional armies and cost over five million lives; helping to conduct the first democratic elections in 40 years in 2006–7; and overseeing the return of more than one million refugees and internally displaced persons in 2009.[19]

Verwey describes the term 'humanitarian' as one of the most contested, legally controversial and obscure concepts in international law.[20] The MONUC intervention was morally required, where the use of force is intended to stop the slaughter of human beings. This intervention was justifiable for the purpose of using force to protect the people in the DRC. MONUC entered the DRC under the Responsibility to Protect. The International Commission on Intervention and State Sovereignty (ICISS) argues that humanitarian intervention is associated with justifiable means of using force for the purpose of protecting the people within another state.[21] However, Lemarchand poses an important question: 'when considering the magnitude of the humanitarian crisis in eastern Congo, one must ask why MONUC has failed so egregiously in protecting human lives?'[22] Despite the positive aspect of the presence of MONUC – blocking the advance of rebels on key towns, transportation and protection of humanitarian NGOs and their protection, it has failed to protect human life. The case of Kiwanja in the east DRC where 150 people were killed by the CNDP between 4 and 5 November 2008 with a 120-member UN peacekeeping force only half a mile away illustrates the shameful performance of the MONUC. The east of the DRC has seen many such cases and MONUC has failed to stop them.

The current UN peace keeping force and humanitarian intervention, like the one that intervened to quell the civil war in the 1960s, seems to be manipulated by great powers. Military intervention as a humanitarian action can only succeed when there is consensus on the goals and on how to end the war by key international powers. When the UN Security Council authorized the deployment of UN troops, there was no consensus between the US, UK and France on the cause of the war and how it should be resolved. For the US and Britain, Rwanda was in the DRC for its own security. The US and Britain had tacitly accepted the presence of Rwandan and Ugandan troops on the DRC soil as legitimate. But for the French, Rwanda and Uganda invaded DRC territory. The lack of consensus made it difficult for the humanitarian intervention to respond effectively. For this reason President Laurent Kabila refused to allow the deployment of UN peacekeeping force. Kabila was concerned that the West were plotting to force him out of power. As Congresswoman Cynthia McKinney puts it, 'The Lusaka Peace Accord was not a good thing for the government; Kabila was forced to accede by implicit and explicit threats of even greater assistance to the rebels and an endless war.'[23] Kabila refusal to allow the UN to deploy a peacekeeping forces was in tune with the long-standing conventional wisdom surrounding norms of state sovereignty and the corollary principle of non-intervention, which have been the fundamental norms of international relations, recognized in customary international law for centuries and reaffirmed in the UN Charter. But he was too small to go against the wish of powerful states.

Kabila's distrust of the UN reflected the fact that, for many Congolese, MONUC – and particularly the idea of deploying armed troops – was reviving memories of the UN blue helmet army force that was involved in Congo's civil war during 1960–4.[24] The humanitarian intervention could not possibly work because of the contradiction between Western powers on how to handle the conflict. The situation took a new dynamic when the reading of the causes of the war changed with UN resolution 1341, drafted by the French. Resolution 1341 for the first time condemned Rwanda's and Uganda's invasion of the DRC. It stipulated that the invasion was 'as akin to the 1991 Iraq's invasion of Kuwait'.[25] More dramatically, the resolution recognized Laurent Kabila as the legitimate national leader of his country. Unfortunately there were no mechanisms to enforce the resolution – MONUC at the time had a much reduced force on the ground.[26] Other events such as the war between Rwandan and Ugandan troops in Kisangani for the control of the gold trade and the UN Expert Panels' report on the illegal exploitation of Natural Resources, which named and shamed all those who were involved in 'conflict trade' especially Rwanda and Uganda, were the catalyst factors that forced the two countries to consider a tactical withdrawal of the troops but remaining in the DRC through proxies. According to Lemarchand, a more useful perspective is to underscore the continuing role of Rwanda as the central actor in any attempt to bring peace (or war) to the region.[27] Because of the UK's and US's protective position on Rwanda, the intervention of the UN to try to unearth the atrocities in eastern Congo has not made significant headway.[28]

It is clear that Rwanda has been in the Congo as part of a long-term strategic plan to control the mineral resources. It is not surprising that 'despite claiming a death toll far greater than that of Dafur, the crisis in eastern Congo receives only a fraction of the media attention devoted to the conflict in Western Sudan'.[29] Equally the UN peace mission has not been seriously engaged, as part of its humanitarian response to crisis in the DRC, in trying to curtail access to resources revenues for potential 'peace spoilers'. As Phillipe Le Billon puts it 'during the peace-building phase, mission staff should seek to address broader linkages between resource extraction and conflict; where needed, this assistance should include deployment of peacekeeping forces in resource produc-tion areas and transportation hubs to help control exploitation and address resource-related conflicts'.[30]

This is what happened in Sierra Leone. The UN mission (UNAMSIL) actively engaged in diamond-sector regulation. From 2003 onward, UNAMSIL conducted aerial surveys and foot patrols and targeted conflict-settlement interventions in the diamond sector. The UN mis-sion intervention in resource sector seems to be limited to sharing information collected on illegal logging with UN agencies, NGOs and government structures. Rwanda has also used the inability of the Congolese state to project its power across and continues to maintain its presence through proxies M23/CNDP. But the war in the DRC is com-plex, characterized by the presence of many regional and local actors including militia, paramilitary and warlords with links to outside actors, which illustrate the globalization of the conflict and which makes it dif-ficult to manage. This is why securing and maintaining peace in the DRC will require a more complex approach that broadens the solution to include regional players and dynamics. By adopting this approach the humanitarian intervention will also have to include effort to address trade-offs inherent in the regional war economy.

Humanitarian interventions in the DRC have also included the assistance provided by international non-governmental organizations (INGOs). In 1998 the UN General Assembly adopted Resolution 43/131 which acknowledged the rights of citizens to international humanitarian assistance and the role of NGOs in humanitarian cri-sis.[31] This entails the provision of aid by foreign donors. Described as helping to shine light on the world's trouble spot, celebrity activism has been part of the DRC humanitarianism. The humanitarian sector has been privatized through media celebrities in the DRC. Celebrities like Jessica Lange, Angelina Jolie and Ben Affleck have all worked with international humanitarian organizations such as UNHCR and Save the Children. They have all called for action to end suffering in the DRC, but the war continues. The biggest concern has been the ineffective-ness of MONUC to be the catalyst for peace in the DRC. Some have blamed its internal weaknesses to explain its effectiveness. Concerns about the mission's ineffectiveness in establishing security in eastern Congo have been compounded by allegations of its involvement in plundering resources, running guns in exchange for minerals or ivory, and sexual exploitation and abuse.

MONUC has also been accused of creating opportunities for power-ful Western nations to advance their parochial interests in the DRC. Some fear that peacebuilding in the DRC is being used as a 'Trojan horse' to advance rapid neo-liberal political and economic transforma-tion of the country in line with the interests of the World Bank. There are also the huge salaries and adventurous lifestyle and special privi-leges of international humanitarian workers which almost take a huge size of the humanitarian budget in the presence of massive poverty in the DRC. Most of the time the provision of education and health to the Congolese has been so rudimentary as to undermine the entire human-itarian intervention. Widespread frustration at the mission's continued presence led President Joseph Kabila to request MONUC's withdrawal from the DRC by June 2010. The UN Security Council visited the DRC in May 2010 and has since agreed that MONUC be converted into the UN Organisation Stabilisation Mission in the DRC (MONUSCO), man-dated to remain in the country until 2011. In 2010, before the second general elections, the Congolese government called for MONUC mis-sion to end. In the same year the mandate of MONUC was changed and its name changed to MONUSCO. Thierry Viroulon argues that MONUC has been contaminated by the corruption and impunity inherent in its environment.[32]

Corruption has also affected INGOs. In the eastern region of DRC, the UN Office for Coordination of Humanitarian Affairs (OCHA) with a budget of approximately US$800 million coordinates 126 organiza-tions, including 10 UN agencies and 50 international NGOs. OCHA also works with Congolese governmental officials and donors. Food aid has also been siphoned off the massive 'humanitarian' mission in eastern Congo and being sold in markets.[33] The criminal aspects of the humanitarian enterprise are well established.[34] There have been situations where the people of the DRC have shown their disapproval of MONUC due to unchallenged warlords and impunity for war crimes and massive suffering.

One the biggest paradoxes of the humanitarian interventions in the DRC has been that the structural factors that maintain the on-going instability have never been challenged: from the late nineteenth century to the present that has been the occupation of the DRC by a foreign power – either Belgium, the US by proxy, or Rwanda. Equally, the Western media has consistently covered up the Rwanda occupation in Congo over the past decade, refusing to accept that most of the rebellions identified as Congolese, such the National Congress for the Defense of the People (CNDP) led by Nkundabatware, have been organized and maintained by Rwanda, and have contributed to a reduction of the value of international humanitarian actions. Most of what is being provided through humanitarian interventions is quickly being destroyed and looted by these rebel groups. The West cannot, on one hand, protect the cause of the humanitarian catastrophe – Rwanda and its proxies – in the east of the DRC, and at the same time provide humanitarian support to the population affected by that catastrophe. At the peak of the conflict Rwanda and Uganda were recipients of foreign aid which has contributed to humanitarian tragedy in the DRC.

Despite a clear indication by the UN report of these two countries being involved in atrocities in the DRC, 'their creditworthiness also improved during the same period, which allowed them to obtain debt relief' from Western governments and international institutions.[35] Uganda's debt service fell from approximately US$88.6 million in 1999 to US$47.1 million in 2000 following a substantial debt write-off earlier in the year, while Rwanda paid approximately US$ 30.4 million in debt service in 2000, falling to US$ 14.8 million in 2001.[36] The two countries have used the surplus to finance the war in the DRC. Only Sweden and the Netherlands suspended aid to Rwanda after the UN report.[37] Rwanda instead has blamed the UN for failing to disarm the Hutu militias.

The problem of aid cancellation for these two countries is that they are able to increase their financial investment to maintain their military presence in the DRC. Donors have refused to admit responsibility of their contradictory behaviour in the DRC. This despite the fact that MONUC staff regularly informed the British Ambassador in Kigali of such facts and the report of the panel of experts had formally made the point in a report published in July 2005.[38] In April 2012, Human Rights Watch and the United Nations Organisation Stabilization Mission in the DRC (MONUSCO) accused Rwanda of supplying M23 (or CNDP) with soldiers and arms. Since 1996, the Rwandan government has acted as a major destabilizing force in the east of the Congo undermining international efforts to bring peace. During the CNDP of Nkundabatware rebellion (2008), it was known that he (Nkuda) maintained direct personal communications with the high office in Rwanda. The Rwanda Defense Forces (RDF) dispatched military personnel into Congo, recruited and armed child soldiers and were involved in minerals plunder, racketeering, extortion and war crime.[39] The same is being said about Bosco Tanganda, the leader of M23, which started a new war in 2012.

Conclusion

The humanitarian assistance provided by the international community to resolve the Congolese crisis has been inadequate when considered alongside the scale of human suffering and when compared with the efforts made to address humanitarian crises in other regions of the world, with the exception of Somalia. The magnitude of the Congolese crisis warrants a much stronger and better coordinated response among agencies, donors and international leaders than has so far been the case. Despite the presence of a peacekeeping force, many Congolese in the east of the DRC are hovering on the brink between life and death. MONUC and MONUSCO have not played their role adequately. They have been hesitant to provide accurate and timely information, especially when this information implicates Rwanda and they have not been capable of protecting Congolese lives when it mattered. A major reason for the relatively humanitarian outcome in the DRC is that those who dictate these interventions have left the cause of the crisis unchallenged.

The argument that is advanced in this chapter suggests that insofar as the humanitarian impulse is animated by economic factors, it might remain relatively weak in the DRC, by comparison with other countries. The humanitarian intervention will have to include, if lasting impact is to be made, the political economy of resources extraction beyond the ad hoc intervention of the panel of experts on illegal exploitation of resources in the DRC. In other words, true attempts at state building, real investment in human resources and an end to the exploitation of the DRC's resources by internal and especially external powers. This would require replacing economic imperialism and geopolitical concerns with true humanitarian priorities.

Humanitarian interventions in the DRC from colonial interventions and the two UN military interventions of 1961 and 1998 have not been used to build a functional state that can take care of its citizens. Instead, they have been used to maintain a status quo with regard to economic balances of power, or access to natural resources. Time and again, humanitarian claims have been made to intervene in the Congo region. Military and civilian aid has been promoted, but what has emerged has continually been the destabilization of indigenous structures in favour of Western economic interest. Just as Roger Casement's call for intervention led to handover of Leopold's Congo to the Belgian government, which continued to exploit rather than develop, the recent UN interventions have looked the other way at Rwandan and Ugandan incursions, instead plastering over the problems with humanitarian aid.

Notes

1. J. Di John, 'Conceptualising the Causes and Consequences of Failed States: A Critical Review of the Literature', Working paper 25, Crisis States Research, London (2008), 2.
2. P. Forbath, *The River Congo* (London: Secker & Warburg, 1977), 331.
3. D. W. Nabudere, 'Conflict over Minerals Wealth: Understanding the Second Invasion of the DRC', in Sagaren Naidoo, *The War Economy on the Democratic Republic of Congo*, IDG Occasional paper 37, Johannesburg (2003), 40.
4. W. M. Doyle, *Empires* (Ithaca, NY: Cornell University Press, 1986), 45.
5. D. K. Fieldhouse, *The Colonial Empire: A comparative Survey from the Eighteenth Century* (Basingstoke: Macmillan, 1991), 103.
6. Jean Paul Sartre, *Being or Nothingness* (Washington, DC: Square Press Edition, 1943), 302.
7. Jean-François Bayart, *The State in Africa: the Politics of the Belly* (Boston: Polity, 2009), 3.
8. G. Brausch, *Belgian Administration in the Congo* (Oxford: Oxford University Press, 1968), 3.
9. C. Young, *Politics in the Congo* (Princeton, NJ: Princeton University Press, 1965), 32.
10. B. Jewsiewicki, 'African peasants in Totalitarian Colonial Society of Belgian Congo' in Martin A Klein, ed., *Peasants in Africa: Historical and Contemporary Perspectives* (Beverly Hills, LA: Sage), 45–6.
11. Thomas Pakenham, *The Scramble for Africa* (London: Abacus, 1991), 679.
12. R. C. Good, 'Four Views of the Congo Crisis/June 1961' in Helen Kitchen, *Footnotes to the Congo Story* (New York: Walker and Company, 1967), 45.
13. E. A. Tarabrin, *The New Scramble for Africa* (Moscow: Progress Publishers, 1974).
14. P. Gleijeses, *Conflicting Missions: Havana, Washington and Africa* (Chapel Hill, NC: University of North Carolina Press, 2002), 62.
15. New York, *Herald Tribune*, 24 July 1962.
16. R. Moose, Testimony in the US Congress House Committee on Foreign Affairs, Subcommittee on Africa, Foreign Assistance Legislation for Fiscal Year 1981 (part 7), 96th Congress, 2nd Session, 5 March 1980.

17. Scarlett Cornelissen and Naison Ngola, 'Capacity Building in Humanitarian Assistance Intervention: Evaluation of the role of Non-governmental Organisations in Conflict Environments: A Case Study of Kenya and Tanzania', in Lisa Thompson and Scarlett Cornelissen, eds, *Humanitarian Aid and Development Aid in Southern Africa: Clash or Continuum?* (Centre for Southern African Studies: University of Western Cape, 2001), 124.
18. Hans Hoebeke 'The Politics of Transition in the DRC' (IRRI-KIIB-Africa Policy & Research Notes, 2006), 1.
19. Post-Conflict Reconstruction in the Democratic Republic of Congo (DRC), Policy Advisory Group Seminar (Centre for Conflict Resolution, Cape Town, South Africa, 19–20 April 2010).
20. V. D. Verwey, 'Humanitarian Intervention Under International Law', *Netherlands International Law Review* 32.3 (1985): 357–8.
21. The Responsibility to Protect: Report of the International Commission on International and State Sovereignty (International Development Research Centre, Canada, December 2001), 12.
22. Rene Lemarchand, 'Reflections on the Crisis in Eastern Congo', *The Brown Journal of World Affairs*, 16.1 (2009): 128.
23. Cynthia McKinney, 'Covert Action in Africa: A smoking Gun', *News Briefs*, accessed 2001, http://www.house.gov/mckinney/news/pr010416.
24. 'Scramble for the Congo: Anatomy of an Ugly War', International Crisis Group, Africa Report No. 26 (Nairobi /Brussels 20 December 2000).
25. 'From Kabila to Kabila: Prospects for Peace in the Congo', International Crisis Group, Africa Report No. 27 (Nairobi /Brussels 20 December 2000), 3.
26. The UN has already deployed a contingent of 600 troops in DRC. These were very significant steps which raised hope that peace was possible.
27. Lemarchand, 'Reflections on the Crisis', 119–32.
28. Nabudere, 'Conflict over Mineral Wealth', 1.
29. Lemarchand, 'Reflections on the Crisis', 127.
30. Philippe Le Billon, 'Resources for Peace? Managing Revenues from Extractive Industries in Post-Conflict Environments', *Policy Brief* (Centre for International Cooperation, 2008), i.
31. Concecao Osorio and Terezinha da Silva, 'Aid Versus Solidarity Versus Development in Mozambique: A Gendered Perspective', in Cornelissen and Thompson, eds, *Humanitarian Aid and Development in Southern Africa*, 107.
32. Thierry Vircoulon, 'Reformer le « Peace-making » en Republique Democratique du Congo: Quand le Processus de Paix deviennent des systemes d' actions internationaux' (Paris: Institut Français des Relations Internationales, Programme Afrique Subsaharienne, 2009).
33. 'UN Peacekeepers Attacked in Congo', BBC News, 24 November 2008.
34. Michael Maren, *The Road to Hell: The Ravaging Affects of Foreign Aid and International Charity* (New York: The Free Press, 1997).
35. Timothy Reid, 'Killing Them Softly: Has Foreign Aid to Rwanda and Uganda Contributed to the Humanitarian Tragedy in the DRC', *Africa Policy Journal*, 1.81 (2006) viewed at http://www.friendsofthecongo.org/pdf/killing_softly.pdf.
36. Ibid.
37. Fran Nyakairu, 'Rwanda Dismisses Aid Suspensions over UN Report', December 2008. Accessed on http://uk.reuters.com/article/2008/12/17.

38. Letter dated 15 July 2004 from the Chairman of the Security Council Committee established pursuant to resolution 1533 (2004) concerning the Democratic Republic of Congo addressed to the President of the Security Council. UN S/2004/551.
39. Final Report of the Group of Experts on the Democratic Republic of Congo, UN, S/2008/773, December 2008.

7
Humanitarian Aspects of Interventions by the United Nations in Southern Africa

Christopher Saunders

Introduction

The countries of Southern Africa (to be defined below as the southern half of the African continent) have witnessed numerous external interventions of different kinds.[1] Above all there have been imperialist interventions, as a result of which the entire region was subjected to one or other form of colonialism by the early twentieth century. The armies of colonial powers conquered and dispossessed the indigenous people, then helped enforce colonial rule, in often highly brutal ways, which in places took the form of genocide. In the last quarter of the twentieth century, the entire region saw the yoke of colonial rule lifted, but as that yoke was lifted new forms of external intervention took place. Some of these were military. A Cuban force came to the aid of the Popular Movement for the Liberation of Angola (MPLA) in 1975 and, mainly because of a series of South African military interventions in Southern Angola that force only began withdrawing in 1989. Partially in response to the Cuban intervention, within the Cold War context, the US supplied stinger surface-to-air missiles to the Angolan rebel movement for the Total Independence of Angola (UNITA) from 1986. From 1989, however, as the Cold War rapidly moved towards its end, the main interventions from outside the region involving troops on the ground have not been by any particular country or countries, whether a former colonial power or not, but by the United Nations (UN).[2] Did these interventions, to which all too little attention has been given both in the region itself and in the relevant scholarly literature, take place in part for humanitarian reasons? Did they have humanitarian consequences? This chapter will survey UN interventions in five Southern African countries from 1960 to the present, considering, on a case-by-case basis, whether they may be said to be examples of 'humanitarian interventions'.

The term 'humanitarian intervention' is now, of course, the subject of a vast literature, which is dominated by lawyers and political scientists and they have given the term a technical meaning, confining it to interventions involving the use of military force. As any historian of the region will know, there have been many non-military forms of intervention for humanitarian reasons in Southern Africa, ranging from the Christian mission work that began in South Africa in the late eighteenth century to the current work of, say, the Non-Governmental Organisations active in the Democratic Republic of the Congo (DRC) or of the UN High Commission for Refugees (UNHCR). I shall not be concerned here with that wider humanitarian work, but with the specific so-called peacekeeping missions undertaken by the UN. Their aim was to establish peace and stability in one or other country in Southern Africa and so they inevitably had humanitarian aspects. This was true both during and after the Cold War. The literature on humanitarian intervention often suggests that it was only after the end of the Cold War that international law moved from former prohibitions against forcible intervention in the internal affairs of states towards the acceptance of a right to humanitarian intervention by either the UN or regional actors in situations where civilian populations are threatened.[3] As has often been pointed out, no such right was explicitly stated in the UN Charter, which rejected any intervention in the domestic affairs of member states. But gradually even the UN itself accepted that it should play that kind of humanitarian role in certain circumstances.

The notion of the international community having a 'responsibility to protect' is relatively recent: the failure to prevent genocide in Rwanda in 1994 was one impetus towards it and the phrase only gained wide currency after it was used as the title for the 2001 report of the International Commission on Intervention and State Sovereignty.[4] While the Organisation of African Unity (OAU), formed in 1963, had adhered to the principle of non-interference, the new African Union (AU), which supplanted the OAU in 2000, accepted the right of intervention where crimes against humanity, including genocide, were being perpetrated, whether or not the government of the country concerned – which might of course be the perpetrator of those abuses – approved the intervention.[5] But the AU continues to lack both the capacity and the will to give content to this right of intervention and it has been left to the UN to authorize such interventions, most recently in the case

of Libya in 2011. Security Council Resolution 1973 of 2011, autho-
rizing 'whatever means necessary' to protect civilians in that country,
was supported by the African non-permanent members of the Security Council, at a time when there seemed a direct and immediate
threat to civilians in the town of Benghazi. It seems, however, that
the African members of the council did not anticipate that that resolution would be used to bring about regime change in Libya and
the AU subsequently criticized harshly the actions that were taken by
the North Atlantic Treaty Organisation to that end.[6] Nevertheless the
resolution itself is now often cited as a clear example of an acceptance by at least some in the international community of the right
to humanitarian intervention, meaning the use of force to achieve
humanitarian ends.

Forcible interventions said to be humanitarian may of course take
place for a range of non-humanitarian reasons. Some critics question
the very concept of 'humanitarian intervention', on the grounds that it
is a cloak for other forms of intervention, in particular imperialist med-
dling, and a device for powerful countries of the global north to act
against weak countries of the global south. As Noam Chomsky pointed
out long ago, the concept has been applied very inconsistently.[7] More
recently Mahmood Mamdani, with the case of the Sudanese region of
Darfur particularly in mind, has produced his own critique of the notion
of humanitarian intervention, maintaining that its defining characteristic is that it is 'beyond the law'.[8] But such an intervention may receive
international support, as the intervention in Libya did in UN Security
Council resolution 1973.

This chapter will not follow those who make sweeping generalizations
about humanitarian intervention, pro or con, or those who analyse the
technical meaning of the term. Legalistic discussions of how to interpret what may be, or may not be, called humanitarian intervention are
of little value to the historian. A different approach and methodology
will be used here: an empirical assessment will be made of the extent
to which a particular set of interventions can be said to be humanitarian. This means addressing the motive for the intervention – was it
said to be and was it in fact, humanitarian in motive, in whole or in
part? – but also, and more importantly, the consequences of the intervention: to what extent, if at all, were the outcomes humanitarian? The
set of interventions chosen for this kind of analysis are those of the
UN in Southern Africa. In asking how humanitarian those interventions
were, this chapter may throw light on the possible range of meanings of
the term 'humanitarian intervention' and may suggest a methodology

for assessing the appropriateness of the use of the term in particular historical contexts.

While 'Southern Africa' may be defined in different ways, it will here be taken to be the southern half of the African continent. In mid-1960, when the first UN mission was sent to the country that had just become independent from Belgium as the Congo, that country was usually thought of as being in tropical or Central Africa, not in Southern Africa. In 1997, however, the same country, by then called the DRC, joined the leading regional organization in the southern half of the continent, the Southern African Development Community (SADC), which, since the DRC became a member, stretches from the Cape to the Zaire (Congo) River and embraces all the territories south of the equator. This, then, is the Southern Africa to be discussed here. Ten UN missions have been sent to five different countries in that region since 1960.[9] These missions, whether during or after the Cold War, are usually discussed as peacekeeping ones,[10] and they have usually been justified in the language of peacekeeping. While most had, as we shall see, at least some humanitarian aspect to them, no one has surveyed them from this perspective, raising the question: in what respects were they humanitarian?

Elsewhere in Africa a number of interventions from outside Africa have been undertaken in recent decades outside a UN framework – such as that by Britain in Sierra Leone. In Southern Africa, though there were two brief interventions of this kind in the 1960s, by far the most significant interventions from outside the continent involving military and civilian personnel in the past two decades have been the multinational UN ones (though the UN has used some peacekeepers from within the region in its missions; South African military have served in the DRC). Most of these UN interventions have taken place in the context of a country emerging from, and in some cases still suffering from, a civil war and their main purpose has been to stabilize the country in the aftermath of such a war. To assess to what extent these UN missions had a humanitarian component, let us now look at each in turn in some detail.

United Nations Operation in the Congo (ONUC)

In early July 1960, a few days after the Congo became independent, Congolese troops mutinied and both foreigners and Congolese began to be killed. When this happened, the Belgian troops stationed in the country, who had been confined to barracks, were ordered out of their barracks and troops were flown in from Belgium. Belgium told the UN Security Council that its intervention in what was now an independent country had 'the sole purpose of ensuring the safety of European and other members of the population and of protecting human rights in general'. Britain was one of those countries that accepted that Belgium had performed 'a humanitarian task', but the Soviet Union and Poland insisted that the appeal to humanitarianism was a pretext and that Belgium was furthering its commercial interests. The Soviet Union and Poland added that even the protection of human life could not justify such an intervention in an independent country. African countries with seats at the UN saw the Belgian intervention as neo-colonial and not primarily humanitarian. The UNSC called on Belgium to withdraw its troops and Dag Hammarskjöld, the second UN Secretary-General, argued that a UN military force should be sent to the Congo to help the Congolese government restore law and order. So the UN Operation in the Congo (ONUC) was born. It was a response to an intervention that was explicitly justified on humanitarian grounds and it was itself justified by the UN, at least initially, primarily on humanitarian grounds.[11]

The mandate of ONUC was subsequently extended to include, for the first time in the history of UN peacekeeping, what was called peace enforcement, the use of military force, mainly to prevent the secession of Katanga. The new mandate of February 1961 did not explicitly use humanitarian language, but it implied that the purpose – to ensure the territorial integrity of the Congo – was to help save lives. ONUC grew in size until it had as many as 20,000 personnel, a large number for the UN to assemble but a very small number given the size of the country in which it was operating. By the time ONUC was closed down in 1964, in part because the Soviet Union had come to oppose it as a device by the West to promote Western interests in tropical Africa, Katanga secession was over. Though some have seen this first UN intervention in the southern half of the continent as a failure or 'folly',[12] it helped to maintain the territorial integrity of the Congo and in so doing undoubtedly saved large numbers of lives, even if it was not able to prevent large-scale killing in parts of a country that was the size of Western Europe. As with later UN interventions, critics of ONUC have tended to emphasize its inadequacies and the lives it did not save and have failed to recognize that vastly more lives would almost certainly have been lost had there been no UN intervention.

When rebel forces seized Stanleyville in the north-eastern Congo in 1964, they held Europeans hostage and threatened to execute them.

The joint rescue operation by Belgium and the US to save them was not the result of any UN authorization. The US representative to the Security Council, Adlai Stevenson, told the council that this intervention was 'nothing more and nothing less than a mission to save the lives of innocent people of diverse nationalities'. Though some Europeans were executed before the rescue mission arrived, and others after it had taken place, over 2000 foreigners were successfully evacuated. African countries with seats on the council called this intervention an act of 'naked aggression', claimed that it was designed to promote Western economic and political interests and asserted that it was intended to ensure that the Western countries 'retain a monopoly over the exploitation of enormous wealth'.[13] This was mere rhetoric, for the intervention was manifestly to save lives, but international opposition to it, along with the view that the UN had not been impartial in the four years it had been in the Congo, helped ensure that neither Western countries nor the UN would intervene in Southern Africa again for a long time.

United Nations Transition Assistance Group (UNTAG)

It is not correct to say, as is sometimes implied, that it was the Cold War that prevented any further UN mission, after ONUC, being contemplated in Southern Africa and that it was only when the Cold War ended that another was sent. In September 1978 the UN Security Council approved the sending of another peacekeeping mission to Southern Africa, this time to Namibia, to help arrange a free and fair election in that country as a key step towards its independence from South African rule. In 1978 there was something of a lull in the Cold War, which was to heat up again with the Soviet invasion of Afghanistan the following year. The Soviet Union did not like the idea of the UN intervening to help bring Namibia to independence, especially as the plan for its transition to independence had been developed in negotiations by a Western Contact Group, headed by the US, with South Africa and the South West Africa People's Organisation (SWAPO), the Namibian movement fighting for independence. The Soviet Union did not use its veto to block the Security Council resolution that established the new UN mission to Southern Africa, however, because the mission had the support of the African countries at the UN. And so the council approved the creation of a UN Transition Assistance Group (UNTAG) for Namibia. UNTAG was to help take Namibia to independence through ensuring a peaceful election that it would help supervise. The election would be for a Constituent Assembly that would draw up a constitution for an independent Namibia. To what extent, if at all, was this UN mission designed to be humanitarian in purpose and to what extent was it humanitarian in fact and outcome?

In considering the Namibian case we need to notice both what was intended in 1978 and what happened when the mission arrived in Namibia more than a decade later. While the mission did not arrive until the Cold War was moving towards an end – and the agreement that provided for the implementation of the Security Council Resolution 435 of 1978, allowing UNTAG finally to go to Namibia, was only reached in 1988 because of the winding down of the Cold War – the mission was planned in 1978 and given both a military and civilian role. It was 'the world body's first multidimensional initiative, involving armed peacekeepers, civilian and police units, supervision of demobilization and disarmament, assisting the return of refugees and overseeing a political transition through a UN-monitored election'.[14]

SWAPO had been engaged in an armed struggle against the South African occupation of Namibia since 1966 and from the mid 1970s the war had intensified. UNTAG's arrival was to coincide with a ceasefire between SWAPO and South Africa, which would bring the war to an end and usher in a period of peace. UNTAG was to monitor the confinement of the South African military forces to bases in the north and the mission was meant to end the reign of terror that the civilian population, especially in the north, had had to endure under South African occupation and to ensure peace during the transition period. Once the ceasefire came into effect, SWAPO's People's Liberation Army (PLAN) was not to operate but the Western plan was silent on whether PLAN would be allowed bases in the north.

When the ceasefire did finally come into effect on 1 April 1989 – and the long delay was caused primarily by South Africa's refusal to allow the implementation of Resolution 435 – PLAN sought to establish bases in the north and infiltrated armed guerrilla fighters for this purpose. The SWAPO incursion led to the heaviest fighting in the entire war, in which over 300 PLAN fighters were killed by the South African military, which the UN Special Representative, who headed the UNTAG mission, allowed out of their bases.[15] The agreement that followed to end this new phase of the conflict was primarily made by the regional actors and the US mediator, Chester Crocker, but the UN presence helped stabilize the situation and enabled a relatively peaceful run-up to the election held in November.

A key element in that process was the return of some 40,000 Namibian refugees, mainly from Angola, by the UNHCR, which worked closely with UNTAG. There can be no doubt that it was the UN presence that more than anything brought relative peace to Namibia and provided the conditions for the country to move to independence.[16] So while UNTAG had not initially been justified mainly in humanitarian terms but rather as a means to take Namibia to independence, that process was dependent on the peaceful transition that UNTAG made possible, which meant that the UN intervention in Namibia had profound humanitarian consequences.[17] This was the case despite the many flaws in UNTAG's humanitarian work, caused in part by the constraints under which it operated, for the South African administration remained in place during the transition period. UNTAG was not able to find out what had happened to those who had been detained by SWAPO in Angola and did not return to Namibia; it took months for the UN to act decisively to ensure that members of the notorious, paramilitary police unit *Koevoet*, who had been terrorizing the North, were demobilized; and there was no effective monitoring of SWAPO fighters outside Namibia, while inside the country UNTAG was unable to prevent such 'dirty tricks' by right-wing South African agents as the assassination of a leading SWAPO official, Anton Lubowski, in September 1989. But in the more than 20 years since Namibia achieved its independence the country has been relatively stable. The UN's intervention in 1989–90 helped bring peace and made possible a liberal democratic outcome. The new SWAPO government that came to power in 1990 abandoned any idea of nationalization and adopted neo-liberal economic policies. Some blame those policies for the continuing poverty of half the country's population and suggest that the UN, in helping to promote such a neo-liberal outcome, may have also helped set the scene for some future instability and conflict.[18] Only time will tell if that turns out to be the case.

United Nations Angola Verification Mission (UNAVEM) and Angolan Observation Mission (MONUA)

In both Angola and Mozambique lengthy liberation wars were fought against the colonial power, Portugal, before those two countries moved to independence. In the case of Angola, the months before independence in November 1975 also saw a bitter struggle between rival parties, aided by external intervention by South Africa, the US and Cuba. Further horrific violence followed in the wars that took place after independence in both countries, wars fuelled in part by South Africa to destabilize them. It was not until the Cold War began to wind down that it seemed that the wars would come to an end.

The first UN intervention in Angola was a Verification Mission (UNAVEM I) established in 1989 with the very specific purpose of verifying that the agreement reached between Angola, Cuba and South Africa in December 1988 for the withdrawal of the 50,000 Cuban troops from Angola, as quid pro quo for the implementation of Security Council Resolution 435 of 1978 on Namibia, was observed. There was, then, no humanitarian aspect to UNAVEM 1, which was completed by May 1991, ahead of schedule. But the successful withdrawal of the Cuban forces did not help to bring the conflict in Angola between the ruling MPLA and the rebel UNITA movement under Jonas Savimbi to an end. The second UN mission to Angola, UNAVEM II, had a much wider mandate than the first: sent by the Security Council in 1991, it was to verify the implementation of the Bicesse peace accords reached between the Angola government and UNITA and to monitor Angola's first election.[19] This small mission – at full strength it comprised only 350 military observers, 126 civilian police and 400 election observers[20] – did not have the resources to do this effectively and any hope that the election held in 1992 would bring peace were dashed when UNITA rejected the result of the election and went back to war.[21]

In this new phase of the Angolan civil war, more people were killed than in all the earlier phases and an estimated 3 per cent of the entire population of the country lost their lives. It is not surprising, then, that when the UN secretary-general argued for the creation of a third UN mission to Angola in 1994, he explicitly used humanitarian arguments to justify it. He pointed to 'the severe toll of the conflict on the civilian population' and cited an estimate that during 1993 some 1000 persons had died every day from the direct or indirect effects of the war and that about 30 per cent of the population were refugees or displaced or in need of relief.[22] The mandate of UNAVEM III went far beyond the relatively limited goals of UNAVEM II, for the world body now planned to intervene actively to demobilize UNITA fighters and to bring the parties together. That the name of the mission again suggested mere verification was therefore misleading. One of the five main features of UNAVEM III was explicitly to coordinate, facilitate and support humanitarian activities.[23] UNAVEM III was very substantially larger than the first two UN missions to Angola – it comprised 7000 troops, 350 military observers and 260 police observers and cost $1 million a day – and the humanitarian relief it could bring to a country the size of Angola was minimal, while it could not stop the ongoing fighting between UNITA and the government. From a humanitarian perspective, therefore, it was a failure and it was wound down in early 1997 and replaced by a smaller successor UN mission that was given a new name, suggesting that it was to play no active role but was merely to 'observe': the Angolan Observation Mission (MONUA).

The mandate of MONUA was, nevertheless, broad, being to assist 'the Angolan parties in consolidating peace and national reconciliation, enhancing confidence-building and creating an environment conductive to long-term stability, democratic development and rehabilitation of the country'.[24] Like UNAVEM III before it, MONUA was a failure and it withdrew in 1999 as war between the government and UNITA again escalated, causing further large-scale loss of life. By then the UN had imposed harsh sanctions on UNITA, but it was not the sanctions that brought the war to an end, but Savimbi's death in 2002.[25] Though the various missions the UN sent to Angola failed to bring about peace, however, does not mean that they achieved nothing. True, the humanitarian component of UN intervention in Angola – seen most notably in UNAVEM III – was derisory, given the enormous needs in a very large country, but this failure did not deter the UN from intervening, only months after it finally withdrew from Angola, in an even more difficult situation, in an even larger country, the DRC. Before we turn to that case, however, let us consider Mozambique.

United Nations Operation in Mozambique (ONUMOZ)

In Mozambique the long conflict between the government and the rebel Mozambique National Resistance (RENAMO) drew to an end by the beginning of the 1990s, after perhaps a million Mozambique had died and many more had been displaced. After the two parties agreed to a peace settlement, the UN Security Council in December 1992 authorized a UN Operation to Mozambique (ONUMOZ, from the Portuguese name), of 7000 personnel, with four components: political, military, electoral and humanitarian. By the end of 1992, in part as a consequence of the collapse of Somalia into chaos, the UN had come to accept an expanded doctrine of humanitarian intervention and ONUMOZ was the first UN peacekeeping mission to emphasize that these four components were interlinked. Humanitarian work was now explicitly seen to be an integral part of the mission because there could be no stability and peace without humanitarian assistance and that assistance required military protection. So humanitarian assistance was 'seen to be part to be part of peacemaking and peace-keeping'.[26] An important part of the work of ONUMOZ was to return people who had been displaced by war and hunger to their homes. Unlike Somalia, Mozambique was not a failed state and ONUMOZ was effective in stabilizing the situation and bringing humanitarian relief to millions.[27]

By the time ONUMOZ was wound up in January 1995, it had lasted twice as long as UNTAG in Namibia and had cost $500 million.[28] That ONUMOZ was successful was in part because the UN learnt the lessons of Angola, not only in relation to the necessary size and mandate of the mission, but also in accepting that the electoral phase should not begin before military disengagement had reached an appropriate stage. The UN secretary-general, Boutros Boutros-Ghali, who visited Mozambique in October 1993, helped to get both parties to agree to move the process forward. As the need for UN military personnel declined, more civilian police were sent to the country. RENAMO lacked the tight discipline of UNITA, while its leader, Alfonso Dhlakama, was more amenable than Savimbi to the kind of inducements provided by the activist UN Special Representative, Aldo Ajello.[29] The key, however, was, as Norrie Macqueen has said, the existence 'of a fundamental desire on the part of both protagonists to extricate themselves from the conflict'.[30] That ONUMOZ was relatively well resourced was essential, but was not the main reason for its success. Both the FRELIMO government and RENAMO were sufficiently committed to the process for it to work and RENAMO did not have the kind of resources available to UNITA to go back to war after it lost the election. In the Mozambique case, then, humanitarian work was carried out alongside political work and the successful outcome of the mission brought peace to Mozambique. That peace remains in place in 2012, though as in Namibia the government's neo-liberal economic policy has brought both economic growth and great inequality and much of Mozambique's population is still mired in deep poverty.

United Nations Observer Mission in South Africa (UNOMSA)

South Africa was the last country in the region to be decolonized, in the sense of moving to majority rule. In the transition from apartheid to democracy in South Africa, the UN did not intervene with a military force, but sent observers whose task it was to help stem the political violence that intensified after the transition began. This violence was seen by most people in the country as the greatest threat to the process of negotiating a settlement that would usher in a new democratic order. Over 14,000 people are thought to have died in political violence in South Africa between 1990 and 1994, more than in the previous decade of struggle against apartheid. By 1992 it was clear that the country's security forces were either unable or unwilling to act to contain the violence. The UN Security Council feared that if the violence grew and full-scale civil war erupted, not only would the peace process in South Africa itself be disrupted, but peace in the larger Southern African region would be jeopardized, for South Africa as the regional hegemon had shown that it could destabilize much of the region.[31] UN Security Council Resolution 772 of 17 August 1992, which provided for the deployment of UN observers in a mission to South Africa (UNOMSA), made specific reference to the Boipatong massacre of mid June in which over 40 people had been murdered. After that massacre, negotiations between the government and the African National Congress (ANC) were broken off. Resolution 772 authorized the UN secretary-general to deploy personnel urgently to strengthen the mechanisms and structures established in the National Peace Accord that had been signed by all the main parties the previous year. The UN intervention was small – only 50 observers were dispatched by September. 1992 and 100 by December 1993 – but they helped monitor flashpoints of violence and the scholar who has made the closest study of UNOMSA concludes that it played 'an important role in addressing political violence in the pre-election period and thereby helped to facilitate the transition process', so preventing greater violence.[32] This UN mission, then, had humanitarian consequences. Once the election had taken place in April 1994, the violence decreased and even the low-intensity civil war in KwaZulu-Natal petered out. South Africa has remained relatively stable ever since, though in recent years numerous so-called service delivery protests against government have taken place, reflecting the ongoing inequalities and poverty, along with increasing unemployment, now thought to stand at over 40 per cent of the workforce.

United Nations Organization Mission in the DRC (MONUC) and United Nations Organization Stabilization Mission in the DRC (MONUSCO)

Only months after withdrawing from Angola in 1999, the UN Security Council in November authorized a new mission, again to the Congo, this one called MONUC (UN Organization Mission in the DRC). Security Council Resolution 1291 of February 2000 then provided that MONUC would have 5537 troops, 500 military observers and a civilian component, with its chief mandate to supervise the ceasefire, but also 'to facilitate humanitarian assistance and human rights monitoring, with particular attention to vulnerable groups including women, children and demobilized child soldiers, as MONUC deems within its capabilities and under acceptable security conditions, in close cooperation with other US agencies, related organizations and non-governmental organizations'.[33] Four years later, another Security Council Resolution, 1556 of 2004, saw MONUC's role as

> to assist in the promotion and protection of human rights, with particular attention to women, children and vulnerable persons, investigate human rights violations to put an end to impunity and continue to cooperate with efforts to ensure that those responsible for serious violations of human rights and international humanitarian law are brought to justice, while working closely with the relevant agencies of the United Nations.[34]

MONUC grew larger over time. Security Council Resolution 1856 of July 2007 provided for 22,016 uniformed personnel, made up of 19,815 military and 760 military observers, along with police and civilian components. In June 2010 MONUC had over 20,000 uniformed personnel on the ground in the DRC. Its military personnel were drawn from over 60 countries and by then over 100 troops and 10 military observers had died since the establishment of the mission. From 2006 on MONUC cost over $1 billion a year. Though violence continued, especially in the eastern provinces, the UN mission ensured, as had ONUC in the early 1960s, that the country did not fall apart and it helped reduce the extent of conflict, if only to some degree. In her recent study of MONUC, Severine Autesserre is highly critical of it for not having prioritized grassroots peacebuilding, but that was beyond its capabilities.[35] One can agree with Adekeye Adebayo's conclusion that the UN peacekeepers in the Congo 'tried their best under very difficult circumstances and took more robust military action from 2007', but also that 'for the most part MONUC observed the decade-long slaughter in the Congo rather than intervened decisively to stop it'.[36] As of 1 July 2010, MONUC was renamed the UN Organization Stabilization Mission in the DRC (MONUSCO). In 2012 its 20,000 personnel remain in the DRC, scattered fighting continues in the east and there are thought to be at least 1.7 million displaced people.[37] With reports of UN troops being engaged in raping and even murdering local people in the Kivu provinces in the east, the government of the DRC asked MONUSCO to withdraw, but the Security Council authorized it to help supervise the election held in November 2011 and then to remain to help stabilize the country. When it does finally withdraw, it is unlikely that the DRC's own security forces will be able to achieve more, in humanitarian terms, than the UN has been able to and it is at least possible that the humanitarian situation will deteriorate sharply in the country's eastern provinces.[38]

Conclusion

The UN interventions considered here are not usually examined in analyses of humanitarian intervention. They took place at least initially with the consent of the host governments. Over time these interventions took on a more humanitarian dimension, though there were, as we have seen, humanitarian aspects to the first intervention in the Congo in the early 1960s. The methodology adopted here has been to consider, on an individual and ad hoc basis, whether particular interventions can be said to be humanitarian, whatever was said at the time. It is not suggested that humanitarian considerations were the major ones behind these UN missions in Southern Africa, only that such considerations were often present, even if not stated explicitly. Some interventions were explicitly justified in humanitarian terms, such as those in Mozambique and the Congo, but those that were not so justified, such as that in Namibia, had humanitarian consequences, consequences that have been insufficiently recognized in the relevant literature.

Initially keeping peacekeeping activities separate from humanitarian ones, the UN moved to integrate the two, doing so explicitly in the Mozambique case for the first time. At the same time, other UN agencies, in particular the UNHCR, continued to be primarily concerned with humanitarian work. The technical legal meaning of humanitarian intervention should not be allowed to obscure the fact that humanitarian interventions have a long history and have taken many different forms. The concept, then, needs to be broadened. The failure of US intervention in the cases of Iraq and Afghanistan to bring a 'liberal peace' to those countries does not negate the real benefits that can accrue from the kind of intervention discussed here. The alternative – not intervening – would probably have had disastrous consequences.[39] One can of course be critical of the often totally inadequate resources that the UN deployed, given the vast humanitarian needs, but the UN can nevertheless be given credit for what it accomplished in Southern Africa in helping to bring peace and stability to the region.

Will such interventions continue? Within the region one now hears frequently that 'African problems need African solutions'. There is a deep suspicion of imperialism and even the UN is seen to be manipulated by imperialist powers. The wish is therefore expressed in some quarters that all external interventions, even by the UN, cease. Any future intervention on humanitarian grounds, it is suggested by these critics of external forms of intervention, should be from within the region. Is there the capacity for that? The proposed SADC Standby Force is untested and problematic and when operational will be a fraction of the size of the UN presence in the DRC.[40] The SADC force is being developed as one of the five components of the proposed African Standby force, but no regional force is likely to have the capacity and resources to act where humanitarian intervention is required, even if the will were there. While an intervention from within the region, or even from another part of the continent, would be able to draw on local knowledge and be more credible and perhaps have greater legitimacy, it is doubtful that any such intervention could avoid favouring the interests of local actors, such as the regional hegemon. While the UN missions surveyed in this chapter were by no means always impartial in their actions, external intervention may well be less partial than one from within the region or from another part of the continent. While the particular reasons why UN missions in the past took place – the ending of internal conflicts and the transition to democracy – may not prevail in the future, it would be rash to assume that there will be no need for external interventions in future. We should not forget these earlier interventions, their limitations and what they achieved in humanitarian terms.

Notes

1. This chapter is concerned with interventions from outside the subcontinent. Other interventions have taken place from one part of it into another: South Africa invaded Angola in 1975 to try to influence who came to power there, while in the last decade of apartheid rule in South Africa, which was a form of colonialism of a special type, the apartheid army, known as the South African Defence Force, fought and instigated wars in a number of neighbouring countries in an ultimately vain attempt to prevent liberation movements from coming to power in South African-ruled Namibia and South Africa itself. In 1998 a military force from South Africa and Botswana intervened in Lesotho to stabilize that country, and in the same year Angola, Namibia and Zimbabwe sent military forces to the DRC.
2. There are only a few cases of other external interventions, such as Operation Artemis by the European Union in the Ituri region of the Congo in 2003. This was almost entirely a French mission.
3. Cf. e.g. Jeremy Levitt, 'Humanitarian Intervention by Regional Actors in Internal Conflicts: The Cases of Ecowas in Liberia and Sierra Leone', *Temple International and Comparative Law Journal*, 12.2 (1998): 333–76. UN Security Council Resolution 688 of April 1991, which provided for protection for the Kurdish population of northern Iraq, set a precedent for interfering in

the internal affairs of a state and explicitly acknowledged the humanitarian dimension of UN intervention: B. E. Louw, 'United Nations Humanitarian Intervention and the New World Order' (unpublished PhD thesis, University of the Witwatersrand, 1999), 180.

4. The commission argued that the international community had a 'responsibility to protect' the citizens of a state where that state has failed to protect its own citizens. It suggested a code of conduct for humanitarian intervention and advocated reliance on non-military measures if possible.

5. See, for example, Thelma Ekiyor, *Implementing the 'Responsibility to Protect' Doctrine in Africa*, FES Briefing Paper, 2007, available at http://www.ccr.org.za/images/stories/FESBP1_R2P.pdf.

6. Sapa-AFP, 'AU Set to Demand End to NATO Libya Strikes', *The Times* (Johannesburg), 26 May 2011.

7. Noam Chomsky, 'Humanitarian Intervention', *Boston Review*, December 1993–January 1994.

8. Mahmood Mamdani, *Saviours and Survivors: Darfur, Politics and the War on Terror* (Cape Town: HSRC Press, 2009), 274.

9. The UN has been involved in the region in other humanitarian ways, of course, but the more general work of, say, the UN Development Program and the UN High Commission for Refugees is not discussed here.

10. There is a large literature now. Notice, for example, Norrie Macqueen, *United Nations Peacekeeping in Africa since 1960* (London: Pearson, 2002); G. A. Dzinesa, 'A Comparative Perspective of UN Peacekeeping in Angola and Namibia', *International Peacekeeping*, 11.4 (2004): 644–63; Dennis C. Jett, *Why Peacekeeping Fails* (New York: Palgrave, 2001); P. Sibanda, 'Lessons from UN Peacekeeping in Africa. From UNAVEM to MONUA', in J. Cilliers and G. Mills, eds, *From Peacekeeping to Complex Emergencies* (Johannesburg: South African Institute of International Affairs, 1999).

11. Thomas G. Weiss and Don Hubert, *International Commission on Intervention and State Sovereignty, the Responsibility to Protect. Research, Bibliography, Background* (Ottawa: IDRC, 2001), 49–51.

12. Adekeye Adebajo, *UN Peacekeeping in Africa* (Johannesburg: Jacana, 2011), Chapter 3.

13. *International Commission on Intervention*, pp. 51–3. It is surprising to find this report endorsing such a view, by saying that 'Colonial powers misused humanitarian justifications to mask self-interested motives', 53.

14. Adebajo, *UN Peacekeeping*, 110.

15. Sam Nujoma, founding president of SWAPO, slates the UN Special Representative, Martti Ahtisaari, for his decision, saying he 'betrayed our cause': Sam Nujoma, *Where Others Wavered* (London: Panaf Books, 2001), 397. A leading UNTAG official, Cedric Thornberry, accepts that the UN 'bore some subsidiary responsibility for what ensued' and suggests that the UN could have considered delaying implementation: Cedric Thornberry, *A Nation is Born: The Inside Story of Namibia's Independence* (Windhoek: Gamsberg Macmillan, 2004), 140. Cf. also the discussion in Brian Harlech-Jones, *A New Thing? The Namibian Independence Process, 1989–1990* (EIN Publications, Windhoek, 1997).

16. As UNTAG withdrew, the UN Secretary-General, Javier Perez De Cuellar, was, appropriately, 'master of ceremonies' at Namibia's celebration of independence on 21 March 1990.

17. G. M. Rocha, *In Search of Namibian Independence: The Limitations of the United Nations* (Boulder, CO: Westview Press, 1984); L. Cliffe R. Bush, J. Lindsay, B. Mokopakgodsi, D. Pankhurst, and B. Tsie, *The Transition to Independence in Namibia* (Boulder, CO: Rienner, 1994); Thornberry, *A Nation is Born*; Henning Melber, 'Decolonization and Democratization: The United Nations and Namibia's Transition to Democracy', in E. Newman, *The UN Role in Promoting Democracy: Between Ideals and Reality* (Tokyo: UN University Press, 2004); Roger Hearn, *UN Peacekeeping in Action: The Namibian Experience* (Commack, NY: Nova Science Publishers, 1999); William J. Durch, *The Evolution of UN Peacekeeping: Case Studies and Comparative Analysis* (New York: St. Martin's Press, 1993); L. M. Howard, 'UN Peace Implementation in Namibia: The Causes of Success', *International Peacekeeping*, 9.1 (2002): 99–132.

18. Roland Paris, *At War's End, Building Peace after Civil Conflict* (Cambridge: Cambridge University Press, 2004), 137.

19. Its original mandate, for 17 months, was merely to observe and verify the implementation of the Bicesse agreement of May 1991 between the MPLA and UNITA.

20. Macqueen, *United Nations Peacemaking*, 126.

21. Margaret Anstee, the chief UN official involved, blames the international community for a lack of resolve in dealing with the Angolan issue in the aftermath of the Cold War: see her *Orphan of the Cold War. The Inside Story of the Collapse of the Angolan Peace Process* (London: Macmillan, 1996).

22. Adebajo, *UN Peacekeeping*, 121.

23. Louw, 'UN Humanitarian Intervention', 127–8.

24. Quoted in Jett, *Why Peacekeeping*, 164.

25. On the end of the Angolan war see Justin Pearce, *An Outbreak of Peace. Angola's Situation of Confusion* (Cape Town, David Philip, 2005) and Michael Comerford, *The Peaceful Face of Angola. Biography of a Peace Process (1991–2002)* (Luanda, n.p., 2005). A small UN presence remained in Luanda after the end of MONUA, mainly for humanitarian purposes.

26. Louw, 'UN Humanitarian Intervention', 140. The UN Office for Humanitarian Assistance Coordination (UNOHAC) was made the humanitarian component of ONUMOZ by the Security Council in resolution 797 (1992). Through a Consolidated Humanitarian Programme, it addressed the emergency needs of between 4 and 5 million internally displaced persons, 1.5 million returning refugees and some 90,000 demobilized soldiers. See, for example, the Secretary-General's report to the UN Security Council of 28 January 1994 (S/1994/89): http://daccess-dds ny.un.org/doc/UNDOC/GEN/N94/047/14/PDF/N9404714.pdf?OpenElement.

27. Cameron Hume, *Ending Mozambique's War: The Role of Mediation and Good Offices* (Washington, DC: US Institute for Peace, 1994).

28. By comparison, UNTAG cost US$416 million, about half the UN's regular annual budget at the time: Macqueen, *United Nations Peacekeeping*, 114–15, 166.

29. Aldo Ajello, 'Mozambique: Implementation of the 1992 Peace Agreement', in C. Crocker, F. Osler Hampson, and P.R. Aall *Herding Cats: Multiparty Mediation in a Complex World* (Washington: United States Institute of Peace, 1999), 615–642; Richard Synge, *Mozambique: UN Peacekeeping in Action 1992–94*

(Washington, DC: US Institute for Peace Press, 1997); *The United Nations and Mozambique, 1992–1995* (New York: United Nations, 1995).

30. Macqueen, *United Nations Peacekeeping*, 165 and N. Macqueen, 'Peacekeeping by Attrition: The United Nations in Angola', *Journal of Modern African Studies*, 36.3 (1998): 399–422.
31. UN Security Council Resolution 765 of July 1992.
32. Muna Ndulo, 'United Nations Observer Mission in South Africa (UNOMSA): Security Council Resolutions 772 (1992) and 894 (1994) and the South African Transition: Preventive Diplomacy and Peacekeeping', in A. Yusuf, ed., *African Yearbook of International Law* (1996), 224. This paper is available on the Internet as Cornell Law Faculty Publications. Paper 61.The mandate of UNOMSA was expanded by UNSC Resolution 894 of January 1994 to include election observance. In April 1994, 1485 election observers joined UNOMSA, 232.
33. UN Security Council Resolution 1291 of February 2000.
34. UN Security Council Resolution 1556 of 2004.
35. Severine Autesserre, *The Trouble with the Congo: Local Violence and the Failure of International Peacebuilding* (Cambridge: Cambridge University Press, 2010).
36. Adebajo, *UN Peacekeeping*, 16.
37. SC Resolution 1925 of 28 May 2010.See also http://www.un.org/en/peacekeeping/missions/monuc/facts.shtml and the blog of Jason Stearns: http://congosiasa.blogspot.com/.
38. On MONUSCO see http://monusco.unmissions.org/.
39. Oliver Ramsbottom and Tom Woodhouse, *Humanitarian Intervention in Contemporary Conflict. A Reconceptualization* (London: Polity Press, 1996), conclusion.
40. The SADC Standby Force, launched in Lusaka, Zambia, in 2007, is, when operational, to consist of a force of some 3–5000 military personnel.

8
The Nigerian Civil War and 'Humanitarian Intervention'

Michael Aaronson

Introduction

The 1967–70 Nigerian Civil War (also known as the 'Biafran War') was notorious for the prolonged suffering of the civilian population in the secessionist enclave of 'Biafra' and the failure of repeated international attempts to bring about an early end to the conflict. At the time the term 'humanitarian intervention' was used to denote the international emergency relief operation, rather than a military intervention – which is how the term has subsequently come to be used. Ironically this humanitarian relief operation may have contributed to the prolongation of the war and thereby added to the human suffering. In this chapter, based partly on my experience working on the ground in this conflict, I argue that other forms of intervention, which could just as reasonably be described as 'humanitarian', were neglected by the principal international actors engaged with the conflict. I compare this state of affairs with subsequent approaches to intervention in Africa and elsewhere and conclude by suggesting that the lessons from 'Biafra' could be used to inform a more enlightened approach to 'humanitarian intervention' in present-day crises.

Background

At the time of Biafran secession the Federal Republic of Nigeria consisted of four regions: northern, western, mid-western and eastern. Since pre-independence days Nigerian politics had been dominated by ethnic rivalries across and within these regional groups. The war began on 30 May 1967 when, following a long period of political crisis across the country, including military coup and counter coup and reprisal killings of mainly Igbo civilians originating from the Eastern Region, Col Ojukwu, the region's governor, declared secession and the establishment of the 'Republic of Biafra'. The Federal Government of Nigeria (FGN) which had already imposed an economic blockade of 'Biafra', responded by launching an armed attack against 'the rebels'. Despite a number of internationally supported initiatives to bring an end to the conflict, it dragged on for 30 months. Although the Nigerian armed forces enjoyed overwhelming military superiority the Biafrans succeeded in prolonging the fighting – as much by political as military means. The result was a long, slow, inefficient war of attrition, which the international community appeared powerless to end. The most salient feature of the war was a massive and controversial international relief operation to support the civilian victims of the conflict – on both sides, but mainly inside Biafra. Despite this, by the time of Biafra's surrender on 12 January 1970, an estimated 600,000 people – the vast majority of them civilians – had died.[1]

From August 1969 until October 1971 I worked in Eastern Nigeria as a member of Save the Children UK's[2] international relief and rehabilitation programme. I was, therefore, a participant in the 'humanitarian intervention' that took place. At the time we were in no doubt what the term 'humanitarian' meant: it signified that we were motivated solely by a concern to bring relief to the civilian victims of the conflict, aside from any political or other objectives. As this perception was shared by both parties to the conflict it meant we were able to act relatively freely and independently, within the constraints of working in a war zone. We organized food distributions to rural communities that had spent up to two months hiding in the 'bush' because they feared genocide by the advancing Nigerian Army and who were, when they were eventually persuaded to emerge, in very poor condition indeed. We ran intensive feeding programmes for the most severely malnourished children and organized emergency sick bays to treat the most seriously ill.[3] We could reasonably claim to have saved many lives and, perhaps unsurprisingly, I acquired a passionate belief in humanitarian values and the importance of neutral, independent, humanitarian action.

From 1988 to 2005 I worked again for Save the Children UK, first as overseas director and then as the charity's chief executive. During this period 'humanitarianism' became a more contested concept and 'humanitarians' lost some of their self-confidence, for a variety of reasons that I shall explore later in this chapter. This was reflected in the fact that the term 'humanitarian intervention' came to be used by politicians and scholars alike to denote military intervention for ostensibly humanitarian purposes, rather than humanitarian assistance in the classic sense with which I was familiar. I say 'ostensibly' because as I have argued elsewhere[4] the combination of motives behind this more coercive form of intervention renders the use of the word 'humanitarian' a distortion of what it means in the English language. Over time this misuse of the term also blurs the distinction between the kind of neutral, independent, humanitarian action I have described above and the more politically driven interventions to which the term has come to be applied. In consequence the effectiveness of true humanitarian action becomes diminished by its perceived association with political and/or military objectives.

I shall return to this discussion later, but I highlight it at the outset of my account to show how much the use of the term 'humanitarian intervention' has changed over the last 40 years. My aim is to explore the concept as it was understood at the time of the Nigerian Civil War and to ask whether this historical appreciation might help us arrive at a better application of the idea of 'humanitarian intervention' in today's world. Fortunately the history of the conflict is well documented and accessible; I shall therefore draw heavily on published accounts, supplemented by my own recollections. I shall also refer to subsequent discussions about 'humanitarian intervention' that have preoccupied scholars of international law and international relations alike in the years since the war took place. My overriding aim is to join the dots: to make the connection between a now historical conflict and contemporary debates about intervention and to ask what we may learn from this particular episode in history. Above all it is an attempt to suggest how 'humanitarian intervention' might be practised better in future conflicts in Africa and elsewhere.

Key features of the Nigerian Civil War

As stated above, the events of the war have been well chronicled and analysed by a number of different authors. I shall draw in particular on John De St Jorre's account based on his experience covering the war as a journalist and writer[5] and on John Stremlau's comprehensive research into the relationship between local and international actors in the conflict.[6] More recently, researchers have benefited from the release of archive material that gives new insights not available at the time, for example from the National Archive in the UK,[7] and also in the US.[8] I shall draw on the accounts of these authors in order to pick out the key features of the conflict that are relevant to the present discussion.

The central issue, as Stremlau puts it, was 'whether the survival of the Biafran state was a necessary condition for the survival of the Igbo people'.[9] In order to appreciate this it is necessary to understand the nature of the colonial creation that was 'Nigeria'. The British had bolted together different nations with very different traditions and systems of governance. In the North, which was mainly Muslim, feudal and with low education rates, they had ruled indirectly, through the Emirs and other traditional leaders. In the South, which had been extensively colonized by missionaries and was mainly Christian with high levels of educational achievement, there was a more actively democratic political system. As an illustration of the disparity between the two halves of the country, although at independence the North and South were of comparable population size (29.8 million in the North and 25.8 million in the South) there were only 41 secondary schools in the North against 842 in the South.[10] Because the South was in this sense more advanced most of the posts in the federal civil service, the military and academia were held by southerners, particularly the Igbos, who had embraced missionary education wholeheartedly and who had the highest levels of attainment; they were also dominant in commerce. Thus many of them lived in parts of the country outside their home region.

Following the 1966 massacres of large numbers of Igbos in other parts of Nigeria (mainly in the North) and the resulting influx of an estimated 1.5 million refugees back into the eastern region,[11] Ojukwu argued that the only way to achieve security for his people was through separate sovereignty. However the FGN under Col Gowon argued that security for the Igbo people could be provided within the Nigerian state; for them the preservation of Nigerian unity was the primary goal. On 27 May 1967, in an attempt to pre-empt the imminent announcement of secession by the East, the FGN announced that the country was to be divided into 12 states, thus splitting the power of the old regions. It is important to understand that the there were significant numbers of ethnic minorities among the peoples of all the regions, including the Eastern Region; even according to official figures (census data in pre-war Nigeria having been notoriously unreliable and usually manipulated in favour of the majority) the Igbos only comprised 64 per cent of the total population.[12] Gowon's move divided the Eastern Region into East-Central, South Eastern and Rivers states; the only state where the Igbos remained in a majority was East-Central. Thus Gowon succeeded in undermining Ojukwu's position by doing away (in theory) with the old regional power blocs and by offering a degree of self-governance to all parts of the country, in the process responding to the fear of Igbo domination felt by the other peoples of the old Eastern Region. Unsurprisingly, Gowon's plan (described by some as 'the third coup'[13]) was not accepted by the Biafrans and was followed immediately by Ojukwu's declaration of secession.

Thus there was a fundamental opposition in the political perspectives of the two sides. These were more than negotiating positions and every single attempt at negotiation or mediation failed at this first hurdle: the Nigerians would only talk on the basis of a commitment by the Biafrans to national unity; the Biafrans would only talk on the basis of no pre-conditions, accompanied by a ceasefire; the Nigerians rejected a ceasefire on the grounds that it would allow the Biafrans to regroup and resupply militarily. No one succeeded in helping the parties break out of this impasse. I shall return below to the central question of whether a different approach could have secured a better outcome.

In addition, the two sides were in effect fighting on different battle-fields. The Nigerians argued that this was an internal rebellion; their strategy was to prevent the internationalization of the conflict, which included not allowing the Biafrans parity at the negotiating table. After it became apparent that Ojukwu was not willing to compromise on this basis the Nigerians pursued an essentially military strategy which, how-ever, they were not very good at implementing. The Biafrans' strategy, on the other hand, was mainly a political one and consisted of mobiliz-ing international public opinion, initially around the threat of genocide and later around the extent of the suffering within the enclave, in order to put pressure on world leaders to recognize Biafra's right to exist and to sit at the negotiating table with the Nigerians. Ojukwu knew he could never achieve a military victory; with inferior numbers and lim-ited resources his best hope was to exploit the difficulties of the terrain and the long supply lines of the Nigerian Army in order to keep the war going as long as possible – whatever the consequences for the people living inside the enclave. As he told his people in September 1968, the aim was 'to delay the enemy until the world's conscience can effectively be aroused against genocide',[14] and he consistently followed this policy, aided by a public relations operation that was much more sophisticated than anything the Nigerians could muster.

Thus any effective third-party mediation would have needed to find a way around these apparently irreconcilable positions. Success-ful exercises in conflict mediation in other contexts have depended on a number of elements that were conspicuously missing in the Nigeria/Biafra case. First among these was the lack of a truly impar-tial and effective mediator. The bulk of the mediation work was carried out by the Organisation of African Unity (the OAU) which, however, in Article III (2) of its charter had a clear statement in favour of 'non-interference in the internal affairs of states'.[15] Therefore its initial mediation efforts were framed using the language of 'placing the services of [the OAU] Assembly at the disposal of the FGN' and 'the Assembly's desire for the territorial integrity, unity and peace of Nigeria'.[16] Throughout the many phases of its mediation efforts and notwithstanding the desire of OAU heads of state to see a negotiated solution, the OAU was unable to break free from a position that explicitly favoured the federal government over the Biafrans.

Because the OAU was seized of the problem the United Nations, which was still licking its wounds from its coercive and highly controversial intervention in the Congo (1960–4), was able to ignore it; not once in the period 1966–70 did Nigeria feature in General Assembly or Security Council Resolutions. In the US the Johnson Administration was preoccupied with Vietnam. Very early in the crisis the US Secretary of State, Dean Rusk, declared 'we regard Nigeria as part of Britain's sphere of influence'.[17] As a result US involvement, other than in the provision of relief aid – which was substantial – remained limited. President Johnson did take a personal initiative with General Gowon in an attempt to open relief corridors and offered eight large transport aircraft to fly in supplies, but the offer was not taken up and the US was as impotent as everyone else in bringing an end to the conflict.[18]

Key European powers had considerable vested interests and were therefore hardly impartial. France had always been wary of the threat posed by a powerful Nigeria to its former colonies in Francophone West Africa. French oil companies were also actively involved in seeking to exploit Nigeria's huge oil and gas reserves. As a result the French played something of a double game; in its public statements the government of General de Gaulle offered words of encouragement to Biafra, while France continued to enjoy a substantial and favourable trade balance with Nigeria. Portugal was still attempting to hold on to its African colonies and given Nigeria's strong support for the liberation struggle in Southern Africa had every reason to support the Biafrans. As a result Lisbon became the setting-off point for the airlift into Biafra, which also used the island colonies of Sao Tome (Portuguese) and Fernando Po (Spanish) as staging posts.

The obvious potential force for good, as the former colonial power with strong cultural, economic and military links with Nigeria, was the UK. However, the history of British involvement in the Nigerian Civil War is not particularly honourable. In the early days, for example at the Aburi meeting in Ghana in January 1967 – where Ojukwu out-smarted Gowon and secured an agreement that was promptly torn up once Gowon returned to Lagos – Britain did try to play a mediating role. But its policy appears to have been crippled by a number of weaknesses. First, in the early stages, there was genuine uncertainty as to how successful Ojukwu's rebellion might be and a consequent fear of backing the wrong horse. Second and linked to this, there was a desperate desire not to lose access to Nigeria's oil and gas (10% of all British oil imports at the outbreak of the war came from Nigeria and most of the fields were situated in the eastern region).[19]

Third, the British feared losing influence in Nigeria to the Soviet Union, which had shown itself ready to supply arms to the federal government; however this had to be balanced against the UK government's reluctance to supply heavy weaponry in the face of UK public opinion that was strongly against the war. Fourth, the UK was vulnerable in Africa over Rhodesian UDI, which had been declared in 1965; this weakened its moral authority vis-à-vis the OAU and its members.

Fifth and probably most importantly, as the former power which as recently as 1960 had bequeathed Nigeria its boundaries and its constitution Britain found it hard to maintain a neutral position; there was a strong lobby in the UK that argued that this would have been tantamount to supporting Biafra and this pushed the government in the direction of supporting the FGN. Thus Britain had too many interests at stake to act as an impartial mediator and in general it could be argued that British policy was geared to assuaging an increasingly concerned public at home rather than to intervening effectively to bring the warring parties to the table.

In addition, for the Western powers as much as for the members of the OAU, the issue of secession was a difficult one. The outside world was genuinely perplexed as to whether Biafra had a right to exist as a separate state or not.[20] The norm that had prevailed since the formation of the UN was decolonization; most African countries had by this time achieved their independence and the international community was embarrassed by situations where one part of a newly independent state wished to secede from the rest. In the case of Katanga's secession from the Congo in 1960 the Congolese government had sought UN support and the UN had after initial reluctance intervened decisively against the secessionists. However the UN's experience had not been a happy one and furthermore the cases of Biafra and Katanga were very different. First, the Nigerian government did not request such support; second, there was a natural nervousness on the part of the UN about becoming involved in another internal conflict in an African state; and finally Gowon's move to create 12 states out of the four regions critically weakened the Biafran argument to a separate sovereignty.[21]

Against this background of weak and ineffective diplomacy from the major external powers the most significant interventions came not from governments or multilateral bodies such as the UN or OAU but from private organizations such as the International Committee of the Red Cross (ICRC), the churches – comprising missionaries on the ground and church organizations mainly in Europe and North America – and the international NGOs (INGOs). These were responding to – and mobilizing – public concern at the growing and increasingly visible human cost of the conflict in terms of displacement, hunger, sickness and death. The Igbo heartland that by the end of 1967 was all that was left of 'Biafra' had always been dependent on trade to meet its food requirements and this had from the early days of the conflict been disrupted by the Federal blockade. In addition the most agriculturally productive areas had been the first to fall to the advancing Federal army.

Particularly poignant was the sight of seriously malnourished children, many close to starvation and highly vulnerable to disease, staring apparently helplessly at the camera. Biafra was the first such situation where, thanks to modern media and the awareness-raising activities of the aid agencies, images of massive suffering penetrated the consciousness of ordinary people in the West. These images have become almost a commonplace in recent times, but 40 years ago they were a huge shock to the conscience of the Western world. This led to an outpouring of support for the relief agencies and a massive scaling up of their operations in Nigeria.

Much of the drama surrounding the war centred on this huge relief operation. Once Biafra was surrounded and cut off, the only way to bring in relief supplies was by air from staging posts in Dahomey, Sao Tome and Fernando Po. Given that the air bridge was already being used to bring in arms and ammunition this was immediately controversial. Relief planes chartered by the ICRC or a coalition of the churches had to compete with the arms flights for night-time landing slots at the improvised airport at Uli inside Biafra and also had to dodge the same Nigerian bombs. Some flights carried both arms and relief supplies. The scale of this operation was remarkable; at its height Uli was said to be the second busiest airport in the whole of Africa, after Johannesburg.

For large periods of the war the politics of this relief operation provided the main issue of contention. The Nigerians were unhappy with the night flights because they knew they provided cover for imports of arms and ammunition. They argued for day flights starting in Lagos and supervised by the ICRC, or land corridors with observers at both ends. The Biafrans rejected both options partly on political grounds – this would have implied Nigerian control and sovereignty over the relief operation – but also because the Nigerians would then have had *carte blanche* to bomb the arms flights at night. Gowon himself was happy for humanitarian assistance to be provided to people within Biafra – not least to counter the Igbos' fears of genocide – and this was reflected in public statements made by the FGN.[22] Thus the federal government initially allowed the ICRC to operate night flights, but at their own risk (the churches acted independently). But as the war dragged on, there was increasing resentment from hardliners in Gowon's administration that the relief operation was prolonging the war. By December 1969 even the Nigerian Commissioner for Foreign Affairs – in general a dove on humanitarian intervention – was saying to a visiting British minister: 'A complete military defeat of the rebels is the only answer to the relief situation.'[23]

The charges against the relief agencies were (a) that they were one-sided in their understanding and characterization of the conflict (giving credence to Biafran allegations of genocide, portraying the war as a religious struggle between Christianity and Islam, providing access to Biafra for foreign journalists and politicians who could not fail to be shocked by the extent of the suffering but who inevitably saw only one side of the story, making emotional appeals for funds and thereby helping to build political support for the secessionists, supporting on humanitarian grounds Ojukwu's essentially political calls for a ceasefire); (b) that the airlift was providing both political and material support to the rebels (undermining the Nigerian position on relief, providing cover for arms flights); and (c) that by importing large amounts of foreign currency to finance the relief operation they were prolonging the war (I return later to this last issue).[24]

On the other side of the argument the relief agencies argued they had a moral duty to make the world aware of the extent of the suffering inside Biafra and to bring aid to starving and dying people by whatever means – in other words, that there was a 'humanitarian imperative' to intervene. However, striking the correct balance between the rights of victims of a disaster to humanitarian assistance and the rights of a sovereign state to control affairs within its own jurisdiction is not straightforward. Nigeria was still a young state and not all those who intervened from outside were as respectful of its sovereignty as they might have been. In retrospect it is remarkable how much ground the Nigerians were prepared to give with regard, for example, to relief flights (see below). The balance of power between interveners and host governments is very different 45 years on, at least in principle if not always in practice. Nowadays, unless interveners are prepared to use military force they have to be much more respectful of host government sensitivities than was the case with regard to Nigeria. With the benefit of hindsight I can also see that as relief workers we were accorded an exaggerated amount of respect not just because of our impartial, neutral, role but also as expatriates working in what had until relatively recently been a British colony. This postcolonial dimension must be recognized in any comparison of the Nigerian situation with more recent ones.

For the missionaries on the ground, many of whom had lived in the East of Nigeria for many years, relieving the suffering of the people was an obvious just cause. To the extent that the churches were in this sense less concerned about neutrality they certainly paid the price at the end of the war when all their people were expelled from the country, their places taken by the agencies – including Save the Children – that had during the war chosen to work exclusively on the Federal side of the line (because the FGN would not allow them to be on both sides).

The ICRC's position was more complicated. Traditionally the organization seeks to practise strict neutrality, which necessitates securing the consent of both parties to any intervention it might make. In the case of Biafra this was very difficult, for a number of reasons, the first of which was the public expectation that relief would be provided to the suffering people within the enclave, whatever the political difficulties. Given the consistent refusal of Ojukwu to allow daytime relief flights or land corridors with inspections by the Nigerians the ICRC was led down the route of flying relief in semi-illegally (i.e. without the formal consent of the Nigerians) until June 1969, when their position was made impossible by the shooting down by the Nigerians of a Swedish Red Cross relief flight. Subsequently the ICRC reverted to a position of strict neutrality, but this did not stop the federal government from taking away from the organization its overall responsibility for coordination of the relief operation (which was passed initially to the Nigerian Red Cross and then, when the relief phase was declared over, to the National Rehabilitation Commission).

One historian of the ICRC has described this as their 'failure to develop a well-considered humanitarian diplomacy in the face of brutal power politics',[25] adding:

> The organisation...vacillated and departed from the principles of international humanitarian law in trying to deal...with the civilian population in secessionist Biafra...the ICRC did not handle well the

complexity it faced... Ojukwu was prepared to sacrifice the welfare of 'his' people by opposing international relief supervised by Lagos (an opposition which symbolised his independence and sovereignty); but the Geneva Conventions provided for a right of supervision over relief leaving a belligerent's territory. The solution Geneva chose, to proceed with relief at its own risk, because of its concern for civilians in need but also because of competition with other relief agencies, led to a debacle for the organisation. The ICRC was widely seen as unfaithful to the principles of [International Humanitarian Law] and to Red Cross neutrality.[26]

However, although it was the issue of neutrality that generated much of the heat at the time, the charge that the importation of foreign currency prolonged the conflict is probably most telling in terms of the actual conduct of the war, why it lasted so long and whether the suffering of so many ordinary people could have been avoided. Stremlau makes a persuasive case that the Biafrans were able to finance their arms purchases – and thereby keep the war going – from the foreign exchange that the relief agencies were obliged to deposit in the bank controlled by the Biafran administration in order to fund their operations inside Biafra.[27] Thus the agencies were depositing hard currency with the Biafran authorities in exchange for Biafran currency that they could only use inside the enclave to purchase goods and services for the relief operation. Meanwhile the Biafran authorities were using the hard currency to procure military equipment that kept the Nigerians at bay. If this analysis is correct it is indeed devastating and illustrates sharply some of the dilemmas of humanitarian action, to which I return in the next section.

As I have already remarked, what is striking when one looks back from the twenty-first century at the literature about the Nigerian Civil War is the fact that the term 'humanitarian intervention' was used in a way that is quite different from what it came to mean in the period following the end of the Cold War. It referred, quite simply, to the relief operation; there was an assumption and an acceptance that this was the business of the aid agencies while diplomats and politicians intervened in other ways. Governments in the UK and elsewhere did, of course, support the relief agencies financially and to a certain extent this addressed the growing unhappiness among the public at the level of suffering inside Biafra. What I want to argue here is that other forms of intervention would almost certainly have been more effective in bringing an end to the conflict and the suffering and in that sense would have better merited the label 'humanitarian'. I turn now to an examination of what these other measures might have been.

Other forms of 'humanitarian intervention'?

In the case of the Nigerian Civil War, although the external use of force does not appear to have been considered, there was considerable debate about the sale of arms and ammunition to the parties to the conflict, which it was assumed would have a crucial role in determining the outcome. The main area for leverage by the major powers (and their main area of vulnerability in terms of public opinion in their own constituency) was exercised in their arms sales policies. Thus, as stated above, the UK government was reluctant to supply heavy weaponry (although nervous about losing influence to the Soviets as a result) and frequently embarrassed at home by its continuing supply of small arms and ammunition – it was only in the closing months of the war that the level of UK arms sales to Nigeria increased substantially.[28]

However, the Nigerian military was largely unprepared to fight the Biafra campaign – at the outset it numbered only 8500 and although by the end of the war this had become 200,000, most of its troops had only the most rudimentary training and were not very effective, to put it mildly.[29] Given this, it is open to question whether a policy of increased arms sales could ever have been justified as an effective way of relieving the suffering. Some of the highest profile atrocities – fuelling the claims of impending genocide – involved the bombing of civilian targets inside Biafra by inexperienced or just plain incompetent Nigerian or Egyptian pilots flying Soviet and Czech jets (the Russians would not allow Western pilots to fly their planes)[30]; certainly on the Federal side the ability of the troops to use the arms effectively was as important as the issue of the arms supplied. Thus, although the Nigerians' superior weaponry undoubtedly did play a part in their military victory[31] it must remain doubtful whether additional arms sales could on their own have brought an early end to the conflict.

This, of course, leaves aside the issue of whether it is morally right to supply arms to bring a conflict to an early end. Indeed, there were many who argued for a complete arms embargo to both sides and some who imposed it. The US, for example, announced early in the conflict that it would not sell arms to either side (a move that was deeply resented in Lagos),[32] and for a brief period under the Prague Spring the Czech government took the same position until arms sales to the FGN were resumed following the Soviet invasion of Czechoslovakia in August

1968.[33] However, given the lack of any effective regulatory regime for arms sales at that time and the proliferation of arms in the context of the Cold War and the continuing liberation wars in Africa, it is highly unlikely that an arms embargo could have been effective.

The most obvious alternative intervention to save lives would have been more determined diplomacy by the major powers and the OAU, combined with effective third-party mediation. Interestingly, when in April/May 1968 Tanzania, Gabon, Ivory Coast and Zambia broke ranks with their fellow OAU members and recognized Biafra they all to a greater or lesser extent justified their action on humanitarian grounds. Although they did not necessarily support Biafra's right to a separate existence they were critical of the Nigerians' position on negotiations and expressed the hope that their action would force the Nigerians to agree to a ceasefire and to come to the negotiating table – and thereby relieve the suffering of the Biafran people. But these four countries – despite the international standing of leaders such as Tanzania's Nyerere, Ivory Coast's Houphouet-Boigny and Zambia's Kaunda – were always a minority voice in the OAU and even Nyerere and Kaunda to an extent moderated their own positions as the prospect of anything other than a Nigerian military victory eventually receded.

It is of course easy at a distance to argue that more effective diplomacy and mediation would have saved lives. But what is indisputable is that the personalities of both Gowon and Ojukwu – particularly the latter – played a major role in the course of the war. They had a shared background as British-trained Army officers, but in terms of personality they were very different people. Ojukwu was a natural politician; Gowon a straightforward soldier. Gowon was a dove in his own camp, whereas Ojukwu was a hawk in his. Gowon's position was relatively weak domestically but strong internationally; Ojukwu's the exact opposite. Anyone attempting to reconcile the positions of the two men would have needed to understand them as individuals and the constraints under which they were operating. And yet it is striking that after the abortive Aburi discussions before the outbreak of hostilities they never once met throughout all the attempts at mediation during the 30-month armed conflict.[34] The inability of the OAU, the UK, the US and the UN to bring the two principals together represented a disastrous failure of diplomacy and effectively doomed the mediation efforts.

It is salutary to contrast this failure with the example of the intervention in Kenya in response to the political violence following the December 2007 elections. The disease affecting the body politic in Kenya was chronic – as it had been in Nigeria 40 years earlier – and the post-election violence following allegations of vote-rigging could easily have descended into civil war. As in Nigeria, politics was split along ethnic lines. As in Nigeria much rested on the personality of the two opposing leaders: Mwai Kibaki and Raila Odinga: former political allies now at each others' throats. Like Nigeria Kenya was a former British colony of considerable strategic significance in Africa – too important to fail. However, in the intervening 40 years the OAU had been succeeded by the African Union (AU), which had adopted a much more robust commitment to humanitarian intervention in the event of human rights abuses.[35] And, unlike the rather feeble attempts at mediation in the Nigerian case, in Kenya the AU not only appointed a mediator of real substance – the former UN secretary-general, Kofi Annan – but also gave him the mandate and the resources to intervene decisively to prevent a slide into chaos. In addition, both the US and the UN made it clear that they supported his efforts. Annan decided to play the role of a strong mediator and was able to do so effectively. For the most part he worked with negotiating teams mandated by the two sides, but when (on 28 February) the negotiations reached a critical stage he insisted on the presence of the two principals and would not allow them out of the room at the office of the president in which discussions were taking place until they had reached the key agreement on a power-sharing arrangement that defused the immediate crisis.[36]

The Kenya mediation was not unequivocally successful – while Annan succeeded in brokering a deal to end the immediate crisis the parties made much less headway on the underlying structural issues that he had insisted also be addressed – and in any case it has to be set within a context of many years of neglect of crisis prevention in Kenya by the AU, UN and others. But as an example of effective diplomacy supporting a determined effort at mediation it stands in strong contrast with the Nigerian example of 40 years earlier and – I would argue – offers a much better model for effective 'humanitarian intervention' in Africa in future.

One other relevant intervention in the Nigerian conflict was the deployment of an International Observers Team – the Observer Team in Nigeria (OTN), comprising representatives from Britain, Canada, Sweden, Poland, the OAU and the UN. A British suggestion, but willingly adopted by Gowon, its purpose was to reassure the Igbos and the outside world about the behaviour of the Nigerian army in Igbo areas. Between August 1968 and the end of the war the OTN produced a series of reports, none of which supported the increasingly implausible hypothesis of Nigerian genocidal intent. Although the main purpose of this mission was political, if one allows it may also have had a deterrent effect in moderating the behaviour of the Nigerian Army it could conceivably be said also to have had a humanitarian dimension.

'Humanitarian intervention' in the aftermath of Biafra

People in all countries were shocked by the scale of the human suffering in Biafra and the apparent inability of the outside world to intervene to bring it to an end. One consequence was a 1969 memorandum written by two US international law scholars, who argued that there was a right of unilateral military intervention and recommended that the International Law Association (ILA) be asked to draft a protocol for eventual adoption by the UN.[37] This was indeed taken forward by the ILA and fed in to a growing debate over the next 30 years among scholars of international law and international relations alike on the subject of 'humanitarian intervention'.[38] This discussion is yet to be concluded, as the debate as to whether the 2011 NATO intervention in Libya was 'humanitarian' or not demonstrates.[39]

Before coming back to this question it is worth noting that the Biafran war also sowed the seeds of a more muscular humanitarianism among the aid agencies, exemplified by the formation following the conflict of Médecins Sans Frontières (MSF) by Bernard Kouchner and other French doctors who had been working for the French Red Cross/ICRC in Biafra and were dissatisfied with what they perceived as an overly neutral approach taken by the ICRC. (Indeed internal pressure from the French Red Cross and some of the Nordic Red Cross societies contributed to the ICRC's difficulties during the conflict.[40]) MSF went on to become one of the most powerful and outspoken advocates of its own version of humanitarianism, often at odds with others who preferred a more discreet approach. From the Biafran war MSF and other aid organizations also learnt the lessons of using the media to good effect to raise awareness of human suffering, to generate public support through fundraising and to put pressure on political leaders in the West to take more effective action to intervene (sometimes with unintended consequences, as in Somalia in 1992–3). From Biafra stems the now familiar image of the aid worker on the front line, delivering life-saving assistance and speaking with apparently unimpeachable authority about the actions needed to bring an end to the suffering. The power conferred by this moral authority and the ethics of its uses and abuses – often in a highly politicized environment – were little understood at the time of the Biafran crisis, but have created new dilemmas for aid agencies as well as engendering a whole new area of academic debate.[41] I return to this below.

With the Cold War continuing, the 1970s and 1980s were in many respects the high point of old style 'humanitarian intervention' in Africa and elsewhere. Following on from Biafra, if political action to resolve armed conflict was deemed too difficult – usually for reasons of super-power rivalry – humanitarian action was often used as a proxy. Thus, for example, in the war in Ethiopia between the Tigrayan and Eritrean liberation movements and the Mengistu government, humanitarian intervention to assist the people of Tigray and Eritrea was left to the aid agencies, operating across the border from Sudan illegally and at some risk to themselves. In the repeated food crises in the Horn of Africa in these two decades – caused at least in part by continuing internal armed conflict – massive and very visible relief operations involving an expand-ing community of international agencies were launched. INGOs claimed an increasingly high profile, their funds grew both from private sources and from government donors and their ranks were swelled with willing new recruits. The culmination of this in 1985 was the landmark Band Aid event, which had a profound impact on a whole new generation for whom the memory of Biafra was already a distant one.

However, it would seem that some of the hard lessons from the humanitarian operation in Biafra took longer to learn. Relief work always throws up complex and difficult ethical dilemmas, from deci-sions about triage – whom to save and whom to leave – to whether to collaborate with those known to have committed atrocities in order to access vulnerable populations. In Save the Children's case in Nigeria one such dilemma, already referred to above, was whether to continue to try to work on both sides of the conflict – in the end it decided to work exclusively on the Nigerian side of the line and the organization closed its operations within the secessionist enclave. Then, because of very limited resources during the latter stages of the conflict, it decided it could only provide intensive care to severely malnourished children; we relief workers were therefore in the uncomfortable position of telling desperate adults that we could not help them. In addition, a large part of our job consisted of negotiating access to newly liberated areas where we knew many thousands of people were hiding and in need of help but were too scared to come out; this involved regular socializing with the Nigerian military, which might have been seen as compromising our neutrality, but without which we would have been able to achieve very little. These are the kind of tough practical choices that have to be made by agencies when they are trying to provide relief in emergencies.

A further dilemma is whether there are circumstances in which it is better to withhold aid. By adopting an uncompromisingly 'humanitarian' approach – providing relief to the victims of conflict regardless of any other consideration – INGOs become more exposed to charges of exacerbating or prolonging the conflict. Although such criticism was relatively muted at the time of the Nigerian Civil War, it became more insistent in subsequent years. As a result some theorists and practitioners argued for a more consequentialist approach; accepting the need for certain restrictions on humanitarianism if adverse consequences were to be avoided. This was conceptualized by some as 'the new humanitarianism', which was supposed to be more politically sophisticated but which for others represented a dangerous step along the road to instrumentalization of humanitarian action for political purposes, where humanitarian objectives become confused with – or subordinate to – political and military ones.[42]

This threat became more acute following the end of the Cold War and the increasing participation in conflict of Western countries, intervening ostensibly for humanitarian reasons, as a consequence of the so-called liberal interventionist foreign policy pursued by the US and her allies in the new world order. Initiated by Operation Provide Comfort in 1991 in Northern Iraq, supported by UN Secretary-General Boutros Ghali's 'Agenda for Peace' in 1992, it included armed interventions in conflicts in Somalia (1993), Bosnia (1992–5), Kosovo (1999), Sierra Leone (1999) and others. All of these to a certain extent posed difficulties for independent aid agencies to the extent that politicians increasingly expected them to contribute to the success of the intervention while from their perspective they needed to distance themselves from the political and military objectives that sat alongside their humanitarian ones. On the other hand there were shocking examples of ineffective intervention or no intervention at all in, for example, Rwanda in 1994 and Darfur in 2005,[43] which laid the West open to charges of selectivity, inconsistency and hypocrisy.

Following 9/11, the increasing prominence of the securitization agenda and the interventions in Afghanistan and Iraq, the challenges facing neutral, independent, humanitarian action in situations of armed conflict have seemed more daunting than at any time since the pioneering work of Henry Dunant and others nearly 150 years ago. Aid agencies believe that aid – whether emergency relief or long-term development assistance – is an end in itself, not to be given in support of any political or military objective. Although improved security may be a necessary condition for long-term development to take place, it does not follow that humanitarian assistance or development aid should support security objectives. Yet in situations such as Iraq and, particularly, Afghanistan there has been considerable pressure from 'our' governments to put aid at the service of the overall mission objective. One of the most egregious examples was the comment of the then US secretary of state, Colin Powell, that international NGOs in Afghanistan would be 'a force multiplier... such an important part of our combat team' (a remark for which he later apologized).[44] The UN's drive in the direction of 'integrated missions' – which brought UN humanitarian, political and military action together under a single command structure – while offering the welcome prospect of improved coordination within the UN system, contained similar threats to the independence of humanitarian action.

Faced with this challenge, there is a temptation for relief agencies to describe themselves as 'humanitarian actors' in order to distinguish themselves from, for example, the military. This, however, fails to recognize that anyone can carry out a humanitarian act – there are in fact no humanitarian actors, only humanitarian actions. Most actions, whether taken by individuals or by institutions, involve a range of motives, but provided there is a demonstrable intent to produce a beneficial outcome for other people purely on the basis of our shared humanity – and that this intent is translated into action consistent with it – there is no reason in principle why any action by any actor should not qualify as a humanitarian intervention. (There is, of course, the additional question of how the act is perceived by those affected by it; it may be harder for some actors – such as the military – to have credibility as 'humanitarians', however worthy their motives may be.)

A new attempt to formulate the principles of 'humanitarian intervention' without attracting some of the difficulties of the latter term came in 2001 with the launch of the concept of 'The Responsibility to Protect'.[45] By placing the emphasis on the responsibility of the state where the crisis is taking place, rather than on the right of an outside actor to intervene, it was hoped that a more acceptable and effective framework could be developed, with a stronger emphasis on prevention and capacity building both locally and internationally. R2P, as it is widely known, offers, as Lee Feinstein has put it, an alternative to the hard choice between 'doing nothing or sending in the Marines'.[46] This is work in progress, but offers a useful framework for the kind of actions I have been advocating in this chapter. However, as the case of the NATO intervention in Libya in 2011 shows, Western states still find it hard to work out how to fill the gap Feinstein identifies. Too often the choice seems to present itself precisely as one of doing nothing or sending in the Marines (or, in this and most other recent cases, NATO bombers). Arguably, in the Libyan example, there was a range of alternative policy options available: trying to broker a ceasefire between Gaddafi and his opponents, securing access by the ICRC and other agencies to civilians affected by the conflict and exploring the potential for third-party mediation. However, none of these was seriously attempted before the intent to enforce a no-fly zone was declared.[47] The subsequent deadlock in the UN Security Council over Syria in 2011/12 provides an even sharper example.

A more enlightened approach to 'humanitarian intervention'?

If we compare Biafra and Libya a curious irony presents itself. In this chapter I have argued that in Biafra 'humanitarian intervention' (i.e. an emergency relief operation) proved to be less effective at relieving suffering than other, more 'political', measures could have been had they been pursued vigorously. More forceful diplomacy by the major powers, more determined mediation by the OAU targeted directly at the personalities of Ojukwu and Gowon rather than their representatives, a UN mandate for an enhanced Observer Team – policing relief corridors as well as human rights abuses; all these would have increased the likelihood of a resolution of the conflict and saved many lives. I accept that in the world of 1967 some of these ideas would have been ahead of their time and my aim is not to prove the counterfactual – rather to demonstrate the lessons from this example and suggest how things might be done differently in future.

In Libya, by contrast, in the face of threatened and actual atrocities, 'humanitarian intervention' – although it did include an arms embargo – consisted in the main of a hastily put together and very speculative bombing campaign, in the absence of a political strategy, informed by very little local knowledge and with a high potential risk that it would create more problems than it solved. This will remain the case even if the eventual outcome appears to make the risks seem justified. The lesson from Biafra is that effective humanitarian intervention should mean a lot more than sending in food and medicines. But the lesson from Libya is that it does not have to mean the military option, either. Between these two extremes lies a wide range of policy options, preventative as well as reactive, from which a 'humanitarian intervention' can be crafted. The ability to intervene effectively as an outsider, under the humanitarian banner, essentially requires one to have credibility that one's interest is primarily to relieve human suffering, rather than the pursuit of a geopolitical agenda. It is above all about knowing how to use power wisely. In the case of the Nigerian Civil War power was not used wisely by those who could have done so. There are still lessons to be learnt from this massive human tragedy, 45 years later.

Notes

1. John De St Jorre, *The Brothers' War* (London: Faber, 2009), 412.
2. 'Save the Children UK', accessed 12 October 2012, www.savethechildren. org.uk.
3. J. Paul Miller, 'Medical Relief in the Nigerian Civil War', *The Lancet* (20/06/70): 1330–4; Roger Hickman, 'The Relief Operation in Former Biafra', *The Lancet* (17/10/70): 815–16.
4. For example, Michael Aaronson, 'Libya: Did We Have a Choice?': PSA Plenary lecture, 21 April 2011, accessed 12 October 2012, http://www. uniofsurreyblogs.org.uk/cii/category/libya/.
5. De St Jorre, *The Brothers' War*.
6. John Stremlau, *The International Politics of the Nigerian Civil War 1967–70*, (Princeton, NJ: Princeton University Press: 1997).
7. For example: Chibuike Uche, 'Oil, British Interests and the Nigerian Civil War', *Journal of African History*, 49.1 (2008): 111–35.
8. For example, Nathaniel H. Goetz, 'Humanitarian Issues in the Biafra Conflict' (UNHCR Working Paper, 2001).
9. Stremlau, *The International Politics*, xii.
10. De St Jorre, *The Brothers' War*, 58.
11. Ibid., 15.
12. Charles R Nixon, 'Self-Determination: The Nigeria/Biafra Case', *World Politics* 24.4 (1972), 480.
13. Walter Schwarz, *Nigeria* (London: Pall Mall Press, 1968), 230.
14. Cited in Stremlau, *The International Politics*, 320.
15. 'OAU Charter', accessed 8 October 2012, http://www.au.int/en/sites/default/files/OAU_Charter_1963.pdf.
16. Stremlau, *The International Politics*, 93.
17. *West Africa*, 22 July 1967, cited in De St Jorre, *The Brothers' War*, 179.
18. Goetz, 'Humanitarian Issues'.
19. Uche, 'Oil, British Interests', 113.
20. K. W. J. Post, 'Is There a Case for Biafra?', *International Affairs*, 44.1 (1968): 26–39; S.K. Panter-Brick, 'The Right to Self-Determination: Its Application to Nigeria', *International Affairs*, 44.2 (1968): 254–66.
21. Nixon, 'Self-Determination', 480.
22. Stremlau, *The International Politics*, 283, 337.
23. Ibid., 361–2.
24. Laurie S Wiseberg, 'Christian Churches and the Nigerian Civil War', *Journal of African Studies*, 2.3 (1975): 297–331, cited in Stremlau *The International Politics*, 281–2.
25. David P. Forsythe, *The Humanitarians: The International Committee of the Red Cross* (Cambridge: Cambridge University Press, 2005), 201.
26. Ibid., 287.

27. Stremlau, *The International Politics*, 238–42.
28. Suzanne Cronje, *The World and Nigeria* (London: Sidgwick and Jackson, 1972), Appendix 2.
29. De St Jorre, *The Brothers' War*, 281; also personal observation by the author.
30. Ibid., 181.
31. Ibid., 279.
32. Ibid., 181.
33. Ibid., 184.
34. Ibid., 91–4.
35. See for example Article 4h of the Constitutive Act of the AU, amended in 2003, 'African Union: The Constitutive Act', accessed 12 October 2012, http://www.africaunion.org/root/au/aboutau/constitutive_act_en.htm#Article4.
36. Meredith Preston McGhie and Serena Sharma, 'Kenya' in Jared Genser and Irwin Cottler, eds, *The Responsibility to Protect: The Promise of Stopping Mass Atrocities in Our Time* (Oxford: Oxford University Press: 2011).
37. Michael Reisman and Myres S. McDougal 'Humanitarian intervention to protect the Ibos', (1969) referred to in R. B. Lillich, *Humanitarian Intervention and the United Nations* (Charlottesville, 1973), 177. Cited in Nicholas Wheeler, *Saving Strangers* (Oxford, OUP: 2000): 42.
38. See, for example Jennifer M. Welsh, ed., *Humanitarian Intervention and International Relations* (Oxford: Oxford University Press, 2006); Aidan Hehir, *Humanitarian Intervention: An Introduction* (Basingstoke: Palgrave Macmillan, 2010).
39. A. Bellamy, S. Chesterman, J. Pattison, T. Weiss and J. Welsh, contributions to 'Roundtable on Libya and Humanitarian Intervention', *Ethics and International Affairs*, 25.3 (2011): 271–7.
40. Forsythe, *The Humanitarians*, 66.
41. Michael Barnett and Thomas G. Weiss, eds, *Humanitarianism in Question: Politics, Power, Ethics* (Ithaca, NY: Cornell University Press, 2008).
42. The debate is well covered in Barnett and Weiss, *Humanitarianism in Question*.
43. Michael Barnett, *Eyewitness to a Genocide: The United Nations and Rwanda* (Ithaca, NY: Cornell University Press, 2002); Alex De Waal, 'Darfur and the Failure of the Responsibility to Protect', *International Affairs*, 83.6 (2007): 1039–54.
44. Secretary of State Colin Powell, Remarks to the National Foreign Policy Conference for Leaders of Nongovernmental Organisations, 26 October 2001, cited in Barnett and Weiss, *Humanitarianism in Question*, 25.
45. 'The Responsibility To Protect: Report of the International Commission on Intervention and State Sovereignty, December 2001', accessed 12 October 2012, http://responsibilitytoprotect.org/ICISS%20Report.pdf.
46. 'Darfur and Beyond: What Is Needed to Prevent Mass Atrocities: Council on Foreign Relations', Council Special Report No 22, accessed 12 October 2012, http://www.cfr.org/international-law/academic-module-darfur-beyond-needed-prevent-mass-atrocities/p13708.
47. Michael Aaronson, 'Libya: Did we have a Choice?', 61st Annual International Conference of the Political Studies Association, 'Transforming Politics: New Synergies', 18 April 2011.

9
Building State Effectiveness: Evolving Donor Approaches to Good Governance in Sub-Saharan Africa

Claire Leigh

Introduction

In 2010, Ellen Johnson Sirleaf, president of Liberia, wrote that 'Africa's crisis is a failure of leadership and management. Sub-Saharan Africa is rich in resources, talent, energy and spirit. But it has not been rich in leadership. It is made up of rich countries that have been poorly managed and the results have been disastrous.'[1] The implication is that development has stalled in Africa primarily because of a failure of governance and institutions. It's a view that an increasing number of people in the development community share, partly informed by a better understanding of the political economy of development, and a clear 'governance turn' can be observed over the last decade in both the rhetoric and spending priorities of the major development actors.

There is also a more pragmatic reason why state capacity-building is *a la mode* at present. With aid budgets frozen as a result of the economic crisis and new questions being asked about the value of aid, donors have converged around the narrative of a 'post aid' future and the importance of building the capacity of recipient states to lead the delivery of public goods and services for themselves.

In what follows I first look at the understandings of 'good governance' that have dominated the development debate since the 1990s and briefly explore the factors driving the new significance placed on state capacity by development actors, in particular why donors have recently been channelling more resources into the area. Secondly, I examine some of the practical challenges of implementing donor-led governance work, including the ways in which donor-led approaches continue to undermine effective governance and emerging understandings of what works and what doesn't. In particular I look at some of the opportunities presented by a new class of 'arm's length' governance-focused initiatives and organizations that have appeared in recent years. Finally, I consider the broader implications of a renewed focus on governance in Africa, including some of the normative challenges raised and prospects for the future.

Why the new emphasis on governance?

The current preoccupation with good governance among donors has its origins in two separate and potentially conflicting forces at work within the development sector. The first is an emerging consensus that sustainable economic development in Africa depends on the ability and willingness of African governments to shape, lead and deliver change for themselves, a consensus expressed in evolving terms through the various *High Level Forums on Aid Effectiveness* in Paris, Accra and most recently Busan.

The millennium, with its eponymous development goals, also heralded a decade of soul-searching by multilateral and bilateral donors. This process found its first formal articulation in the Paris Declaration on Aid Effectiveness in 2005.[2] The Paris Declaration reflected lessons learnt over several frustrating decades of aid activity, which led donors to conclude that sustainable development depends primarily on efforts at the state (as opposed to international or sub-national) level and that aid needs to focus on facilitating country-led efforts, not on trying to replace them.[3]

The resultant 'Paris Declaration' saw donors sign up to five core principles. These were:

1. Ownership: Developing countries should set their own strategies for poverty reduction, improve their institutions and tackle corruption;
2. Alignment: Donor countries should align behind these objectives and use local systems;
3. Harmonization: Donor countries should coordinate, simplify procedures and share information to avoid duplication;
4. Results: Developing countries and donors should shift their focus to development results and results get measured;
5. Mutual accountability: Donors and their country partners should be jointly accountable for development results.[4]

The subsequent 'Accra Agenda for Action' in 2008 went even further and – through pressure from developing countries themselves – donors agreed that the concept of 'ownership' should be extended to mean recipient country leadership on aid coordination itself and more use of country systems for aid delivery. The implications of the Accra Agenda were significant; whereas in the past donors could run a programme in practical isolation from a recipient government and hence insulated from its dysfunctionality, the Accra principles required donors not only to work in partnership with host governments and their line ministries but indeed to allow their work to be led by these national agencies.[5]

However, Paris and Accra contained a paradoxical logic. In states – particularly post-conflict states – where the current capacity of state institutions and civil servants is often very low, the expectation that aid be increasingly channelled through state structures under the command of local officials was in clear contention, at least in the short term, with the demand that aid achieve better results and is spent more efficiently and accountably.

The second factor at work has been an increasingly vocal demand from taxpayers in donor nations themselves for better accountability and demonstrable results from aid. As donor nations struggle to achieve the international aid target of 0.7 per cent of Gross National Income by 2013[6] and in circumstances of greater fiscal austerity at home, development organizations are painfully aware of the need to justify money spent in terms of concrete results, while at the same time mitigating taxpayer fears that the same money is lining the pockets of government officials or politicians.

The effort to resolve these two competing imperatives – to hand the reins of development to recipient country governments and at the same time to demonstrate more value and accountability for the money spent – is driving ever greater involvement by donors in recipient state institutions and ministries. For most donors the solution to the ownership/results paradox inherent in Paris and Accra has been an upsurge in governance and capacity-strengthening activities to complement or precede any shift towards greater use of country systems.

The impact on the donor *modus operandi* has been dramatic, in terms of the spread of now-ubiquitous ways of working, including joint donor and government coordinating structures such as sector working groups, ministry-based programme management units (PMUs), the rise of direct budget support and in terms of massive amounts of additional donor support to build governance systems and state institutions able to cope with the new expectations placed upon them. The total proportion of

ODA funds spent on governance programmes today has tripled since 1993.[7] Consequently, the great irony of the 'country ownership' agenda is that Western actors are perhaps more directly involved in supporting the administration of government in sub-Saharan Africa than at any time in the postcolonial period.

Good governance as accountability

Aid agencies have often been accused of privileging process over outcomes and the same could be said of the renewed drive for good governance. Process dominated the Paris Declaration, informing four of its five main principles and since 2005 donors have arguably done more to change how things are done rather than what is achieved as a result.

Good governance in business or in public sector contexts is usually taken to mean two things; governing *successfully* (i.e. achieving stated objectives) and governing *accountably* (i.e. doing so in an appropriate, accountable way). Within the development discourse, however, good governance has arguably acquired a narrower meaning and has been used as shorthand for efforts to eradicate corruption, to promote the rule of law and otherwise create a positive environment for the free market economy. On its website the UN says 'In the community of nations, governance is considered "good" and "democratic" to the degree in which a country's institutions and processes are transparent.'[8]

This somewhat one-sided interpretation of good governance is perhaps unsurprising, reflecting aid organizations' dual accountabilities to both aid recipients and to taxpayers at home, as discussed above. These dual accountabilities have created what Alan Hudson and Paolo de Renzio have called the 'impossible geometries' of aid.[9] Accountability to recipients' interests require donors to strengthen state institutions, offer more money in terms of direct budget support and programmes run with or through government structures and crucially to take greater risks, including the risk that a proportion of spend will be wasted through inefficiency or corruption. Accountability to taxpayers instead requires donors to act cautiously and to demonstrate measurable results.

In other words, while development partners have come a long way in recognizing the importance of country-led development, underpinned by a capable state, too often this has – for reasons that frequently have more to do with the concerns of domestic taxpayers than those of recipient countries – meant a focus on improving governance processes rather than governance outcomes, in other words a 'good governance as accountability' approach. While this undoubtedly matters, the capacity of recipient states to plan and deliver development programmes has been comparatively neglected as a result.[10] In the World Bank Governance Strategy of 2007, for example, corruption is mentioned 576 times, whereas references to the term 'governance' in its 'successful government' usage appear just 32 times.[11]

Good governance as effectiveness

'Good governance as effectiveness' represents an important second pillar of the country ownership agenda. Without effective state institutions able to take the lead in the planning and delivery of development programmes, the ambitions of donors set out at Paris and Accra will remain just that.

Lately the development sector has started to show signs of widening the scope of governance programmes to encompass the objective of improving state capacity to deliver public goods and services. A renewed emphasis on the impact of aid was reflected in the theme for the 2011 iteration of the fourth *High Level Forum on Aid Effectiveness* at Busan, the successor to Paris and Accra, with its emphasis on improving development outcomes as opposed to donor processes.[12] The increasing importance placed on state effectiveness and capacity in international development is also evidenced by the series of global summits that have taken place since 2009.

UNDP's global conference in 2010 addressed the theme 'Capacity is Development' and governance and public-sector capacity have been elevated to one of the three themes that make up the World Bank's 2011 Africa Strategy.[13] Callisto Madavo, former World Bank vice president for the Africa Region, endorses this more holistic conception of good governance: 'An effective poverty reduction strategy process and a productive partnership can only be built on a platform of strong public sector capacity: Capacity to formulate policies, to build consensus, to implement reforms and the capacity to monitor results, learn lessons and adapt accordingly.'[14]

This trend is also reflected in the programming of the major bilateral donors. GTZ, USAID and DFID now regularly include a government capacity-building element across their African programming. USAID administrator Rajiv Shah, in his landmark June 2011 speech at the Conference on Democracy, Rights and Governance, explained the shift, saying that 'In the end, our assistance is no substitute for the capacity necessary to drive through reform. We must promote, build and nurture leadership and institutions so that governments have a realistic chance to provide results.'[15]

The importance of state effectiveness to development

Arguably, a broader understanding of good governance as implying state effectiveness is on the rise because the major development partners increasingly see that their own impact is dependent on the capacity of their partner governments, and because it is becoming ever more apparent Paris and Accra presupposed capable state infrastructures which at present do not exist. But there is also an emerging empirical foundation for the new emphasis on state effectiveness within the good governance discourse, with recent research highlighting the ways in which a lack of state capacity can undermine political stability in young African democracies, in turn undermining socio-economic progress.

Paul Collier provides a helpful model for understanding why this is. His argument is that while democracy is generally assumed to increase stability and reduce conflict, that logic does not hold for poor democracies. This is because the chief mechanisms through which democracy contributes to peace are legitimacy – that is, that leaders have an elected mandate – and delivery, whereby a government earns the right to rule through its performance and provision of the things that people want.

The latter mechanism approximates to the 'effectiveness' pillar of good governance – the ability of a regime to achieve its stated aims. Collier's argument continues that conflict is often perpetuated in poor democracies in part because governments lack the capacity – in terms of the ability to collect taxes, prioritize and implement programmes effectively – to perform and live up to election promises.[16] If a government does not know how to succeed, if it lacks the skills to overcome the already difficult constraints it faces, then the next election cannot possibly be fought on the grounds of policy choices or performance. Instead, self-interested politicians will be encouraged to lie, cheat and bribe their way to electoral victory. They will often turn to violence, as will their outraged opponents and the results of this have been seen in Nigeria, Cote D'Ivoire and Kenya (to name but a few) in recent years.

In summary, Collier argues that 'in encouraging elections, we have landed these societies in an unviable halfway house that has neither the capacity of autocracies to act decisively nor the accountability of a genuine democracy'.[17] Donors hope that if poor, young democracies can be supported to govern effectively (and the 'if' part of that sentence is critical) then just maybe the cycle of underdevelopment and conflict in

LDCs identified by Collier can be broken. That alone should be enough to make state effectiveness the Holy Grail of development.

How donor activities can undermine state effectiveness

It is worth pausing for a moment to reflect on how traditional ways of working in the aid industry have in the past acted to actually undermine both country ownership and government capacity. A major problem with how donors have tended to work in the past, and often still do, is that they have focused on the direct provision of tangible public goods and services such as roads, schools and hospitals. The focus on straight-to-citizen outputs has rightly been criticized for being paternalistic – playing into Western constructs of African victimhood, charitable magnanimity and shouldering the 'White Man's Burden' – as well as for undermining local capacity and ownership.[18] Again, dual accountabilities to domestic taxpayers/political masters may partly explain donor preference for direct provision. Schools and hospitals are what voters in donor countries expect their money to be spent on, not on subsidizing African Big Men or bankrolling core state functions.[19]

A second explanation pertains to the respective timeframes involved in delivering directly versus delivering through dysfunctional state institutions. State-building takes time and is notoriously difficult. Political changes in the recipient country can unexpectedly reverse years of work. Meanwhile humanitarian needs in particular demand urgent responses and donors have understandably been unwilling to hang around. As a consequence aid agencies have arguably sought shortcuts to poverty reduction that avoid state-building altogether.

The temptation to bypass the state has been compounded by growing demands from donor headquarters that field programmes demonstrate fast, measurable results. This has further deterred donors from the slow, painful and hard to measure business of state capacity building.[20] The impact of stronger government institutions takes years to take root and end results are hard to attribute to upstream capacity-building work that in and of itself produces nothing but better-designed ministries or more competent civil servants.

Finally, it has simply been easier for donors to operate independently than to engage meaningfully with the byzantine complexities of befuddled bureaucracies. Donors often struggle to reconcile their programming priorities and internationally set budget cycles with local priorities and budget cycles, creating practical barriers to working through state institutions. Unsurprisingly most have instead opted to take the path of least resistance in such circumstances and to work independently in contexts where they can control inputs and risks.

The preference of donors to operate outside of state institutions and to deliver developmental programmes directly has of course acted to emasculate and weaken those very institutions. The by-products of the resultant parallel delivery infrastructures are well documented, including the brain drain they incentivize, whereby local talent drifts from the civil service into donor organizations.[21] Salaries are raised as ministries attempt to woo people back, but only enough to encourage the poorest performers never to leave and to inflate recurrent budgets at the cost of project funds. In the Ministry of Agriculture in Liberia, for example, 80 per cent of the core annual budget is typically spent on recurrent costs (mainly wages) leaving almost no money to actually do anything or deliver projects.[22]

The decision by donors to bypass government has been short sighted and counterproductive to the long-term strengthening of state institutions for other reasons. Unintended negative consequences are both operational and political in nature – operational because the institutions and public sector staff being bypassed are demotivated and de-skilled in the process and political because the public quickly becomes aware that their elected leaders are not the ones delivering core public goods and services.

Returning to Collier, the persistent lack of state capacity means leaders are rendered incapable of earning legitimacy through delivery on their electoral promises.[23] It is difficult to win loyalty and respect as a leader, or to build belief in the state and the political system, if taxes are seen to be wasted on government institutions that seem to achieve nothing but ever more ingenious methods of corruption while all the things that people want and like – the roads, schools and hospitals – are being delivered by foreign organizations.

Where angels fear to tread?

Since the public self-flagellation of the High Level Forums on Aid Effectiveness in Paris and Accra, all of the aforementioned issues have been acknowledged by the major aid players and there have been significant moves recently to work with and through developing country governments to deliver aid programmes and to build capacity within state institutions so that they can start to undertake some of the heavy lifting. But these early efforts have been patchy at best and have raised issues of their own.

Traditional donors are partly constrained by who they are and what they are perceived to represent, as agents of Western powers with vested interests. Because of this, where donor-led programmes have attempted to address capacity weaknesses in state institutions, they have generally ignored the 'centre of government' (including presidents/prime ministers offices and cabinet functions) in favour of supporting line ministries; those budget-spending ministries that are (in theory) in charge of delivering public goods and services. The centre of government presents many barriers to entry for traditional donors. They are either denied access to the quarterdeck by a country's leadership, who feel that intervention in, for example, the president's office would be an incursion too far, or donors themselves make the decision that central institutions of state are too politically risky, or too upstream, for their tastes.

In the Government of Liberia, for example, there are a growing number of programmes dedicated to state capacity building. The German aid agency GTZ (now GIZ) has undertaken a major programme supporting the Public Works Ministry, which is responsible for road construction.[24] Meanwhile USAID has just completed the TASMOA programme of capacity-building support to the Ministry of Agriculture.[25] But not one major development partner works with the Ministry of State for Presidential Affairs. In countries where frequently power and decision making are concentrated around the person of the president, this often leaves their efforts in line ministries unavoidably and fatally weakened.

The exceptions to this bias towards line-ministry support are Ministries of Finance, which often host the largest number of donor-funded consultants and capacity-building programmes. However, this can be better explained by the concern, discussed above, to minimize the risk of corruption and to ensure accountability, rather than a concern for enhancing a government's central delivery capacity. Where capacity-building support programmes have been undertaken, efforts by donors have exposed a variety of persistent issues and there are signs that in reality less has changed in donor approaches than they would have us believe.

There are many concerns with current development partner approaches to capacity development. Donors often succumb to the temptation to quickly disburse their newly inflated governance budgets by hiring temporary international consultants to give training or write reports under the banner of technical assistance (TA). TA tends to focus on providing specialist policy advice and on supporting policy design rather than policy delivery. This means priorities and strategies frequently fail to take full account of local political concerns, interests and constraints, hence go undelivered. Donors prefer to support the direction-setting end of the policy supply chain for obvious reasons. But a commensurate lack of support for implementation means that these policies can often simply gather dust on the shelf. Capacity-building programmes done badly can also impose priorities and processes that overlap and sometimes conflict with a government's own agenda and systems, adding ever new layers of complexity and placing a huge coordination burden on country officials.

Another common temptation for donors is to achieve gains in effectiveness in state institutions by 'gap-filling' key posts with international staff and bringing in international consultants to do the work of local civil servants for them. This can achieve results and certainly has its uses in terms of quickly driving forward priorities, but is ultimately unsustainable and can be just another means of bypassing internal government infrastructures.

Finally, when ministries are given control of donor-funded programmes or trust funds, donors' main concern is often to ensure that the ministry's processes meet their organization's own global standards. Thus development partners can ostensibly meet their Paris commitments while in practise maintaining control and making no significant changes to their ways of working, making the ministry or agency adapt rather than vice versa. At worst there are multiple donors doing this in the same ministry at the same time. This adds a huge administrative burden to already weakened institutions.

In Liberia, for example, Programme Management Units (PMUs) are now commonly bolted on to ministries as delivery vehicles for donor programmes. However, donor programmes are integrated into government systems only in the loosest sense. In the Ministry of Agriculture, for example, one major co-funded programme that is being run through the PMU has two funders, two sets of reporting and accounting requirements and two sets of staff, none of which match the ministry's own systems.[26] And the PMU is in charge of several programmes at any one time. The added complexity of multiple accountabilities and ways of working imposed on developing country ministries under the auspices of country ownership is a perverse outcome of the Paris Agenda that its architects presumably did not anticipate.

Arms' length capacity-building initiatives

The constraints on the ability of traditional donors to deliver effective and direct capacity-building support within recipient country governments has led to the emergence of a new cluster of niche NGOs and initiatives that specialize in governance support and are able to operate at arm's length from (although often still funded by) donors. These include the Africa Governance Initiative (AGI), which was set up by former British Prime Minister Tony Blair in 2008 with the ambition of working with African states where weak institutions are seen to be holding back progress on ambitious government development agendas. The Overseas Development Institute's Budget Strengthening Initiative, the International Budget Partnership, the Africa Capacity Building Foundation and the International Growth Centre are among other examples.

The AGI in particular emphasizes the importance of state effectiveness as a necessary complement to efforts to improve accountability. It regards an effective government as having a strong strategic centre (i.e. strong coordinating and direction-setting centre of government institutions), a capable set of line or delivery ministries, senior civil servants skilled in the dark arts of bureaumancy and a leader able to provide strategic direction and unity.[27] AGI promotes three key aspects of governance effectiveness, which it sees as particularly weak in many African governments:

1. Prioritization of the most important objectives and to focus central government resources on these;
2. Effective planning for the implementation of policies to achieve priorities; and
3. Performance management to provide an evolving picture of the progress that is being made, in order to inform future decisions.

This approach to effective governance, lifted from common private sector management practises, is reminiscent of the managerialist approach of the UK's Labour Government between 1997 and 2010.[28] The application of managerialist approaches to African governments is particularly useful for international actors. Managerialism is predicated on the universal applicability of subject-neutral tools and methods to improve efficiency, helping donors to avoid accusations of introducing 'westernized' approaches to developing country governments, while turning a lack of deep knowledge of a particular country context into something of a virtue.

As an example of the managerialist approach in action, AGI worked with the senior leadership of the Government of Rwanda to support its annual leadership retreat. Each year at the 'Kivu retreat' the president sets out his strategic priorities for the year ahead. Rather than supporting the president's office on the substance of the government's priorities, AGI instead advised senior officials on agreeing a process for selecting priorities across government and designing the system and tools necessary to drive and monitor implementation after the retreat. As a result, the number of goals set at Kivu fell from 134 in 2009 to just 6 in 2011, allowing the government to focus on a small number of carefully chosen goals. These were subsequently overseen by a new Joint Delivery Committee, which project managed and monitored implementation of the chosen priorities. This kind of substance-neutral implementation support is in stark contrast to the capacity-building interventions typical of many traditional donors, which tend instead to focus on the provision of expert policy advice.

Interventions by this new breed of niche capacity-building initiatives also aim to be collaborative, sustainable and sensitive to local circumstances and demands. Some of the most successful governance interventions follow what is often called the 'Botswana model' of capacity development, where practitioners are bought in on a longer-term basis as embedded employees of state institutions to work alongside local counterparts.[29] Under the Botswana model, through a gradual process of skills transfer, formal training, coaching and mentoring of senior staff, along with the introduction of systems, tools and processes to enable effective delivery, the overseas practitioner can in theory eventually step back. Supporters of the Botswana Model argue this is ultimately both more sustainable, ensuring local ownership and developing local capacity and politically more viable, as it works from the premise that the intervention should enable leaders to achieve their own goals rather than imposing goals from the outside.

For example, in Rwanda between 2008 and 2010 the AGI worked in the Coordination Unit in the prime minister's office, which is responsible for producing quarterly reports on the progress of a small set of presidential priorities. AGI advisors worked intensively with the local team in the first iteration of reports to agree methods, standard templates and tools, then purposely became less involved with each successive quarter, until they were able to exit altogether from the process and unit.[30]

Emerging lessons

Although there is still a long way to go in working out how and if sustainable capacity development can be accelerated by external support, from AGI and other similar organizations' experiences in doing this kind of work, five emerging lessons can be identified about how to increase the impact and sustainability of external capacity-development interventions:[31]

Offer independent, embedded advice. First, capacity development is perhaps better undertaken by small specialist operators able to credibly demonstrate that they are working on the side of the recipient government. It is arguably harder for a major donor to undertake state capacity development work, as a large portfolio of in-country programmes will mean it brings with it its own agenda and potential conflicts of interest. Embedding advisors in government institutions improves contextual understanding, builds trust and allows advisors to act as enablers and coaches of local counterparts, rather that coming for short periods to do the job themselves.

Work from the inside out. Second, in political contexts where power is often concentrated at the centre and around a handful of people, it is vital to gain the trust and visible support of a country's leadership, without which any capacity-building intervention will likely fail. For this reason, organizations like the AGI maintain that it is vital to work with the centre of government as well as line ministries. Central institutions may work upstream, but they provide the necessary coordination and influence to get the rest of government pulling in the same direction.

Close the implementation gap. Third, AGI has found that the focus of capacity development should be on closing the implementation gap between the plethora of strategic plans in existence and the relative lack of delivery on the ground, rather than drafting new high-level strategies. Moving from priorities to delivery requires planning and project management skills that are often lacking in many developing country civil services.

As discussed above, this managerialist approach to capacity building is premised upon the universal applicability of standard management techniques in improving the effectiveness of any organization. If the premise is accepted, it enables external actors to support government effectiveness through a focus on systems, soft skills and structure, as opposed to substance. Thus boundaries are, in theory, maintained between intervention and interference in domestic policy. In other words, the ideal is for the external advisors to be a force magnifier for the recipient government's ability to pursue its own priorities in its own way.

Demonstrate tangible results. Fourth, the effectiveness of capacity development should be measured by its outputs not its inputs. Capacity has to be *for* something. If it does not deliver change on the ground then why do it? Achieving real results will mean that a country's leadership (be they ministers or presidents) will continue to be bought in. It makes them look good to each other and to voters and means that officials all along the delivery chain see the purpose of changing the way they do things. It also makes measuring the success of the intervention easier and enables the rigorous monitoring and evaluation that most donors and funders demand.

AGI maintains that focusing on outputs means working back from what you want to achieve, identifying capacity gaps that are preventing the relevant institutions from implementing priorities and then targeting capacity-building efforts accordingly. For example, AGI supported the Government of Sierra Leone to launch its Free Healthcare Initiative in 2010, which ended user fees for new mothers and under-fives. Capacity development was targeted at points of weakness in the healthcare delivery chain. The programme has already had some impressive results. Since its launch, there has been 85 per cent drop in the malaria fatality rate for children treated in hospitals and a 214 per cent increase in the number of children accessing medical care.[32] This has won the capacity-building programme credibility with leaders and officials and has been shown to have an ongoing impact of the capacity of the Ministry of Health.

Avoid gap-filling. Fifth, the sustainability of capacity development rests on whether outside TA can avoid the temptation to simply fill gaps. Instead, AGI believes that capacity builders should focus on developing, in partnership with counterparts, skills, systems and structures that will outlast the lifespan of the given capacity-development intervention. A good example of where gap-filling can badly go wrong comes from Liberia, where the UN's Mission in Liberia (UNMIL) has arguably created a dependency on the UN Police Force to provide civilian policing and has retarded the development of a capable home-grown police force. The UNMIL drawdown now raises serious concerns over the ability of domestic police services to take over.[33]

Persistent constraints

However, while these five lessons can arguably help to improve the effectiveness of capacity-building interventions, they are not silver bullets and carry with them their own challenges. Working from the inside out and as independent advisors embedded in a government, is easier said than done when donors control most of the funding for governance projects, even if actual interventions are implemented by specialist, independent organizations. Focusing on outputs rather than inputs makes it treacherously difficult to measure a specific intervention's effectiveness and not 'gap-filling' involves resisting the pressure to demonstrate quick results to funders.

Perhaps most difficult challenge of all is the question of how far external organizations are willing to go on the country ownership agenda. NGOs and donors who genuinely place themselves at the disposal of the country's leadership and who follow a truly demand-led approach to capacity building, are faced with the dilemma of what to do when a recipient government makes decisions with which they disagree. This tests to the limits the extent to which NGOs and donors are willing and able to remain impartial advisors and exposes potential weaknesses in the much-lauded commitment to country ownership.

Normative constraints

Beyond the practical challenges facing external actors engaged in capacity-building interventions, there remains a set of normative questions and controversies about the export of governance norms to the African context. Critics have pointed to the danger of imposing Western modes and in the process eroding the normative principle of self-determination.[34] At worst governance interventions could be suspected of being Trojan Horses to advance a neo-colonial agenda and discourse, or as a way for donors to maintain influence without conditionality, in an era when tied aid is frowned upon.

The first normative issue, around the 'Westernization' of African governance practices, is perhaps the most challenging. The claim that a managerialist approach to capacity development uses tools and techniques which are somehow 'culture neutral' and applicable across contexts and organizations is a contentious one and requires rigorous analysis and debate going forward. Donors and NGOs operating in this area should note that some of the best governance innovations emerging from Africa combine indigenous modes and traditions of governance with Western approaches to form hybrid systems.[35]

In Rwanda, for example, the government has revived various forms of governance that trace their origins to the pre-colonial era. The *gacaca* system of community courts was famously revived to cope with the huge backlog of genocide cases after 1994. Meanwhile in 2006 the Government of Rwanda started using the traditional *imihigo* system as an equivalent of management-speak 'performance contracts' or Public Service Agreements. *Imihigo* is a long-standing cultural practice in Rwanda whereby two parties publicly commit themselves to the achievement of a particular task. All ministers are expected to sign *imihigo* contracts annually, committing them to key objectives over the year.[36] Some exciting new research programmes are developing research into hybrid solutions, such as Africa Power and Politics (APP) and the Institute for Development Studies' 'Working with the grain' programme.[37] The APP advocates a move away from best practise towards 'best fit', building on what works and modifying approaches to the local context and culture.

The second normative concern is around the question of sovereignty and whether interventions in state institutions constitute an affront to state autonomy. 'Country ownership' may be the watchwords in development these days. But as we have seen, the great irony of the concept is the fact that the agenda may be driving ever deeper incursions into state institutions by donors and NGOs.

Defenders of governance programmes have met this concern by emphasizing that donor incursions into the governance sphere are part of a temporary and necessary effort to address key market failures in the short term in order to restore the recipient state's sovereignty and independence in the long term. Paul Collier, for example, argues that

> [j]ust as the high-income world should provide a vaccine against malaria for the citizens of the bottom billion, so it should supply them with security and accountability of government. All three are public goods that will otherwise be chronically undersupplied. Only once they are properly supplied can the societies of the bottom billion achieve their aspirations of genuine sovereignty.[38]

In other words governance interventions to strengthen the ability of states to govern successfully, rather than undermining sovereignty, are seen by their supporters as a means to return genuine sovereignty to developing country governments, a sovereignty currently crippled by a reliance on donors to supply the most basic functions of the state.

Conclusion

The recent governance trend in donor programming in Africa has its origins in three insights: that good governance means governing *successfully* as well as *accountably*; that state ineffectiveness drives instability and underdevelopment in important ways; and that to enable African states to govern successfully involves fundamental changes in the current *modus operandi* of the aid regime, which until recently has arguably done more to undermine than to promote effective state institutions.

Effective governments have the potential not only to make real improvements to people's lives but to enhance stability and belief in the political system and to reassert their sovereignty. Since the Paris Declaration and Accra Agenda it has been in donors' interests to turn state institutions into effective delivery vehicles. Under moves towards country ownership, donors realize that their own effectiveness as organizations is increasingly bound up in the effectiveness of the state institutions in recipient countries and that they need to support, not just exhort, institutions to become better functioning.

In practice the challenges of supporting state effectiveness are manifold and donors and NGOs are only starting to learn how to do so effectively and sustainably. Questions remain around the appropriateness of deeper incursions into the realm of the state by Western organizations. These could be seen as neo-colonial at worst or at least reminiscent of paternalistic attitudes to the continent that have persisted for some 200 years.

Donors have to show that they can work in and with recipient governments in a way that genuinely leaves their sovereignty intact, in a way that takes seriously and respects indigenous forms of governance and that builds genuine and sustainable capacity. If they cannot, then they risk fostering a new form of dependency that will undermine country ownership in the long run. The emergence of a new breed of niche initiatives, enabling donors to support capacity building at arm's length, may offer a way to overcome many of the pitfalls and barriers, but the challenges are still prodigious.

Notes

1. Ellen Johnson-Sirleaf, 'Introduction', in Steven Radelet, ed., *Emerging Africa: How 17 Countries are Leading the Way* (Center for Global Development, 2010), 5.
2. OECD, *The Paris Declaration on Aid Effectiveness and the Accra Agenda for Action* (OECD, 2008), accessed 7 October 2012, http://www.oecd.org/development/aideffectiveness/34428351.pdf.
3. The evidence-base for the Paris principals included, among others surveys by: Nicolas Van de Walle and Timothy A. Johnston, *Improving Aid to Africa* (Washington, D.C.: Overseas Development Council, 1996); David Booth, ed., *Fighting Poverty in Africa: Are PRSPs Making a Difference?* (London: ODI, 2003);

and Stefan Koeberle, Harold Bedoya, Peter Silarsky and Geor Verheyen, eds, *Conditionality Revisited: Concepts, Experiences and Lessons* (Washington, D.C.: World Bank Publications, 2005).

4. For an overview of the Paris and Accra panel outcomes, see 'Aid Effectiveness', OECD, accessed 31 October 2011, http://www.oecd.org/document/18/0,3343,en_2649_3236398_35401554_1_1_1_1,00.html.

5. OECD, *The Paris Declaration*.

6. In 1970, the 0.7 per cent ODA/GNI target was first agreed and has been repeatedly re-endorsed at the highest level at international aid and development conferences. For example in 2005, the 15 countries that were members of the European Union by 2004 agreed to reach the target by 2015. The 0.7 per cent target also served as a reference for 2005 political commitments to increase ODA from the EU, the G8 Gleneagles Summit and the UN World Summit. For more information see the OECD's explanation at 'The 0.7% ODA/GNI target – a history', OECD, accessed 30 October 2011, http://www.oecd.org/document/19/0,3746,en_2649_34447_45539475_1_1_1_1,00.html.

7. OECD, *Development Aid at a Glance: Statistics by Region/ Africa* (OECD, 2011), accessed 7 October 2012, http://www.oecd.org/investment/aidstatistics/aidstatisticsstatisticsbyregion2012aidataglance.htm.

8. See, 'Governance', UN.org, accessed 29 November 2011, http://www.un.org/en/globalissues/governance/. The webpage goes on to say 'Good governance promotes equity, participation, pluralism, transparency, accountability and the rule of law, in a manner that is effective, efficient and enduring. In translating these principles into practice, we see the holding of free, fair and frequent elections, representative legislatures that make laws and provides oversight and an independent judiciary to interpret those laws.'

9. Alan Hudson, *Impossible Geometries*, Presentation to the Overseas Development Institute, available at http://www.odi.org.uk/events/documents/2715-presentation-alan-hudson.pdf, accessed 27 October 2011.

10. The tensions inherent in these competing imperatives were explored at the ODI event 'A results take-over of aid effectiveness? How to balance multiple or competing calls for more accountability' (London, 25 July 2011), accessed 20 September 2012, www.odi.org.uk/events/report.asp?id=2715&title= results-take-over-aid-effectiveness-balance-multiple-competing-calls-more-accountability.

11. World Bank, *Governance and Anti-Corruption Strategy* (Washington, D.C.: World Bank Publications, 2007).

12. For an overview of the High Level Forum at Busan in November 2011 see, 'Busan 2011', accessed 29 November 2011, http://www.aideffectiveness.org/busanhlf4/en/about/about-busan.html.

13. World Bank, *Africa's Future and the World Bank's Support to It*, accessed 29 November 2011, www.worldbank.org/africastrategy.

14. Frannie A. Leutier and Callisto Madavo, 'Foreword' in Brian Levy and Sahr Kpundeh, eds, *Building State Capacity in Africa: New Approaches, Emerging Lessons* (World Bank Institute, 2004), v– vi.

15. Raj Shah, USAID Administrator, 'An Expansion of Human Welfare' (paper presented at the Democracy, Rights and Governance Conference 2.0, Arlington, Virginia, 20 June 2011).

16. Paul Collier, *Wars, Guns and Votes: Democracy in Dangerous Places* (London: Bodley Head, 2009).
17. Collier, Ibid., 49.
18. For a discussion of prevailing attitudes towards Africa in the West, which cast Africa as the theatre for charitable acts and its citizens as passive victims to be 'saved', see Maria Eriksson Baaz, *The Paternalism of Partnership: A Postcolonial Reading of Identity in Development Aid* (London: Zed Books, 2005). Baaz looks at the eurocentric nature of development and an aid discourse that still assumes images of the superior, initiating, efficient 'donor' as opposed to the inadequate, passive, unreliable 'partner' or recipient. For a comparison with eighteenth- and nineteenth-century British attitudes and motivations for intervention in the continent, see Philip Curtin, *The image of Africa: British ideas and action, 1780–1850*, Vol. 1 (Madison, WI: University of Wisconsin Press, 1973).
19. For some statistics on public attitudes to aid in the UK, for example, see Action Aid, *Opinion Poll on Public Attitudes to Aid* (Action Aid, 2006), accessed 30 November 2011, http://www.actionaid.org.uk/doc_lib/poll_summary.pdf.
20. For a discussion of the bureaucratic pressure to demonstrate measurable results, often at the cost of long-term development, pressure placed on the country offices of donor organizations by their metropolitan headquarters, see Andrew Natsios, 'The Clash of the Counter-Bureaucracy and Development', in the Centre for Global Development essay series (Washington, D.C.: Centre for Global Development 2010).
21. Nancy Birdsall, 'Do No Harm: Aid, Weak Institutions and the Missing Middle in Africa', *Working Paper 113, Center for Global Development*, accessed 30 November 2011, http://www.cgdev.org/content/publications/detail/13115. In the article Birdsall discusses the effects of the 'internal brain drain' by donors and NGOs in developing countries.
22. Government of Liberia, Ministry of Agriculture, Budget 2010–11 (unpublished).
23. Collier, *Wars, Guns and Votes*, Ch. 1.
24. For more information see: 'Capacity Building in the Infrastructure Sector in Liberia', GIZ, accessed January 14, 2013, www3.giz.de/imperia/md/content/ainternet2008/ portaliz/wirtschaftundbeschaeftigung/capacity_building_in_the_infrastructur_sector_in_liberia.pdf.
25. For more information see 'Technical Assistance and Support to the Ministry of Agriculture', USAID, accessed 30 November 2011, http://liberia.usaid.gov/node/39.
26. For details of the jointly funded IFAD and African Development Bank project, see 'The Agricultural Sector Rehabilitation Project (ASRP)', Republic Of Liberia, Ministry Of Agriculture, accessed 30 November 2011, http://www.afdb.org/fileadmin/uploads/afdb/Documents/Project-related-Procurement/EOILiberiaASRP %20%205-11_01.pdf.
27. For the Africa Governance Initiative's approach to building effective government see 'Our approach', Africa Governance Initiative, accessed 30 November 2011, http://www.africagovernance.org/africa/pages/our-approach.

28. 'Managerialism' refers to the belief that organizations have more similarities than differences and thus the performance of all organizations can be optimized by the application of generic management skills and theory. For a discussion of the rise of mangerialist approaches in the British Public Sector in the late 1990s, see Mark Exworthy, *Professionals and the New Managerialism in the Public Sector* (Oxford: Oxford University Press, 1999).
29. For a description of the Botswana model and a comparison to other approaches, see 'Pooling of Technical Assistance', Capacity.Org, accessed 30 November 2011, http://www.capacity.org/capacity/export/sites/capacity/documents/journal-pdfs/CAP0201_12_ENG_LR.pdf.
30. See a description of AGI's Rwanda Project at 'Rwanda', Africa Governance Initiative, accessed 30 November 2011, http://www.africagovernance.org/africa/pages/rwanda/.
31. These lessons are taken from the author's own experience of working for the Africa Governance Initiative and from Tony Blair, *Not Just Aid: How Making Government Work Can Transform Africa* (Washington, D.C.: Center for Global Development, 2010).
32. Figures supplied by DFID and reported in Adam Nossiter, 'In Sierra Leone, Heartening Progress for Pregnant Women', *New York Times*, 17 July 2011.
33. For GTZ's analysis of the challenges facing Liberia's security forces, see 'The challenges of re-starting the Liberian police force', available at www.inwent.org/ez/articles/194123/index.en.shtml (accessed 30 November 2011).
34. Jennifer Welsh and Ngaire Woods, *Exporting Good Governance: Temptations and challenges in Canada's Aid Program* (Ontario: Wilfred Laurier University Press, 2007).
35. Richard Crook and David Booth, eds, 'Working with the Grain? Rethinking African Governance', *Institute of Development Studies* (2011), accessed 30 November 2011, http://www.ids.ac.uk/go/idspublication/working-with-the-grain-rethinking-african-governance.
36. 'Rwanda: Performance contracts (Imihigo)', Budget Strengthening Initiative, accessed January 14, 2013, www.budgetstrengthening.org/storage/country-learning-notes/Rwanda%20performance%20contracts.pdf
37. 'Africa Power and Politics', accessed 30 November 2011, http://www.institutions-africa.org/ (accessed 30th November 2011); and David Booth, 'Governance for Development in Africa: Building on what Works', *Africa Power and Politics*, Policy Brief 01.
38. Collier, *Wars, Guns and Votes*, 11.

10

Beyond Humanitarian Imperialism: The Dubious Origins of 'Humanitarian Intervention' and Some Rules for its Future

Richard Drayton

The problem of humanitarian intervention sits at the crossroad of ideas of human rights, theories of sovereignty and Just War theory. Any respectable argument for such collective violence depends on the assertion that international military intervention is necessary where a polity either causes or allows mortal danger to the life and liberty of its citizens such that its sovereignty is suspended. What remains absent from both international law and practice, however, are clear rules on how we decide when such collective violence is justified, whose obligation and right it is to intervene and what limits and sanctions exist to restrain the behaviour of those who intervene, or to punish those who intervene without international agreement. The problem in all humanitarian interventions is that those powers with the capacity to apply force at a distance for humanitarian or other ends are generally also those with economic and strategic interests overseas and are often also states which refuse any cosmopolitan restraint on their own military action. From the nineteenth century to the twenty-first, 'humanitarian' interest has repeatedly been used by Britain, France and the US to justify what to critics appeared to be the naked prosecution of selfish national foreign policies.[1] Ryan Goodman may ultimately be right that legalizing unilateral humanitarian intervention would 'discourage wars with an ulterior interest' but only if the international community makes rules which specifically protect against the risk of imperialism wearing a humanitarian mask.[2]

This chapter seeks to confront this entanglement of humanitarian intervention and imperialism and to ask if and how the idea of cosmopolitan action for human rights might be rescued from the grip of Great Power interests? It shall first examine the origins of 'humanitarian intervention' in the nineteenth-century context of the European domination of the world. Second, it will turn to the span from 1918 to 1989 and to the emergence of postcolonial doctrines of humanitarian intervention. Third, we shall look at the current period, from c. 1989 to the present, in which serious crises, a collapse in confidence in the United Nations as an efficient actor, expanded ideas of human rights and a critique of national sovereignty, have made 'humanitarian intervention' and, after 2000, 'the Responsibility to Protect' – or R2P, its UN abbreviation – into significant problems for international relations. Last, we shall examine the dangerous relationship of intervention with civil war and the erosion of national sovereignty and suggest some new protocols which might be applied to all theatres of proposed 'humanitarian intervention'. It is in particular my aim here to urge the case that all powers who propose such collective action should be compelled to make a full declaration of their interests, that those who seek to prosecute 'humanitarian' ends should seek international approval for the weapons and tactics they will apply and all participants should submit to the supervising and if necessary punitive discipline of the International Criminal Court.

European and American Imperialism and the origins of the claim of the right to intervene, c. 1815–1914

The doctrine of humanitarian intervention may, if one wishes, be traced to Vattel, Grotius and Roman precedent and to European state relations after the Peace of Westphalia.[3] But in its modern form it emerged more from the practice than the theory of international relations in the decades after the Congress of Vienna. Clearly it depended upon nineteenth-century doctrines of human rights.[4] But it was part of a world order in which Europe in general and Britain, in particular, had acquired a temporary ascendency over the rest of humanity and expressed the Vienna idea that the powers of Christendom had the right to organize cosmopolitan peace. Its partners were the linked British campaigns for the enforcement of anti-slavery, the expansion of free trade and the spread of Christianity, in the name of which merchants and missionaries sought the protection of gunboats in China and Africa. One kind of right flowed easily into another: as John Bowring, whose manoeuvring would later lead to the Second Opium War, put it when campaigning for parliament: 'Free Trade was Jesus Christ and Jesus Christ was Free Trade.'[5] The morality and legitimacy of the collective action of 'civilized' nations, by which contemporaries understood white European and Christian nations, was never in doubt.

Even in the nineteenth century, the new discipline of International Law was unhappy with the way in which the idea of humanitarian intervention infringed on the principle of national sovereignty, arguing it was more a 'high act of national policy' than a matter of law.[6] 'On the strict legalistic principles', wrote Oscar Straus, the jurist and diplomat, when lecturing on 'The Humanitarian Diplomacy of the United States' in 1912, 'it is very doubtful if humanitarian intervention can be justified'.[7] The solution, however, was to argue that less civilized communities did not enjoy a claim to sovereignty equivalent to that of Europeans and their overseas diasporas. The rule of law was premised on European norms and its frontier was coextensive with that of European power.[8] Few were the voices which objected with the French jurist Gaston Jèze that 'civilized powers have no more right to seize the territories of savages than savages have to occupy the European continent [and that] the law of nations does not admit any distinction between the barbarians and the so-called civilized'.[9] Far more common was the view that the option to intervene was the prerogative of the 'civilized', as the representatives of a higher constitutional and legal regime. The most complete example of this tendency, expressing a claim the outlines of which resurface in the twenty-first century idea of the 'failed state', was the assertion of the Roosevelt Corollary to the Monroe Doctrine (1904) that

> chronic wrongdoing, or an impotence which results in a general loosening of the ties of civilized society, may in America, as elsewhere, ultimately require intervention by some civilized nation and in the Western Hemisphere the adherence of the United States to the Monroe Doctrine may force the United States, however reluctantly, in flagrant cases of such wrongdoing or impotence, to the exercise of an international police power.

European and American norms were to stand as the measure of a 'civilized society', with the dominant imperial power in any region of the world having the duty and right to decide if abuses justified intervention.

No audit was done then or later of the the destructive impact of these European and American 'humanitarian' invasions of Africa, Asia and Latin America. That perhaps half of the population of the Congo died in the generation after the Berlin Conference consigned them to Belgium is blamed on King Leopold alone, when the European nations were collectively responsible. The aftermath of intervention was often brutal wars of counterinsurgency, as in Cuba and the Philippines, and generations of colonial tyranny. In the Congo, the Balkans, the Levant many future humanitarian crises would be direct consequences of nineteenth-century interventions. It is clear too that no reciprocal obligations and rights were extended to non-European nations for their intervention in defence of human rights in Europe. Only briefly, in the Congo, was there even the glimmer of a chance that the international community might combine against human rights abuses committed by Europeans. Extra-European custom and law always had to yield to European principle and adjudication, a principle given its starkest expression in the doctrine of extra-territoriality which denuded the Chinese state, even on its own territory, of any right to police abuses committed by Westerners.[10]

It might be argued, following Lauren Benton, that much of the infrastructure for postcolonial 'humanitarian intervention' was laid in the late nineteenth century. The prerogative, indeed the responsibility of imperial powers to intervene against slavery, or the collapse of order, in areas under their supervision created a system of precedents for the weakening of the claims of sovereignty at the periphery of European power.[11]

'Humanitarian Intervention' and the international system, 1918–89

War in 1914 and 1939, the Russian Revolution of 1917 and the rise of a global anti-colonial movement opened divisions in the consensus bequeathed by the age of Imperialism, during and after the great crisis of 1914–45. In its aftermath the universe of sovereignty and human rights was radically extended and doctrines of 'just war' tightened, with contradictory consequences for the doctrine of humanitarian intervention.[12] Attempts to regulate the international system, in particular through the League of Nations and the United Nations, the rise of the Soviet Union, the emergence of non-European political elites able to argue for rights in European terms and languages and the closing of the arms gap which once existed between Europe and the rest, placed new limits on the agency of the Great Powers. But at the same time, the experience of genocide and the horrors of wars and dictatorships and expanded ideas of human rights provided a slow but ever-growing international consensus that there were universal rights which both preceded and went beyond national sovereignty.[13] On the one hand, the exclusive prerogatives of a state within the territories it administered was acknowledged by Article 2(4) of the Charter of the United Nations which required members to 'refrain in their international relations from the threat of use of force against the territorial integrity or political independence of any state'. Its authors, after all, were supremely aware that Adolf Hitler had invoked the humanitarian 'defence of oppressed minorities' when he dismembered Czechoslovakia in 1938 and invaded Poland in 1939. But, on the other hand, the 1948 Genocide Convention created an international responsibility to intervene and punish perpetrators of crimes against humanity and to rescue civilians in danger. The United Nations, however, was understood to be the instrument through which the international community responded to humanitarian crises.

Decolonization after 1945 represented a new Westphalian moment of proliferating claims to exclusive national rights which collided with many of the economic and strategic interests of the Great Powers. Within its immediate shadow, at least as long as the Soviet Union represented a counterweight to Europe and the US, the principle of nonintervention in the internal affairs of other nations was respected in theory until late in the twentieth century. But in practice, old imperial habits, the need to protect interests and the new imperatives of the 'Cold War' created from the 1950s a practice of open and covert intervention in the former colonial world. New leaders, such as Patrice Lumumba in his famous speech of 30 June 1960, on the day of independence of the Congo, understood themselves to be achieving strict equality with the formal colonial powers. Their former masters, it might be argued, merely considered they were conceding local internal sovereignty within a system in which the West set the norms, much as the Victorian Raj acknowledged the sovereignty of the princely states of India. Among the nations of the world certain powers, identified by their permanent presence on the Security Council of the United Nations, would be more equal than others, with the right to veto any collective action by the international community and an unanswerable right to act. And yet, it was commonly asserted that national actors were prohibited from intervening in other nations and only collective action constituted by the United Nations was legitimate, as Peter Falk put it in 1964, 'Basic doctrines of sovereignty, territorial jurisdiction, equality of states, independence, non-intervention and recognition each acknowledge this primacy of the nation state.'[14]

A critical breach in this post-war consensus and the first example of a pattern of 'humanitarian intervention' which would characterize the very end of the century, started much as the modern version of humanitarian intervention had begun in Africa with the Congo crisis. In July 1960, Lumumba had been forced by the mercenary-backed insurrection in Katanga to seek intervention from the United Nations. After his capture and murder, his former allies rallied their forces from Stanleyville, in the east of the country. On 9 December 1964, US and Belgian forces acted beyond United Nations sanction, intervening unilaterally for 'humanitarian' purposes, attacking Stanleyville putatively to protect whites who were being held there as hostages.[15] After the Congo debates in the Security Council, Weisberg argues, the legal principle of Article 2(4) remained, but 'there was now an unwillingness on the part of the world community to read it as an absolute prohibition on the use of force in humanitarian intervention'.[16]

Yet the assumption of the primacy of national sovereignty still prevailed. In 1970, the General Assembly of the United Nations passed unanimously 'The Declaration on Principles of International Law concerning Foreign Relations and Cooperation among States' which affirmed that 'No state or group of states has the right to intervene, directly or indirectly, for any reason whatsoever, in the internal or external affairs of any other state.' The majority opinion among international lawyers remained that the United Nations Charter had made force illegal except in self-defence or if commanded by the Security Council.[17] But a series of crises in postcolonial Asia and Africa, from the late 1960s into the 1970s – the Biafran war and famine in Nigeria (1968–70), India's intervention in East Pakistan in the Bangladesh war of independence (1971), Vietnam's intervention against the Pol Pot regime in Cambodia (1978) and Tanzania's removal of power of Idi Amin in Uganda (1979) – generated new debates about the limits of sovereignty and new supporters of humanitarian intervention.[18]

By the 1980s, from a variety of directions, there were complaints that the United Nations and the international community had not proved itself able to act effectively on humanitarian issues. While the Left pointed at the repeated vetoes of the Western powers in the Security Council of proposals for collective action against the apartheid regime in South Africa and US support for brutal dictatorships in Latin America, the Right complained of state repression in the Communist bloc. The deaths of perhaps three million Ibos in the Nigerian Civil War and the horrors of Cambodia, where perhaps one in five people died under the Khmer Rouge regime, awakened a concern that genocides could happen again. Even before the end of the Cold War, there was a growing number of voices arguing that the commission of major human rights abuses in any polity should dilute the prohibition against foreign humanitarian intervention.[19]

After 1989: The collapse of national sovereignty and the 'Responsibility to Protect'

The scope for humanitarian intervention would however be dramatically transformed by the collapse of the USSR and the connected emergence, temporarily, of a de facto unipolar world. Coming into the 1990s, there was no significant strategic or ideological opposition to the norms of the US and Western Europe becoming the rules of the international system. This was clear in the domain of international political economy where the Reagan-Thatcher attack of the 1980s on the Keynesian and welfarist orthodoxies of the post-1945 era and the 'Washington Consensus' culminated in the neo-liberal logic of the World Trade Organisation of 1996. At the same time technical and industrial developments of the late twentieth century, particularly in computer and space technologies, opened up a significant military power gap between the core powers of the West and the rest of the world, as exemplified in the First Gulf War (1991).

Into this context of a significantly increased confidence in the West, both about its moral and institutional centrality and its capacity to intervene, came the collapse of Yugoslavia into a bloody civil war and the Rwandan genocide. The protection of Kurds by a 'no fly' zone in northern Iraq, the NATO war on Serbia (1999) and the British intervention in Sierra Leone (2000) appeared to present practical demonstrations of how the West's military power might be applied to solve what appeared to some as genocides.[20] In a linked process over the 1990s, old ideas of national sovereignty came under ideological attack just as humanitarian intervention acquired an unprecedented legitimacy.[21]

Precedents set in the 1990s hardened rapidly into orthodox doctrines about humanitarian intervention in the early twenty-first century. In 2000 the Canadian government organized the International Commission on Intervention and State Sovereignty (ICISS). Its co-chairs Gareth Evans of the International Crisis Group and Algerian diplomat Mohamed Sahnoun wrote candidly in *Foreign Affairs*: 'The issue must be reframed not as an argument about the "right to intervene" but about the "responsibility to protect."'[22] The commission's 2001 report argued that where 'a state's population is suffering serious harm, as a result of internal war, insurgency, repression or state failure and the state in question is unwilling or unable to halt or avert it, the principle of non-intervention yields to the international responsibility to protect'.[23] While the United Nations' version of 'Responsibility to Protect' restricted the power to use military means to the Security Council and the General Assembly, the doctrine still represented a dramatic renegotiation of the meaning of Article 2(4) of the United Nations Charter.[24]

The dangerous potential of the 'Responsibility to Protect', particularly in the train of the precedents set in the Kosovo War by NATO acting outside of the mandate of the United Nations, was apparent around the world. In the Havana declaration of 2000, the Group of 77 nations declared:

> We reject the so-called 'right' of humanitarian intervention, which has no legal basis in the United Nations Charter or in the general principles of international law ... humanitarian assistance should [only] be conducted in full respect of the sovereignty, territorial integrity and political independence of host countries and should be initiated in response to a request or with the approval of these States.[25]

The Non-Aligned Nations meeting of February 2003 in Kuala Lumpur repeated this rejection and noted explicitly the potential threat which the doctrine of the 'Responsibility to Protect' posed to the 'principles of non-interference and non-intervention as well as the respect for territorial integrity and national sovereignty of States'.[26]

International concern about possible abuse of the 'Responsibility to Protect' was not diminished by the assertion of the Bush and Blair administrations, supported by some influential theorists of 'humanitarian intervention' such as Fernando Tesón, that the invasion of Iraq, which took place without United Nations sanction and against the opposition of the vast majority of members of the United Nations, was justified by the need to protect Iraqis from Saddam Hussein's regime.[27] While in 2006 R2P was invoked in a UN resolution on the crisis in Darfur, no collective action was proposed and no powers chose to act beyond the UN mandate. The true human cost of the Iraq War was by then apparent, with estimates, by the same reliable epidemiological methods used for civilian deaths in Bosnia and Darfur, to be somewhere around 600,000 unnecessary deaths from the violence and collapse of state and society which accompanied 'humanitarian intervention'.[28]

In 2011, the Libyan civil war, however, provided a case on which France, the US and Britain were finally able to act with the sanction of the United Nations under the doctrine of R2P. Resolution 1973 of the Security Council empowered member states to 'take all necessary measures' to protect civilians under attack via a no-fly zone. This was taken, at the time, as a critical departure, a vindication of R2P and a precedent which could be appealed to in the future.[29] But, from another perspective, the visible mission-creep in 2011 from protecting civilians to regime change, with France, Britain and the US as active allies of one party of belligerents and the aftermath of civil war and the possible partition of Libya, made other powers wary about granting future mandates for military intervention under R2P. If it was true after Iraq that 'regime change was...the ghost at the banquet of humanitarian intervention', after Libya that spectre appeared to preside over the feast.[30] All could see, moreover, how Iraq and Libya had been devastated by Western bombing but not, as the original 2001 R2P manifesto had imagined, rebuilt with Western assistance. Instead, most strikingly in Iraq, the aftermath of 'humanitarian intervention' was the destruction of public health, education and safety. It is easy to understand why the Chinese Assistant Foreign Minister Le Yucheng commented, when the issue of possible intervention in Syria arose in April 2012, 'What we need is not just "the Responsibility to Protect" but also "responsible protection" '.[31]

Humanitarian intervention and the question of civil war

In Libya, as earlier in Rwanda, Biafra and the Congo, as well as in other examples outside of Africa, the question of humanitarian intervention has almost always been linked to civil wars. The proponents of intervention and the 'Responsibility to Protect' argue that it is the duty of the international community to protect minorities in conflicts from the violence of those who command the state and its military power. But what happens, in such a context, to any government's right to use force to protect its territorial integrity or to restrain internal disorder? Should the international community have come to the protection of the confederacy when it faced defeat by Union troops in the 1860s, and when rioters took over the streets of the cities of the UK in August 2011, should Libyan and Iraqi troops been mobilized to protect them from the response of the police and the armed forces? If we assume that the administrations of Lincoln and Cameron had a popular mandate to preserve the territorial integrity of the nation and the rule of law, who then gets to decide when a civil war exists, in which a weaker party needs to be protected from state belligerents, or when instead civil order has broken down and Leviathan is obliged to draw his sword? If, with Machiavelli, Hobbes and every theorist of the state, we accept that political society always emerges out of complex tensions between groups and interests, what are the implications for the social peace and political stability of nations, particularly new ones, of an international understanding that those who rise against the state can count on external assistance if they prove too weak to overthrow it on their own and face annihilation? To what extent therefore does the doctrine of the 'Responsibility to Protect' not make the evolution of civil conflicts into civil wars more likely and in particular encourage the taking up of arms?

The full logical implications of 'Responsibility to Protect' doctrine are, thus, that Great Powers (or at best the United Nations Security Council), become the arbiters of what in other countries constitutes order and disorder, good governance and failed states, legitimate police powers and oppression and can choose to decide when it is fit to replace sovereign governments with foreign protectorates. Great powers which have ulterior economic or strategic interests now might need only to foment disorder or arm covertly local belligerents to acquire the right to invade. Given that, throughout history, imperial powers have always been able to find or make local collaborators, with greater or lesser success, humanitarian justifications could easily become the basis of new de facto colonial order based on cycles of *divide et impera* of permanent revolution from above. At the very least, to the extent that intervention is by definition something the strong do to, or for, the weak and always in their territory and society, it risks entrenching the power differences in international society. There is also, even in a most benign scenario of honest international concern about state violence, a double-sided 'moral hazard'. The decision to intervene and essentially to provide external support for regime change comes with an asymmetry of risk: if the intervention ends in chaos and social breakdown, it is the intervened upon and those who respond to foreign encouragement and not the intervenors, who pay the price. At the same time, Alan Kuperman has identified 'moral hazard' from the other direction: as minority interests seek to provoke state violence knowing that the international community provides insurance against defeat in the event of the failure of an insurrection.[32]

The idea of the 'Responsibility to Protect' has at its core the assumption that nation states only exercise sovereignty with the consent of the international community. This is not only profoundly corrosive of national sovereignty, it might also be seen as profoundly anti-liberal, since it gives external opinion an importance above the internal processes, consensual and non-consensual, through which a regime achieves that coalition of support which allows it to govern. Implicit among the supporters of the doctrine is that the ideal type of good governance and the 'rule of law' is a political system which resembles a Westminster-model parliamentary democracy and which protects a market economy and property rights.[33] Are there any grounds other than narcissistic prejudice for assuming that this is necessarily and eternally the case?[34] Might it be also that violent internal conflict, in which there are significant losses of life, as in seventeenth-century England, eighteenth-century France, nineteenth-century US, or twentieth-century China, are sometimes the foundations of new stable political orders? Tragic always is the loss of human life and the spectacle of violence excites in anyone a desire to end it. But violence may sometimes be a necessary means through which an old order, whose destructive impact on local experience is masked by its entrenched character, is replaced by a new one. If this is the case, then violence should always be at the choosing of those closest to its effects and who will themselves and through their kin bear perpetually its consequences. The intellectuals, statesmen and public of the West, who only know Asia, Africa and Latin America through privileged exiles, computer and television screens and brief tourist adventures, need to learn a kind of humility about taking sides in other people's civil conflicts. The catastrophic legacies of earlier Western interventions in enduring civil wars, weak states, destroyed infrastructure and diminished living standards, from the Congo, to Iraq, to Libya suggest that it is not clear that action necessarily yields better outcomes than inaction.

Some rules for humanitarian intervention and the 'Responsibility to Protect'

If in the spirit of the UN Resolution of 2005 we accept the principle of the 'Responsibility to Protect', how can the international community protect itself from the principle being hijacked by Great Powers for their own interests? We might suggest three rules which should be incorporated into the procedures of global governance. First, much as we accept today in the West that those who make decisions in private and public bodies declare their interests, members of the Security Council should be required, before any meeting in which a matter is discussed, to make a declaration of the strategic and economic interests which they and their nationals have in the territory under discussion. What applies to good corporate governance in civil society today, should also apply to international governance. In 2011, for example, when the provision of air support for the Benghazi rebels in Libya was discussed, the Sarkozy regime in France should, for example, have declared Total Elf Fina's actual and potential future interests in Libyan oil and the negotiations of French actors with the Libyan rebels in the weeks before the matter came to the Security Council.

Second, there should be a similar declaration of means. Great powers should not simply be granted the licence to use whatever weapons and tactics they choose in fulfilling a Security Council mandate. The international community should be allowed before a conflict to decide whether civilian infrastructure and systems of water, electricity, telephone and television systems are legitimate targets. It should be allowed to prohibit cluster bombs, land mines, remote killing by cruise missile or drone and in particular the use of depleted uranium weapons. It should require the protection of captured belligerents and impose the obligation to punish the soldiers and allies of the intervening power when they commit murder, rape and theft in the midst of a campaign. It should prohibit torture, collective punishment and the removal of prisoners from the country without their consent. There should be a declared exit strategy, through which the international community envisions the restoration of national sovereignty within a limited time frame.

Third, there should be a formal process of audit of the implementation of 'protection' during and after the use of violence in the name of the international community. The intervening powers should be required to declare and to prove that they and their nationals have derived no benefit from intervention. From the moment that intervention is commissioned by the Security Council, it should appoint a prosecuting judge, on the European model, to collect testimony and records of how force was used and to what ends, with the aim of bringing prosecutions in the event of delinquencies. All powers who act in the name of the international community should certainly accept the supervisory and punitive powers of the International Criminal Court and not seek to exercise any latter day version of extra-territoriality.

With these three safeguards we might be more confident about humanitarian intervention and the 'Responsibility to Protect' not providing a mask for the abuses of great powers. But, perhaps, were these rules in place to protect the interests of the Global South, the Great Powers might lose their taste for such adventures.

Notes

1. Jean Bricmont, *Humanitarian Imperialism: Using Human Rights to Sell War* (New York: Monthly Review Press, 2006); Richard Seymour, *The Liberal Defence of Murder* (London: Verso Books, 2008).

2. Ryan Goodman, 'Humanitarian Intervention and the Pretexts for War', *The American Journal of International Law*, 100.1 (2006): 107–31. See the rather less sanguine view of Jonathan I. Charney that 'the so-called doctrine of humanitarian intervention can lead to an escalation of international violence, discord and disorder and diminish protections of human rights worldwide' in 'Anticipatory Human Rights Intervention in Kosovo', *American Journal of International Law* 93.4 (1999): 839–44.

3. Francis K. Abiew, *The Evolution of the Doctrine and Practice of Humanitarian Intervention* (The Hague; London: Kluwer Law International, 1999), 21–60.

4. For very different views of the origins of human rights see Lynn Hunt, *Inventing Human Rights: A History* (New York: Norton, 2008); and Samuel Moyn, *The Last Utopia: Human Rights in History* (Cambridge, MA: Harvard University Press, 2012).

5. Sir John Bowring, in 1855 on the eve of the Arrow War. See David Todd, 'John Bowring and the Global Dissemination of Free Trade', *Historical Journal*, 51 (2008): 373–397.

6. William E. Hall, *International Law* (Oxford: Clarendon Press, 1880), 247; F. E. Smith, *International Law* (London: J. M. Dent & Sons, 1911), 64.

7. American Society of International Law, *Proceedings of the American Society of International Law at Its Annual Meeting* (New York: General Books, 2009 [1912]), 5:7, 49.

8. Martti Koskenniemi, *The Gentle Civilizer of Nations: The Rise and Fall of International Law 1870–1960* (Cambridge: Cambridge University Press, 2001), 127–40; Antony Anghie, *Imperialism, Sovereignty and the Making of International Law* (Cambridge: Cambridge University Press, 2005); Andrew Fitzmaurice, 'Liberalism and Empire in Nineteenth-Century International Law', *American Historical Review*, 117.1 (2012): 122–40.

9. Quoted in Fitzmaurice, 'Liberalism and Empire', 122–40. See also Frédéric Mégret, 'From Savages to Unlawful Combatants', in Anne Orford, ed., *International Law and its Others* (Cambridge: Cambridge University Press, 2006), 265–317.

10. Lauren A. Benton, *Law and Colonial Cultures: Legal Regimes in World History, 1400–1900* (Cambridge: Cambridge University Press, 2002); Pär Kristoffer Cassel, *Grounds of Judgment: Extraterritoriality and Imperial Power in Nineteenth-Century China and Japan* (Oxford; New York: Oxford University Press, 2012); Eileen P. Scully, *Bargaining with the State from Afar: American Citizenship in Treaty Port China, 1844–1942* (New York; Chichester: Columbia University Press, 2001).

11. Lauren A. Benton, 'From International Law to Imperial Constitutions: The Problem of Quasi-Sovereignty, 1870–1900', *Law and History Review*, 26 (2008): 595–620.

12. Mark Mazower, 'The Strange Triumph of Human Rights, 1933–1950', *Historical Journal*, 47.2 (2004): 379–98; Erez Manela, *The Wilsonian Moment:*

Self-Determination and the International Origins of Anticolonial Nationalism (Oxford: Oxford University Press, 2007).

13. Philip Caryl Jessup, *A Modern Law of Nations* (New York: Macmillan, 1948).
14. Richard A. Falk, 'The Legitimacy of Legislative Intervention by the United Nations', in Roger Fisher and Roland J. Stanger, eds, *Essays on Intervention* (Columbus: Ohio State University Press, 1964), 31–61.
15. Howard L. Weisberg, 'The Congo Crisis of 1964: A Case Study in Humanitarian Intervention', *Virginia Journal of International Law*, 12 (1971–2): 267–76.
16. Weisberg, 'The Congo Crisis', 274.
17. John Carey, *United Nations Protection of Civil and Political Rights* (New York: Syracuse University Press, 1970); Ian Brownlie, 'Humanitarian Intervention', in John Norton Moore, ed., *Law and Civil War in the Modern World* (Baltimore, MD: John Hopkins University Press, 1974), 217–28.
18. Michael Reisman and Myres S. McDougal, *Memorandum upon Humanitarian Intervention to Protect the Ibos* (s.n., 1968); Richard B. Lillich, ed., *Humanitarian Intervention and the United Nations* (Charlottesville, VA: University Press of Virginia, 1973); Thomas M. Franck and Nigel S. Rodley, 'After Bangladesh: The Law of Humanitarian Intervention by Military Force', *American Journal of International Law*, 67 (1973): 275–305; Laurie S. Wiseberg, 'Humanitarian Intervention Lessons from the Nigerian Civil War', *Human Rights Journal*, 70.1 (1974): 61–98; Richard B. Lillich, 'Humanitarian Intervention: A Reply to Ian Brownlie and a Plea for Constructive Alternatives', in J. N. Moore, ed., *Law and Civil War in the Modern World* (Clark, NJ: The Lawbook Exchange, 2010), 229.
19. Farooq Hassan, 'Realpolitik in International Law: After Tanzanian-Ugandan Conflict: Humanitarian Intervention Reexamined', *Willamette Law Review*, 17 (1980–1): 859–912; H. Scott Fairley, 'State Actors, Humanitarian Intervention and International Law: Reopening Pandora's Box', *Georgia Journal of International and Comparative Law*, 29 (1980): 26–63; W. D. Verney, 'Humanitarian Intervention Under International Law', *Netherlands International Law Review*, 32 (1985): 357–418; Michael J. Bazyler, 'Reexamining the Doctrine of Humanitarian Intervention in Light of the Atrocities in Kampuchea and Ethiopia', *Stanford Journal of International Law*, 23 (1987): 547–619. See in particular the essay by the US State Department lawyer Michael Wolf, 'Humanitarian Intervention', *Michigan Yearbook of International Legal Studies*, 9 (1988): 333–66.
20. On the Kosovo War see Bartram S. Brown, 'Humanitarian Intervention at a Crossroads', *William and Mary Law Review*, 41 (2000): 1683–741; on Sierra Leone intervention see the chapter in this volume by J. Kaplan.
21. For the evolution of doctrine see J. Nafziger, 'Self-Determination and Humanitarian Intervention in a Community of Power', *Denver Journal of International Law and Policy*, 20.1 (1991–1992): 9–40; and V. P. Nanda, 'Tragedies in Northern Iraq, Liberia, Yugoslavia and Haiti – Revisiting the Validity of Humanitarian Intervention under International Law', *Denver Journal of International Law and Policy*, 20.1/2 (1991–1992): 9–40, 305–34; Thomas J. Biersteker and Cynthia Weber, eds, *State Sovereignty as Social Construct* (Cambridge: Cambridge University Press, 1996); S. D. Krasner, 'Rethinking the Sovereign State Model', *Review of International Studies*, 27.1 (2001), 17–42.

For examinations of this period see Nicholas J. Wheeler, *Saving Strangers: Humanitarian Intervention in International Society* (Oxford: Oxford University Press, 2000); J. L. Holzgrefe and Robert O. Keohane, *Humanitarian Intervention: Ethical, Legal and Political Dilemmas* (Cambridge: Cambridge University Press, 2003).

22. Gareth Evans and Mohamed Sahnoun, 'The Responsibility to Protect', *Foreign Affairs*, November/December 2002, accessed 10 July 2012, http://www.foreignaffairs.com/articles/58437/gareth-evans-and-mohamed-sahnoun/the-responsibility-to-protect.

23. Gareth Evans and Mohamed Sahnoun, eds, *The Responsibility to Protect: Report of the International Commission on Intervention and State Sovereignty* (Ottawa, ON: International Development Research Centre, 2001), 11, accessed 1 July 2012, http://responsibilitytoprotect.org/ICISS%20Report.pdf.

24. United Nations General Assembly, 'Draft resolution referred to the High-level Plenary Meeting of the General Assembly by the General Assembly at its fifty-ninth session 2005, World Summit Outcome', September 2005, accessed 1 July 2012, http://responsibilitytoprotect.org/world%20summit%20outcome%20doc%202005(1).pdf.

25. 'Declaration of the South Summit', *Havana*, 10–14 April 2000, accessed 30 June 2012, http://www.g77.org/summit/Declaration_G77Summit.htm.

26. 'Final Document of the XIII meeting of the Heads of State or Government of the Non-Aligned Movement', *Kuala Lumpur*, 24–25 February 2003, accessed 30 June 2012, http://www.nam.gov.za/media/030227e.htm.

27. Fernando Tesón, 'Ending Tyranny in Iraq', *Ethics and International Affairs*, 19.2 (2005): 120.

28. G. Burnham, R. Lafta, S. Doocy, and L. Roberts, 'Mortality After the 2003 Invasion of Iraq: A Cross-sectional Cluster Sample Survey', *The Lancet*, 368, (21 October 2006): 1421–8.

29. Stewart Patrick, 'Libya and the Future of Humanitarian Intervention', *Foreign Affairs*, 26 August 2011, accessed 10 July 2012, http://www.foreignaffairs.com/articles/68233/stewart-patrick/libya-and-the-future-of-humanitarian-intervention.

30. D. Rieff, 'Humanitarian Vanities', *New York Times*, 1 April 2008.

31. Quoted in 'China Saying "No" on Syria Issue is Responsible Move: FM Official', accessed 9 July 2012, http://news.xinhuanet.com/english/china/2012-04/10/c_131518137.htm.

32. Alan J. Kuperman, 'The Moral Hazard of Humanitarian Intervention: Lessons from the Balkans', *International Studies Quarterly*, 52 (2008): 49–80.

33. Jeremy Waldron, *The Rule of Law and the Measure of Property* (Cambridge: Cambridge University Press, 2012).

34. On the (racial) narcissism central to much political thought in the West see Charles W. Mills, 'Racial Liberalism', *Publications of the Modern Language Association*, 123.5 (2008): 1380–97; and Carole Pateman and Charles W. Mills, *Contract and Domination* (Cambridge: Polity Press, 2007).

Conclusion

Bronwen Everill and Josiah Kaplan

This volume, covering perspectives from international relations, politics, history and practical experience, helps to demonstrate a number of continuities in the concepts, debates and ideologies of humanitarian intervention in Africa stretching from the eighteenth century to today. Through the preceding chapters, contributors to this volume have explored the empirical and conceptual linkages between past and present across a wide diversity of Western aid, development and military interventions on the African continent. The presence of such continuities does not mean that the international humanitarian project has failed to evolve since the colonial era. Indeed, the chapters strongly illustrate the significant changes which Western humanitarian engagement with Africa has undergone over several centuries of complex development. Nonetheless, the parallels which these authors identify across these eras are clear and unmistakable and point to the need for both historians and social scientists to reinterpret several fundamental premises in their study and understanding of the phenomena of humanitarian intervention in Africa. In particular, the themes explored in this volume suggest that perhaps a new critical awareness could disrupt the often-dysfunctional cycles of intervention and aid that currently define the West's relationship with Africa.

Continuities

One of the continuing debates over international interventions in Africa has been the role of global governance. Although sovereignty is often raised with relation to the legality of humanitarian interventions, throughout the history of humanitarian engagement with Africa, global actors and organizations – from the United Nations to transnational aid organizations, colonial governments to coalitions of countries from inside and outside of Africa – have preferred to disregard or overstep the state in order to reach the suffering individual. Even in situations where humanitarian military intervention was called for by the international community but not received, the decision rarely proceeded from a concern over the sovereignty of the state, but rather other factors including the likelihood of success and the perception of the potentiality of a quagmire.

Recognition of this tradition is critical for understanding the contemporary international humanitarian project. The implications of Western aid, economic and military assistance and intervention in Africa on the normative foundations of state sovereignty and international rule of law are hotly debated and closely watched topics in the study of international relations. So too are critical questions regarding the degree to which the international humanitarian project is coercive in nature, promulgates hegemonic Western power, authority and forms of knowledge in the global order and encourages dependency within African contexts.

Linking the study of contemporary global governance to its imperial and colonial past, as the preceding chapters have done, provides an invaluable framework of empirical evidence, conceptual perspective and historical context for better understanding such issues. This volume has lent insight into how the present architecture of global governance arose and what best practices and dangers already implemented in past practice might inform future policy and practice in Western and African relations. More broadly, by identifying the long-standing pattern of tension between Western interventionist projects motivated by universalist values on the one hand and their dismissals of African state sovereignty on the other, the contributing authors have demonstrated that the liberal and neo-liberal models upon which current global governance and humanitarianism projects rest belong to a long, problematic and contested tradition.

One central theme common throughout the chapters in this volume, to this end, has been the role of universality in specifically African interventions and aid. From the time of the missionary interventions in the slave trade and their establishment of aid provision in the early nineteenth century, a humanitarian universalism has guided Western policymakers, INGOs and individuals with regard to the provision of military intervention, development agendas and aid. That missionary–humanitarian liberal universalist link becomes clear in the investigations of not only motives but practices throughout this volume. From lobbying to campaigning to on-the-ground aid provision, interventions on behalf of African humanity seem to stem from a common image of African suffering representing world suffering.

This highlights another continuity that emerges from all of the chapters, that is the role of what Philip Curtin and Chinua Achebe call the 'Image of Africa'. Many of the specific interventions described in this book cannot be regarded as useless or unsuccessful; in many instances real lives were changed by the interventions of outsiders through military or more peaceful means. However, given the above-mentioned continuities in the disregard for sovereignty and the liberal universalist ideals that drive Western motivation, it is perhaps unsurprising that interventions and aid provision in Africa continue to shape an image of Africans as either helpless or (in the context of armed conflict) savage and violent and Western interveners as saviours.

The inherent flaws of such reductionist depictions of African and Western identity quickly become apparent under the scrutiny of more detailed scholarship, as the preceding chapters strongly demonstrate. Far from reflecting evidence of African 'helplessness', a number of the chapters in this book have emphasized the central role of local agency in determining the nature of past interventions on the continent. Challenging the image of African states, institutions and people as 'symbols of helplessness' developed by Western cultural imaginations of the eighteenth and nineteenth centuries, the historic reality instead consistently demonstrates examples of Africans acting as political and cultural agents of change and decision-making. While the geopolitical realities of the period show clear asymmetries of power between the West and Africa, that power was itself more consistently negotiated between local and global forces throughout history and in the interventionist projects of today, than might be expected.

The image of the Western agent as 'saviour' has, throughout each case, also been problematized. A very wide diversity of agendas and impetuses – political, ethical, religious – drove each manifestation of intervention studied in this volume. Lofty humanitarian and emancipatory rhetoric coexisted with, and often masked, *realpolitik* goals and ambitions for engagement with the African continent which were anything but salvationary in intent. Western actors also routinely interjected themselves into the same complex conflicts and emergencies in whose roots they themselves held (or continue to hold) varying degrees of complicity. And repeatedly, Western interventions have failed to achieve their goals, either by failing to fully address the humanitarian challenges which they were intended to address, or indeed, by exacerbating the situation through intervention's unintended consequences.

In such instances, the identity of Western actors acting as salvationary agents to the African people has been challenged further by the gap between rhetoric and reality.

Through their chapters, contributors to this volume have also raised important investigations into *why* such constructs have proven so resilient and enduring between the colonial and contemporary eras in the portrayal of Western and African identities. One consistent finding, to this end, has been the means by which self-empowering narratives have served and continue to serve a powerful ideational function for Western audiences. Here, Western agents of humanitarianism in Africa, through their acts of intervention and the discourses surrounding them, create spaces of opportunity in which their own potency, agency and moral and ethical virtue are justified through action. This act of identity-building requires, in turn, the presence of the African 'Other' as a symbol of either helplessness or as a perpetrator of irrational, barbaric violence.

Going forward

So what do these continuities mean? What use is there in pointing them out? Perhaps there are three potential impacts of the comparisons.

First, such continuities between the colonial and contemporary rhetoric and practice demonstrates that the lineages of humanitarian intervention ideologies with regard to Africa have always been shaped in Africa and in European engagement with Africa. With these continuities shaping engagement with Africa, perhaps it is time to better acknowledge and reflect upon, that the way that the West thinks about Africa has been shaped by the colonial and pre-colonial relationships forged in 'humanitarian' intervention and aid. These relationships were shaped by imperial and sometimes colonial engagements, and the types of global governance that have emerged in the postcolonial period are still shaped by many of the fundamental underlying assumptions of enlightenment, and universalist, liberal ideas of humanity. Rather than looking for the roots of African humanitarian intervention in the Red Cross movement, or drawing out arguments about sovereignty from the history of European states' engagement with other European states, perhaps it makes more sense to look to these Western actor's imperial pasts. It is time to understand that intervention and aid have long histories *in Africa* that might differ from the histories of intervention and aid in European contexts – histories which are and have always been shaped by power and assumptions of dependency, premodernity and the liberal idea of an individual's ability to affect change.

Second, this study emphasizes the importance of language and rhetoric in understanding how 'humanitarian intervention' has changed and in other ways, remained the same, across a wide historical spectrum of practice. The preceding chapters have all explored the fluid, often contested, definitions of what constitutes humanitarianism, the nature of 'consent' and 'coercion' as they relate to acts of intervention and whether objective standards of 'success' and 'failure' can be used to judge the impact of endeavours which often combined positive benefits and negative unintended consequences simultaneously. Here, observable continuities in discourse between the colonial and contemporary eras highlight the ways in which conceptualizations of 'humanitarian intervention', international humanitarianism and models of liberal and neo-liberal peace have evolved and remained consistent, over several centuries.

Third, interdisciplinary comparison shows the persistence of problems with interventionist development and aid schemes, first in the nineteenth century, but ultimately over the longer term. Despite the lessons learnt, even in the nineteenth century colonial governors, missionaries and humanitarians ignored the common problems in their model. Some adaptations were made, but the limitations of the model itself prevented too much change, particularly as the humanitarians and missionaries were (and continue to be) reliant on host governments and consciously aiming at 'civilization', 'progress' or 'development' in education, health and civil society. In thinking about refugees, development, aid and the fallout from military interventions, perhaps it is time to move out of this eighteenth-century mould?

What emerges from a study that looks at humanitarian activities in Africa in the *longue durée* are the cycles of intervention. Although calculated military intervention might be useful or necessary, it also brings with it considerations of choosing sides, of providing for displaced people, of participating (in one way or another) in the rebuilding efforts. Although professionals in the aid and development sectors have long tried to distance themselves from the political or military in favour of the purely humanitarian, questions remain about whether this is possible. Considerations of local political conditions – discussed in several places in this volume – reveal the local role in intervention and aid provision, as well as in the rebuilding efforts after interventions.

This point is critical to recognize for contemporary scholars of international relations, development and security, whose own disciplinary engagements with contemporary policy analysis too often lack requisite historical grounding. It is true, as the preceding chapters have certainly acknowledged, that the roles, relationships and identities of Western and African political actors in the post-Cold War, post-9/11 world, the modern and ever-changing structure of the aid and development industries and their approach towards African populations and the evolving practices of military humanitarian intervention, peacekeeping and stabilization operations, all caution against any neat symmetry between colonial and contemporary.

At the same time, however, the very strong continuities in rhetoric and practice between the eras illustrated in this volume represent a clear invitation to study the empirical record and conceptual legacy of past successes, failures, challenges and experiences preserved in the West's long history of interventionist engagement with the African content as part of humanitarian undertakings. Continuities in practice, as well as in the paradigms of power and engagement with Africa demand a closer look at the historical record and demand a focus that takes into account the specificity of the West's engagement with Africa over the past two centuries. While broader imperial and international relations dynamics have been crucial in developing ideas of humanitarian intervention and aid, Africa's unique position in Western thinking about humanitarianism requires an approach that takes historical roots into account.

Moreover, building on the idea of adding historical context to the study of intervention, this volume has also adopted a purposefully broad definition of humanitarian intervention, one which reaches beyond its typical usage in IR to refer only to military interventions. By doing so, a wider breadth of examples highlighting the core dynamic of Western intervention in Africa for humanitarian justifications has been made available, drawn from past and present missionary, aid, development, economic and military interventions. Adopting a similar degree of flexibility, IR scholars primarily interested in the contemporary military manifestations of humanitarian intervention might perhaps find greater opportunities for exploring the intrinsic themes of humanitarian interventions common across this wider taxonomy and locating a longer and larger sample size for measure the role of impact, accountability and cost-benefit assessments of military interventions.

For historians, it may be valuable to look to the contemporary work in interventions and humanitarian work. This discourages the kind of a historical thinking that predominates when thinking about historical 'failed' projects or unintended consequences. By looking at modern parallels, historians can give fuller account of the motivations, personalities, organizational structures and institutional factors at play in eighteenth- and nineteenth-century engagements with Africa. The chapters in this volume from contemporary practitioners also help to demonstrate that although there are core continuities in the paradigmatic constructs of humanitarianism, practices have changed over time. These changes are reflective of the changing international system and the relationships of key concepts of power, race, class and gender to ideas of intervention over time. While it is extremely useful to draw out the practices and constructs that have remained the same for understanding why norms come to dominate global discourse, it is also useful to see how contemporary practitioners conceptualize their engagements with Africa and demonstrate how changing paradigms really can filter into practice.

This volume, in summary, hopes above all else to challenge the widely prevalent perception that Africa can be understood a site for intervention and aid without first possessing critical awareness of the colonial and pre-colonial historical legacies of aid and intervention. Questions should be raised about assumptions held in the West, not only about Africa as a site of intervention, but about the fundamental issues at the heart of 'humanitarianism' and interventionism. Is self-determination a humanitarian issue? Who is accountable for an intervention's effectiveness? Can there really be a 'clinical' in-and-out intervention, or do all come with the need for follow-up interventions into politics, economics and culture, especially now, with the R2P doctrine's 'responsibility to rebuild'? And if so, how do these fit into a cost-benefit analysis of intervention effectiveness? Are human, civil and political rights all subject to intervention? And how do local conditions effect these decisions?

The chapters in this volume have begun to raise and address these questions from a variety of interdisciplinary perspectives and the contributors do not all agree on their answers. This is a contentious debate that requires a balancing of a variety of principles and positions in modern liberal ideology. Consensus is unlikely. However, that does not preclude investigation and collaboration. It is clear that more work is needed. By combining the perspectives of historians, policymakers, NGO workers and international relations experts we hope to present some of the more critical perspectives, while still remaining aware of the fundamental impulse to help. We also hope to invite further interdisciplinary exploration of these themes, so as to generate new research which deepens our understanding of the nature and complexity of humanitarian intervention as a phenomenon firmly rooted in both the past and the present.

Select Bibliography

Abiew, F. *The Evolution of the Doctrine and Practice of Humanitarian Intervention*. The Hague; London: Kluwer Law International, 1999.

Achebe, C. *Hope and Impediments: Selected Essays, 1965–1987*. London: Heinemann, 1998.

Adas, M. *Machines as the Measure of Men: Science, Technology, and Ideologies of Western Dominance*. Ithaca, NY: Cornell University Press, 1989.

Adebajo, A. *UN Peacekeeping in Africa*. Johannesburg: Jacana, 2011.

Amutabi, M.N. *The NGO Factor in Africa: The Case of Arrested Development in Kenya*. New York: Routledge, 2006.

Autesserre, S. *The Trouble with the Congo: Local Violence and the Failure of International Peacebuilding*. Cambridge: Cambridge University Press, 2010.

Ayittey, G. *Africa in Chaos*. New York: St. Martin's Press, 1998.

Bade, K.J., ed. *Imperialismus und Kolonialmission: Kaiserliches Deutschland und Koloniales Imperium*. Wiesbaden: Steiner, 1982.

Barnett, M. *Eyewitness to a Genocide: The United Nations and Rwanda*. Ithaca, NY: Cornell University Press, 2002.

Barnett, M. and T. Weiss. *Humanitarianism in Question: Politics, Power, Ethics*. Ithaca, NY; London: Cornell University Press, 2008.

Barry, J. and C. Jones, eds. *Medicine and Charity Before the Welfare State*. London: Routledge, 1991.

Bass, G. *Freedom's Battle: The Origins of Humanitarian Intervention*. New York: Alfred A. Knopf, 2008.

Beidelman, T.O. *Colonial Evangelism: A Socio-Historical Study of an East African Mission at the Grassroots*. Bloomington, IN: Indiana University Press, 1982.

Benton, L. 'From International Law to Imperial Constitutions: The Problem of Quasi-Sovereignty, 1870–1900', *Law and History Review* 26 (2008): 595–620.

Berman, N. *Impossible Missions? German Economic, Military, and Humanitarian Efforts in Africa*. Lincoln, NB: University of Nebraska Press, 2004.

Bhabha, H. *The Location of Culture*. London: Routledge, 1994.

Biersteker, T. and C. Weber, eds. *State Sovereignty as Social Construct*. Cambridge: Cambridge University Press, 1996.

Blyden, E.W. *Christianity, Islam and the Negro Race*. Baltimore, MD: Black Classic Press, 1994.

Bricmont, J. *Humanitarian Imperialism: Using Human Rights to Sell War*. New York: Monthly Review Press, 2006.

Campbell, G. *Blood Diamonds: Tracing the Deadly Paths of the World's Most Precious Stones*. Boulder, CO: Westview Press, 2002.

Cassidy, R. *Peacekeeping in the Abyss*. Westport, CT: Praeger, 2004.

Collier, P. *The Bottom Billion*. Oxford: Oxford University Press, 2008.

Conklin, A.L. *A Mission to Civilize: The Republican Idea of Empire in France and West Africa, 1895–1930*. Stanford, CA: Stanford University Press, 1997.

240 *Select Bibliography*

Crozier, A. *Practising Colonial Medicine: The Colonial Medical Service in British East Africa*. London: I.B. Tauris, 2007.
Curtin, P. *The Image of Africa: British Ideas and Action, 1780–1850*. Madison, WI: University of Wisconsin Press, 1962.
De St Jorre, J. *The Brothers' War*. London: Faber, 2009.
De Waal, A. *AIDS and Power: Why There is No Political Crisis – Yet*. London: Zed Books, 2006.
De Waal, A. 'Darfur and the Failure of the Responsibility to Protect.' *International Affairs* 83, no. 6 (2007): 1039–54.
Deutsch, J.D. *Emancipation without Abolition in German East Africa, c. 1884–1914*. Oxford: James Currey, 2006.
Durch, W. *The Evolution of UN Peacekeeping: Case Studies and Comparative Analysis*. New York: St. Martin's Press, 1993.
Dzinesa, G.A. 'A Comparative Perspective of UN Peacekeeping in Angola and Namibia.' *International Peacekeeping* 11, no. 4 (2004): 644–63.
Easterly, W. *The White Man's Burden: Why the West's Efforts to Aid the Rest Have Done so Much Ill and So Little Good*. Oxford: Oxford University Press, 2006.
Findlay, T. *The Use of Force in UN Peace Operations*. Oxford: Oxford University Press, 2002.
Forsythe, D.P. *The Humanitarians – The International Committee of the Red Cross*. Cambridge: Cambridge University Press, 2005.
Francis, D., ed. *Civil Militia: Africa's Intractable Security Menace?* Aldershot: Ashgate, 2005.
Gauntlett, D. *Media, Gender and Identity*. London: Routledge, 2005.
Gberie, L. *A Dirty War in West Africa: The RUF and the Destruction of Sierra Leone*. London: Hurst, 2005.
Goodman, R. 'Humanitarian Intervention and the Pretexts for War.' *The American Journal of International Law* 100, no. 1 (2006): 107–31.
Gussow, Z. and G. Tracy. 'Stigma and the Leprosy Phenomenon', *Bulletin of the History of Medicine* 44, no. 5 (1970): 425–49.
Halttunen, K. 'Humanitarianism and the Pornography of Pain in Anglo-American Culture', *The American Historical Review* 100, no. 2 (1995): 303–34.
Hehir, A. *Humanitarian Intervention: An Introduction*. Basingstoke: Palgrave Macmillan, 2010.
Hirsch, J. *Sierra Leone: Diamonds and the Struggle for Democracy*. Boulder, CO: Lynne Reinner, 2001.
Holzgrefe, J.L. and R. Keohane. *Humanitarian Intervention: Ethical, Legal, and Political Dilemmas*. Cambridge: Cambridge University Press, 2003.
Horton, K. and C. Roche. *Ethical Questions and International NGOs: An Exchange Between Philosophers and NGOs*. London: Springer, 2010.
Hume, C. *Ending Mozambique's War: The role of Mediation and Good Offices*. Washington, DC: US Institute for Peace, 1994.
Hunter, S. *Who Cares? AIDS in Africa*. Basingstoke: Palgrave Macmillan, 2003.
Hutchinson, J.F. *Champions of Charity: War and the Rise of the Red Cross*. Boulder, CO: Westview Press, 1996.
International Commission on Intervention and State Sovereignty. *The Responsibility to Protect: Report of the International Commission on Intervention and State Sovereignty*. Ottawa, ON: International Development Research Centre, 2001.
Jett, D.C. *Why Peacekeeping Fails*. New York: Palgrave Macmillan, 2001.

Kabou, A. *Et si l'Afrique refusait le développement?* Paris: L'Harmattan, 1991.

Kaldor, M. *New and Old Wars: Organised Violence in a Global Era,* 2nd edn. Cambridge: Polity Press, 2006.

Kampfner, J. *Blair's Wars.* London: Free Press, 2004.

Kargbo, M. *British Foreign Policy and the Conflict in Sierra Leone, 1991–2000.* Oxford: Peter Lang, 2006.

Keen, D. *Conflict and Collusion in Sierra Leone.* Oxford: Currey, 2005.

Kibicho, W. *Sex Tourism in Africa: Kenya's Booming Industry.* Farnham: Ashgate, 2008.

Korang, K.L. *Writing Ghana, Imagining Africa: Nation and African Modernity.* Rochester, NY: Rochester University Press, 2003.

Lancaster, C. *Aid to Africa: So Much to Do, So Little Done.* Chicago, IL: University of Chicago Press, 1999.

Leo, C. *Land and Class in Kenya.* Toronto, ON: University of Toronto Press, 1984.

Levy, R. *Give and Take: A Candid Account of Corporate Philanthropy.* Boston, MA: Harvard Business School Press, 1999.

Lingelbach, G. *Spenden und Sammeln: Der westdeutsche Spendenmarkt bis in die frühen 1980er Jahre.* Göttingen: Wallstein, 2009.

Macqueen, N. *United Nations Peacekeeping in Africa since 1960.* London: Pearson, 2002.

Mamdani, M. *Saviours and Survivors: Darfur, Politics, and the War on Terror.* Cape Town: HSRC Press, 2009.

Matua, M., ed. *Human Rights NGOs in East Africa: Political and Normative Tensions.* Kampala: Fountain Publishers, 2009.

Mbembe, A. *On the Postcolony.* Berkeley, CA: University of California Press, 2001.

Moyn, S. *The Last Utopia: Human Rights in History.* Cambridge, MA: Harvard University Press, 2012.

Moyo, D. *Dead Aid: Why Aid is Not Working and How There is a Better Way for Africa.* New York: Farrar, Straus and Giroux, 2009.

Nafziger, J. 'Self-Determination and Humanitarian Intervention in a Community of Power.' *Denver Journal of International Law and Policy* 20, no. 1 (1991–2): 9–40.

Nelson, D. *National Manhood: Capitalist Citizenship and the Imagined Fraternity of White Men.* Durham, NC: Duke University Press, 1998.

Nixon, C.R. 'Self-Determination: The Nigeria/Biafra Case', *World Politics* 24, no. 4 (1972): 473–97.

Nujoma, S. *Where Others Wavered.* London: Panaf Books, 2001.

Olonisakin, F. *Peacekeeping in Sierra Leone: The Story of UNAMSIL.* London: Lynne Rainer, 2008.

Orford, A. *Reading Humanitarian Intervention.* Cambridge: Cambridge University Press, 2003.

Panter-Brick, S.K. 'The Right to Self-Determination: Its Application to Nigeria.' *International Affairs* 44, no. 2 (1968): 254–66.

Paris, R. *At War's End, Building Peace After Civil Conflict.* Cambridge: Cambridge University Press, 2004.

Pateman, C and C. Mills. *Contract and Domination.* Cambridge: Polity Press, 2007.

Pearce, J. *An Outbreak of Peace: Angola's Situation of Confusion.* Cape Town: David Philip, 2005.

Pesek, M. *Koloniale Herrschaft in Deutsch-Ostafrika: Expeditionen, Militär und Verwaltung seit 1880.* Frankfurt: Campus, 2005.

Pieterse, J. *World Orders in the Making: Humanitarian Intervention and Beyond.* Basingstoke: Macmillan, 1998.

Polman, L. *The Crisis Caravan: What's Wrong with Humanitarian Aid?* trans. L. Waters. New York: Picador, 2010.

Prochaska, F. *The Voluntary Impulse: Philanthropy in Modern Britain.* London: Faber and Faber, 1998.

Pyenson, L. *Civilizing Mission: Exact Sciences and French Overseas Expansion, 1830–1940.* Baltimore, MD: Johns Hopkins University Press, 1993.

Quataert, J.H. *Staging Philanthropy: Patriotic Women and the National Imagination in Dynastic Germany, 1813–1916.* Ann Arbor, MI: University of Michigan Press, 2001.

Ramsbotham, O. and T. Woodhouse. *Humanitarian Intervention in Contemporary Conflict: A Reconceptualization.* London: Polity Press, 1996.

Razack, S. *Dark Threats and White Knights: The Somalia Affair, Peacekeeping, and the New Imperialism.* Toronto, ON: University of Toronto Press, 2004.

Richards, P. *Fighting for the Rainforest: War, Youth and Resources in Sierra Leone.* Portsmouth: Heinemann, 1996.

Rockel, S.J. *Carriers of Culture: Labor on the Road in Nineteenth-Century East Africa.* Portsmouth: Heinemann, 2006.

Rogers, L. *The Foundation of the British Empire Leprosy Relief Association.* Watford: Voss and Michael, 1945.

Ryan, S.M. *The Grammar of Good Intentions: Race and the Antebellum Culture of Benevolence.* Ithaca, NY: Cornell University Press, 2003.

Seymour, R. *The Liberal Defence of Murder.* London: Verso Books, 2008.

Skidmore, T.E., P.H. Smith, and J.N. Green, *Modern Latin America* (Oxford: Oxford University Press, 2009), http://www.oup.com/us/companion.websites/ 9780195375701/pdf/SPD6_Dollar_Dipl_Central_Am.pdf.

Simms, B. and D.J.B. Trimm, eds. *Humanitarian Intervention: A History.* Cambridge: Cambridge University Press, 2011.

Sparr, P. *Mortgaging Women's Lives: Feminist Critiques of Structural Adjustment.* London: Zed Books, 1994.

Stanley, B. *Bible and the Flag: Protestant Missions and British Imperialism in the Nineteenth and Twentieth Centuries.* Leicester: Apollos, 1990.

Stein, H. *Beyond the World Bank Agenda: An Institutional Approach to Development.* Chicago, IL: University of Chicago Press, 2008.

Stremlau, J. *The International Politics of the Nigerian Civil War 1967–70.* Princeton, NJ: Princeton University Press, 1997.

Synge, R. *Mozambique: UN Peacekeeping in Action 1992–94.* Washington, DC: US Institute for Peace Press, 1997.

Thomas-Emeagwali, G., ed. *Women Pay the Price: Structural Adjustment in Africa and the Caribbean.* Trenton, NJ: Africa World Press, 1995.

Thornberry, C. *A Nation is Born: The Inside Story of Namibia's Independence.* Windhoek: Gamsberg Macmillan, 2004.

Thurow, R. and S. Kilman. *Enough: Why the World's Poorest Starve in an Age of Plenty.* New York: PublicAffairs, 2009.

Uche, C. 'Oil, British Interests, and the Nigerian Civil War', *Journal of African History* 49 (2008): 111–35.

Welsh, J., ed. *Humanitarian Intervention and International Relations.* Oxford: Oxford University Press, 2006.

Welsh, J. 'Implementing the Responsibility to Protect: Where Expectations Meet Reality', *Ethics and International Affairs* 24, no. 4 (2010): 415–30.

Wheeler, N. *Saving Strangers*. Oxford: Oxford University Press, 2000.

Wiseberg, L. 'Christian Churches and the Nigerian Civil War', *Journal of African Studies* 2, no. 3 (1975): 297–331.

Wiseberg, L. 'Humanitarian Intervention Lessons from the Nigerian Civil War', *Human Rights Journal* 70, no. 1 (1974): 61–98.

Index

Printed and bound in Great Britain by
CPI Antony Rowe, Chippenham and Eastbourne